Treatment Approaches for
Body Image in Art Therapy

of related interest

Creative Arts Therapies and Clients with Eating Disorders
Annie Heiderscheit
ISBN 978 1 84905 911 4
eISBN 978 0 85700 695 0

A Clinician's Guide to Gender Identity and Body Image
Practical Support for Working with Transgender
and Gender-Expansive Clients
Heidi Dalzell and Kayti Protos
ISBN 978 1 84905 911 4
ISBN 978 1 78592 830 7
eISBN 978 1 78450 971 2

Eating Disorders Don't Discriminate
Stories of Illness, Hope and Recovery from Diverse Voices
Dr Chukwuemeka Nwuba and Bailey Spinn
ISBN 978 1 78592 830 7
eISBN 978 1 78450 971 2

Treatment Approaches for BODY IMAGE in ART THERAPY

Eileen Misluk-Gervase,
Heidi N. Moffatt, and Taylor McLane

Jessica Kingsley Publishers
London and Philadelphia

First published in Great Britain in 2025 by Jessica Kingsley Publishers
An imprint of John Murray Press

1

Copyright © Eileen Misluk-Gervase, Heidi N. Moffatt, and Taylor McLane 2025

The right of Eileen Misluk-Gervase, Heidi N. Moffatt, and Taylor McLane
to be identified as the Author of the Work has been asserted by them in
accordance with the Copyright, Designs and Patents Act 1988.

Chapter 1 © Eileen Misluk-Gervase 2025, Chapter 2 © Taylor McLane 2025, Chapter
3 © Eileen Misluk-Gervase 2025, Chapter 4 © Liza Hyatt 2025, Chapter 5 © Rachel
Feldwisch and Eileen Misluk-Gervase 2025, Chapter 6 © Mary K. Kometiani and
Cynthia Wilson 2025, Chapter 7 © Linda Adeniyi 2025, Chapter 8 © Chelsea Leeds
2025, Chapter 9 © Deborah Elkis-Abuhoff and Morgan Gaydos 2025, Chapter 10 ©
Alison Silver 2025, Chapter 11 © Joan Alpers 2025, Chapter 12 © Michelle Itczak
2025, Chapter 13 © Heidi Moffatt 2025, Chapter 14 © Charlie Marshall 2025

All rights reserved. No part of this publication may be reproduced, stored
in a retrieval system, or transmitted, in any form or by any means without
the prior written permission of the publisher, nor be otherwise circulated
in any form of binding or cover other than that in which it is published and
without a similar condition being imposed on the subsequent purchaser.

A CIP catalogue record for this title is available from the
British Library and the Library of Congress

ISBN 978 1 83997 884 5
eISBN 978 1 83997 885 2

Printed and bound by CPI Group (UK) Ltd, Croydon, CR0 4YY

Jessica Kingsley Publishers' policy is to use papers that are natural,
renewable and recyclable products and made from wood grown in
sustainable forests. The logging and manufacturing processes are expected
to conform to the environmental regulations of the country of origin.

Jessica Kingsley Publishers
Carmelite House
50 Victoria Embankment
London EC4Y 0DZ

www.jkp.com

John Murray Press
Part of Hodder & Stoughton Ltd
An Hachette Company

The authorised representative in the EEA is Hachette Ireland, 8 Castlecourt
Centre, Dublin 15, D15 XTP3, Ireland (email: info@hbgi.ie)

For every individual's authentic parts of the self, deserving to be heard, understood, accepted, and loved unconditionally, and for the readers who dedicate their time in service of others.

Acknowledgments

EILEEN MISLUK-GERVASE

For Joe, Giada, and Paden—you are my why. I love you the most.

I acknowledge my tribe of people who continuously support and love me in all my ventures. I am appreciative of my students and clients who inspire and challenge me to always strive to be better. Thank you to the contributors whose invaluable clinical work made this book possible. Taylor and Heidi, I am so grateful for your willingness to take a leap of faith with me, and for filling it with laughter.

HEIDI MOFFATT

I gratefully acknowledge Eileen Misluk-Gervase for initiating concept development for this book; Eileen and Taylor McLane for their partnership in authoring and editing this book and encouraging my study; the assistance of Lisa Habegger for completing the searches for my study; Charlie Marshall for reviewing my chapter and partnering to write about men with cancer; authors of this book who committed to research and writing to support their selected client population and advance research in the field of art therapy; Karen Braeckel for her friendship and careful attention to details while proofreading my chapter; my grandparents who taught me how to read and write and encouraged a love of written language; my mother and various family members who share an appreciation for the arts; friends and family for encouragement; the authors referenced in my chapter who work to improve quality of life for individuals; clients I have had the privilege of partnering with; and all other supporters for encouraging this work in coming to fruition. Much gratitude goes out to the team at Jessica Kingsley Publishers for the compassion for and faith in this book from its inception. Finally, I would like to thank the readers of this book for dedicating their time in service of others.

TAYLOR MCLANE

I want to acknowledge and express my deepest gratitude to my parents, Cindy McLane and Walt Glaub, for your endless support of my educational and professional pursuits. I also want to thank all my other loved ones for encouraging me and challenging me to keep striving and who have helped me keep my balance. To my colleagues, and co-workers, thank you for making me laugh while also letting me bounce ideas off you, and for your feedback. A very special thanks to my co-editors, Eileen Mis-luk-Gervase and Heidi Moffatt, for your inspiring dedication and keeping me grounded.

Contents

Contributors 13

Introduction. 17
Eileen Misluk-Gervase, Heidi N. Moffatt, and Taylor McLane

I. Mental Freedom and Social Power: Defining Positive
Body Image 25
Eileen Misluk-Gervase

PART 1: BODY IMAGE AND EATING DISORDERS

II. Body Image in Clients with Eating Disorders: An Overview . 41
Taylor McLane

III. Neuroscience-Informed Art Therapy for Clients with
Eating Disorders 57
Eileen Misluk-Gervase

IV. Returning the Body to Safety: Somatic, Nature-Attuned
Art Therapy with Eating Disordered Adult Trauma Survivors 77
Liza Hyatt

PART 2: BODY IMAGE AND TRAUMA

V. Trauma and the Body: Relationships between Art
and Experience 97
Rachel Feldwisch and Eileen Misluk-Gervase

VI. Treating Body-Based Trauma of Sex Trafficking through
Art Therapy 115
Mary K. Kometiani and Cynthia Wilson

VII. Body Image: From the Victim's Lens 135
Linda Adeniyi

VIII.	Using Art Therapy to Address Body Image with Queer Clients	154
	Chelsea Leeds	
IX.	Art Therapy with Veterans Who Have Experienced a Combat-Related Amputation	173
	Deborah Elkis-Abuhoff and Morgan Gaydos	
X.	Body Image during Peri/Postpartum Period: Reconciling Grief and Betrayal—Mother and Body: Utilizing Creative Arts Therapy	188
	Alison Silver	

PART 3: BODY IMAGE AND MEDICAL DIAGNOSES

XI.	Body Image in Children Who Encounter Medical Conditions and Hospitalizations	205
	Joan Alpers	
XII.	Adolescents and Body Image in Medical Settings	224
	Michelle Itczak	
XIII.	Effective Methods for Art Therapists Partnering with Breast Cancer Survivors to Improve Body Image and Quality of Life: A Literature Review	239
	Heidi Moffatt	
XIV.	Exploring Male Body Image and Considerations for Men with Cancer in Art Therapy	261
	Charlie Marshall	
	Appendix: Search Strategies	276
	Subject Index	280
	Author Index	285

List of Figures

Figure 3.1: Altered book page 65

Figure 3.2: Black-out poetry 66

Figure 3.3: Christina: Spice painting 68

Figure 3.4: Felted brain 73

Figure 4.1: What power do leaves have over me? 88

Figure 4.2: Simply leaves falling from the strong, sturdy trees 89

Figure 4.3: Three-dimensional body shape 89

Figure 6.1: Holes 124

Figure 6.2: Boy knocked over 125

Figure 6.3: Untitled 129

Figure 6.4: And the Rain Wouldn't Come (pages 23–27) 130

Figure 7.1: The controller 150

Figure 7.2a: View of the controller in the box 150

Figure 7.2b: Front view of the box 151

Figure 8.1: Emma 1 161

Figure 8.2: Emma 2 161

Figure 8.3: Emma 3 162

Figure 8.4: Jane 1 163

Figure 9.1: Expressive painting 182

Figure 9.2: Collage-making 184

Figure 11.1: Bird taking flight from a broken tree 214

Figure 11.2: Self-portrait 215

Figure 11.3: Carrying the pain 216

Figure 11.4: Two bone marrow tests 218

All figures can be viewed in full colour at https://digitalhub.jkp.com using the code RZMSRLG.

List of Tables

Table 12.1: The psychological consequences of chronic diseases on adolescents 227

Table 13.1: Extracted data from literature review: objectives, assessment tools, therapeutic approaches, directives, and art media . . 248

Contributors

EDITOR BIOGRAPHIES

Taylor McLane, MA, LMHC, ATR is a Registered Art therapist Licensed Mental Health Counselor. She has a bachelor's of Fine Arts in Drawing and earned her Master's of Arts in Art Therapy in 2022 at Indiana University, Indianapolis. She extensively studied art therapy and contemporary research surrounding clients with eating disorders through her final year of her graduate program. She completed her thesis, *A Literature Review: Addressing Body Image in Clients with Eating Disorders through Art and Somatic Interventions*, compiling studies into a review of art and somatic interventions, exploring various tools and therapeutic approaches art therapists are using to address such a multilayered and complex disorder. Taylor currently provides art therapy services at the Department of Veterans Affairs for the Northern Indiana Healthcare System.

Eileen Misluk-Gervase, MPS, LPC, ATR-BC, LMHC, CEDS is a registered and board-certified art therapist, licensed professional counselor, licensed mental health counselor, and certified eating disorder specialist. She received her Master's in Professional Studies in art therapy and creativity development from Pratt Institute. Eileen is an Associate Faculty, graduate program director, and The Cindy Simon Skjodt Chair in Art Therapy at Herron School of Art and Design, Indiana University, Indianapolis. She maintains a private practice where she has specialized in working with individuals with eating disorders, disordered eating behaviors, and body image concerns for 15 years.

Heidi N. Moffatt, MA, LMHC, ATR, CEC is a board-certified registered art therapist, licensed mental health counselor, and certified embodiment coach. She received her Master of Arts from Indiana University. Heidi has more than ten years of experience in healthcare, working at the intersection of medical and mental health. Her practice focuses on helping clients improve quality of life and overall well-being.

CONTRIBUTOR BIOGRAPHIES

Linda B. Adeniyi, MBA, MA, ATR is an art therapist, muralist, and Army veteran in Indianapolis, Indiana. She has over two decades of experience working with individuals who have experienced violent traumas. Currently, she is employed at Indiana University Health University Hospital providing art therapy for individuals with chronic illness. As the first African American graduate in the first graduating class of Herron School of Art and Design, Indiana University Master of Arts in art therapy's graduate program, Linda is passionate about addressing community trauma via art therapy and supervision and preparing new art therapists to enter the field. She is inspired daily by her two sons and husband.

Joan Alpers, MPS, CCLS, ATR-BC, LCAT is a licensed creative arts therapist in New York, a certified child life specialist, and a Sandplay practitioner for Sandplay Therapists of America. She has worked with medically ill children in hospitals and in private practice for 35 years. Currently, she directs a child life program at Stony Brook Children's Hospital and is an adjunct professor for Hofstra University's graduate art therapy program and for Herron School of Art and Design, Indiana University's art therapy graduate program.

Deborah Elkis-Abuhoff, PhD, LCAT, ATR-BC, ATCS, BCPC is an Associate Professor in the Creative Arts Therapy Counseling program at Hofstra University. She holds both creative arts therapy and psychology licenses in New York, is a registered and board-certified art therapist, an art therapist certified supervisor and certified clinical trauma professional. Her research interests bring together behavioral medicine and creative/medical art therapy and neuroscience, veterans, and trauma. She and her team have published and presented to national and international audiences. She holds an appointment to the NS/LIJ Feinstein Institute for Medical Research in the Center for Neuroscience.

Rachel Paige Feldwisch, PhD, MAAT, LMHC, ATR-BC is a faculty member at the University of Indianapolis. She earned a Master of Arts in art therapy from the University of Illinois at Chicago and a PhD in counseling psychology from Indiana University. She has primarily worked with adolescents, young adults, and women, specializing in the treatment of trauma and disordered eating. Her most recent research focuses on a treatment program for young survivors of domestic sex trafficking.

Morgan Gaydos, MA, LCAT, ATR-BC is a creative arts therapist with expertise in inpatient mental health. She practices within acute hospital settings and is also an adjunct professor within a Master's level program. Ms. Gaydos' research interests revolve around creative arts therapy and neuroscience, as well as neurodegenerative disorders.

Liza Hyatt, LMHC, ATR-BC, ATCS is a therapist for Indiana University Health Charis Center for Eating Disorders and teaches as adjunct faculty for Saint Mary-of-the-Woods College. She is certified in Eye Movement Desensitization and Reprocessing therapy and has over 35 years of experience providing therapy for adults and teens healing from complex trauma. She provides supervision for art therapists working toward credentials and offers continuing education workshops/retreats on eco-therapy, eco-spirituality, and the expressive arts. She has also published several books of poetry.

Michelle Itczak, MA, LMHC, ATR-BC, ATCS is an Associate Professor and Program Director for the Department of Counseling at the University of Indianapolis. Michelle was the founding art therapist of the Art Therapy program at Riley Hospital for Children, where she addressed body image topics with patients on all units. She maintains her clinical work and connection to the medical population through contractual work with Riley Children's Health Grief Services.

Mary K. Kometiani, MA, LPAT, LPCC ATR-BC is a registered board-certified art therapist, licensed professional clinical counselor, lecturer, and author in art therapy. She has over a decade of experience providing art therapy for survivors of sex trafficking, inpatient and outpatient medical patients and their families, and families of hospice patients and the bereaved. As the owner and art therapist of Art Therapy Heals, LLC, she collaborates with community organizations and educates the public about art therapy. She is the editor of *Art Therapy Treatment for Sex Trafficked Survivors: Facilitating Empowerment, Recovery and Hope*, in addition to authoring several journal articles and book chapters.

Chelsea Leeds, MA, ATR-BC, LMHC is a licensed mental health counselor and registered and board-certified art therapist working in private practice in Indianapolis, Indiana. Her clinical population focus is on young to middle-aged adults processing past complex relational trauma and working to detangle the intersection of trauma and identity. Chelsea integrates a systems perspective into her work, including internal family systems, for which she has completed level one training.

Charlie Marshall, ATR-BC, LPAT currently lives in his hometown of Louisville, Kentucky and is a licensed professional art therapist. He received his Master's in art therapy from the University of Louisville in 1992. He is currently practicing art therapy with adults in the psych intensive outpatient program and substance use disorders intensive outpatient program within a medical hospital and in his private practice. He supervises art therapy graduate school students as they see adult clients in the hospital, including an oncology unit. He has a history of doing art therapy in a psychiatric hospital with an eating disorder clinic in Tulsa, Oklahoma.

Alison Silver, MPS, LPAT, ATR-BC, CFTP, PMH is a licensed creative arts therapist in New Jersey, while residing in Delray Beach, Florida. She graduated with a Master's in professional studies from Pratt Institute and a Bachelor of Science from University of the Arts. Alison has worked in a myriad of settings serving diverse populations including veterans, survivors of domestic violence, human trafficking, sexual abuse, brain injuries, postpartum mood and anxiety disorder, children and families undergoing medical hospitalizations, as well as maintaining a private practice. Alison's focus as a trauma specialist is to reassimilate her clients into their bodies while attaining self and body awareness.

Cynthia Wilson, PhD, ATR-BC has been an art therapist for two decades, in private practice working in the office, nursing homes/hospitals or via telehealth with children, adults, groups, and families. She is a clinical art therapy supervisor, author, and speaker. She also volunteers on the board and committees of professional organizations, with schools for emotional development and disaster processing, and in the community for connection, grief and loss, cancer care, dementia care, dissociation support and education, and trauma processing.

Introduction

—— EILEEN MISLUK-GERVASE, HEIDI N. MOFFATT, AND TAYLOR MCLANE ——

The history of the self is the history of the body. In all clinical populations, the body is part of therapy whether it is merely the vessel that enters the room or the central focus of treatment. But what is body image? In our research, we found that body image has nine factors that lead to and interact with one another to develop body image. Foundationally, interoceptive awareness is the understanding of the ways that the body both feels and presents in space. For example, *interoceptive awareness* helps us understand if we can fit in spaces. We have all experienced that time, when we thought we could slide behind a chair someone was sitting in and quickly realized that we could not. Well, that brain process, rooted in the insula, helps us understand our spatial bodies and the perception of how others perceive our bodies in space. This brain process leads to the development of *schemas*, which are outlooks or assumptions. These broader assumptions lead to *self-schemas*. Self-schemas are organized beliefs or information about the self that guide a person's perception of the world. As the body and brain take in information, our interoceptive awareness evolves, leading to the development, modification, or solidifying of schemas and self-schemas that shape our sense of self.

Sense of self is an individual's feelings of uniqueness, self-direction, and identity. A sense of self impacts *self-perception* or the view of the self and *self-concept*, which is the way someone describes and evaluates themselves. These three factors develop into *self-image*, which is one's view or concept of oneself and is crucial to personality development. These are foundational in the development of body perception and body concept. *Body perception* is the mental image created by physical characteristics, while *body concept* is the thoughts and feelings that constitute the way an individual views physical characteristics. The foundation for body image is laid from interoceptive awareness to body perception and concept. Broadly, *body image* is the result of a continuous collection of lived experiences shaped by biological, emotional, psychological, and sociological influences. This continual evolution means that body image is not stagnant and does not remain fixed throughout life. As a result, body image is an essential component in overall wellness, and needs to be prioritized across treatment populations, regardless of diagnosis.

So, when do body and subsequently body image become the focus of therapeutic work independently or embedded within the larger clinical goals? The following chapters explore the concept of body image within a specific clinical population and the unique ways that it is addressed. These chapters guide the conceptualization of body image across clinical populations, making it an essential part of treatment. Case studies and sample directives are provided as examples. Art therapists are uniquely equipped to address the complex foundation of body image that often lives in a place without words. By engaging the body in therapy to explore body image, art therapists use art media and processes to raise awareness of how the body moves in space, creating a visual representation of the body. By consciously bringing the body into artmaking, clients are able to be embodied, challenge maladaptive body perceptions, concepts, and schemas, and build new, healthier paradigms.

Art therapists should use clinical judgment to support individual client needs and treatment goals, and use expertise when selecting materials and processes for body image work. These chapters do not serve as a cookbook of therapeutic recipes, but rather the primary goal is to raise awareness for clinicians working with these populations to prioritize body image as an essential component of overall health. By offering clinical examples and sample directives, we intend to educate and empower clinicians to recognize the clinical need to address body image and engage in this type of work with their clients.

This book is organized into three broad sections: body image and eating disorders, body image and trauma, and body image and medical diagnoses. As clinicians, we understand the complexity of mental health and medical diagnoses. The authors focus on a specific diagnosis within their chapter but recognize that most of these clients have comorbid diagnoses and multiple therapeutic factors that are not explicitly addressed.

The book begins with an understanding of the difference between positive body image and negative body image. Body image is often misconstrued through a singular lens, with the definition landing on how the viewer perceives their body, with a focus on weight and size. This perspective is reductionistic and ignores the complexity of the continuously evolving development of body image. *Positive body image* is a holistic, multidimensional construct where facets are explored in parallel to, or simultaneously with, varying degrees of success. For positive body image, attunement is required—the reciprocal and mutual influence of internal and external systems that support regulation and reciprocity between the individual and the environment. Cognitive, affective, perceptual, and behavioral interventions are necessary. Furthermore, the holistic model highlights the fluidity between the various components. The developmental level focuses on cognitive development, social experiences such as sexual objectification and intimacy experiences, quality and longevity of relationships, educational and occupational opportunities, and physical and psychological wellness.

Positive body image is deeply embedded in *eating disorder research and treatment* because of the diagnostic criteria of body disturbance. McLane, Misluk-Gervase, and Hyatt elucidate this understanding in their chapters on body image work with individuals with eating disorders. McLane highlights the following themes: shame, guilt, control, and disordered eating as a coping mechanism to mediate body image ideals imposed by self and others. The research reveals that individuals with eating disorders redirect psychological pain or distress from a range of external and internal stressors, including comorbid mental health conditions, discrimination, marginalization, and traumatic experiences, into the physical body. Body image is a developmental and transformative experience throughout the lifespan, as those with eating disorders take in input from larger societal and cultural influences. Internally, body ideals involve biological body inheritances and personal emotions, as well as thoughts and attitudes directed towards the self through physical behaviors. Due to the complex nature of body image as it relates to identity, art therapy provides a safe environment to address the complex fragments of body image as it relates to self-image. Art therapy can also increase comfort by exploring body sensations, body boundaries, and emotions from a safe, reflective distance.

Misluk-Gervase explains that body image disturbance is a diagnostic criterion in anorexia nervosa and a clinical concern in bulimia nervosa, binge eating disorder, and otherwise specified feeding and eating disorders, and causes significant psychological distress long after the behavioral aspects are treated. The psychological distress around weight restoration, weight maintenance, and mind/body connectedness negatively impacts the individual long after their behavioral aspects around food have subsided. Body image issues remain constant, impacting potential for relapse. The *neuroscience research on body image* is still in its infancy; Chapter I provides an overview of the brain systems—with a focus on the insula—involved in body image development. The insula is the hub for processing internal and external stimuli and, most important, sensory information. This processing involves brain regions that decode this information into a body schema. Interoceptive awareness supports attunement, self-awareness, learning, and self-assessment to form body image. Body representations arise from multimodal sensory inputs—visual, tactile, proprioceptive, interoceptive, nociceptive, and motor. Engaging the senses (i.e., sight, hearing, smell, taste, touch) helps interpret external stimuli essential in determining the human experience. The ability of art materials to engage multiple senses at one time makes them uniquely capable for addressing body image dissatisfaction on a neurological level. By intentionally focusing on external stimuli and the resulting internal stimulations of art materials, art therapists can intentionally use materials to explore body image.

Hyatt found that *adults recovering from eating disorders* gain an enhanced sense of embodied safety through participation in an art therapy group that incorporates a trauma-informed, somatic, nature-attuned approach. This approach recognizes the impact of childhood trauma and attachment wounds as a significant, underlying cause for the tendency to objectify and dissociate from the body, a common experience of many people with eating disorders. Through artmaking combined with somatic awareness and nature attunement, this approach provides ample opportunities in which group participants experience: 1) increased freedom from habitual disembodied patterns; 2) increased access to felt experience; 3) growth of self-compassion; 4) safe, pleasurable connection of the physical body to the physical sensations of art materials and the living world; 5) access to their body's ability to regulate nervous system arousal; 6) more curiosity and openness towards their own creative process as an embodied expression of authentic self; and 7) enhanced trust in the body as a resource for healing. The necessity that the group facilitator also practice attunement with the natural world and embodied self-compassion is also discussed.

Chapters on trauma focus on *physical, psychological, and sexual trauma* and the impact on body image. In Chapter V, Feldwisch and Misluk-Gervase provide an *overview of trauma*, focusing on how traumatic experiences shape the connection between body and mind. Trauma may not only impact an individual's perceptions of their body but also shift and dramatically alter experiences within the body. An exploration of historical perspectives on trauma and the body and an overview of the Adverse Childhood Experiences (ACEs) studies provide a deeper understanding of psychological disorders associated with trauma and the connections between trauma and body image. Subsequently, treatment recommendations are provided, including the role of psychoeducation on trauma and the body, comorbidity between trauma and body image concerns, and general recommendations regarding art therapy treatment for this population. As the chapter concludes, specific art therapy directives are provided using Herman's Stage Model as a theoretical guide.

In Chapter VI, Kometiani and Wilson report that survivors of *sex trafficking* require extensive trauma-informed care services due to the complicated nature of the physical, emotional, psychological, spiritual, and moral injuries compounded by relational trauma. These grave consequences alter the survivors' perceptions and their sense of and relationship to self and body. The distinct health concerns for survivors of sex trafficking and the effects on survivors' body image are explored. This chapter presents current research, with recommendations for therapeutic care that provides optimum benefits for sex trafficking survivors. Body-based trauma is explored through case vignettes, while special considerations and adaptations are examined. Lastly, this chapter provides concise suggestions for art therapists who treat this complex population.

In Chapter VII, Adeniyi states that *intimate partner violence* (IPV) is not trivial or insignificant, but an immense and wide-ranging problem with grave consequences for victims. IPV relationships have an impact on the victim's body image and include social and cultural influences that reciprocally affect their ongoing relationship with the body. Images created in art therapy invite victims to reframe their feelings, respond to their traumatic experiences of IPV, and work towards emotional and behavioral changes that improve their relationship with their body. Research supports the use of art therapy in individual and group sessions, as an effective psychological intervention for IPV victims to address body image distress, symptoms of post-traumatic stress disorder (PTSD), positive thinking, self-esteem, self-worth, and cognitive distortions.

Leeds' chapter (VIII) explores the relationship between queer identity, oppression, trauma, and resulting body image issues. Different facets of traumatic experiences as a queer person are explored, as well as the influence these facets have on one's relationship to one's own body. These traumatic experiences include but are not limited to stigma, systemic oppression, discrimination, medical trauma, body dysphoria, violence, bullying, rejection, objectification, dehumanization, and maladaptive coping. Counseling theories, specific media and materials, and potential directives appropriate for this population are described. Art therapy goals specific to this population include acceptance of queer identity, decreased gender dysphoria, increased self-awareness and understanding of one's own identity, increasing critical consciousness of systemic influences on the individual, and acknowledgment and processing of trauma. Secondary goals are increasing a sense of control, decreasing self-harm and suicidal ideation, understanding and changing one's relationship to one's body, increasing self-compassion, and enhancing support.

In Chapter IX, Elkis-Abuhoff and Gaydos focus on traumas experienced in combat zones and the impact on body image. In today's combat zones, soldiers are faced with roadside bombings, encountering an improvised explosive device (IED), or having their compound ambushed, among many other dangers. As a result, soldiers risk the loss of life, witnessing friends, comrades, and innocent civilians dying, and experiencing their own traumas as a result of military actions. This includes traumatic brain injuries, burns, and loss of limbs ending their military career, and changing how they perceive themselves and look in the mirror. For veterans who have experienced changes to their physical appearance during their service, a number of factors can contribute to poor body image. These factors may include a decreased sense of masculinity or strength, depleted self-worth, difficulty with relationships, and inability to see themselves as the same individual who once served their country. Individuals who sustain appearance-altering injuries can be prone to psychological symptoms and diagnoses such as depression, generalized anxiety, and social anxiety, as well as decreased emotional well-being and body image distress. A case study demonstrating the implementation of art therapy with a veteran with limb loss whose body and body image were drastically altered because of combat is presented.

In their chapters, Alpers, Itczak, Moffatt, and Marshall focus on the impact of *medical diagnoses* and treatments for body image. Alpers explores body image concepts in *children who have experienced hospitalization* and treatment for medical conditions. The chapter starts by explaining the physical and emotional challenges implicit in medical illness and hospitalization for children, then examines body image as it is understood developmentally for all children and as it is expressed in the artwork and attitudes of children with chronic medical conditions. It proceeds by comparing the ways that illness and body image interface as children use different expressive techniques to cope with their diagnoses and treatments.

Itczak details the intricately intertwined topics of *body image and adolescence* along with medical diagnoses and experiences that create even more complexities within this phase of development. This chapter (XII) provides a brief overview of the impact of medical diagnoses, medications, and treatments on the social, emotional, and physical development of an adolescent body image. Art therapists who work in hospital settings or with adolescents experiencing body image issues related to medical diagnoses will find a summary of art materials that are effective and age-appropriate.

Moffatt's research on *breast cancer survivors* includes the stages from diagnosis and treatment to living beyond cancer. She found emotional, physical, and social considerations in her literature review. Physical changes include potential hair loss or hair texture change, loss of breast or asymmetrical breasts, swelling, body and nutritional changes, loss of muscle definition, fatigue, changes in sexual functioning, nerve pain, among others. Body image is a significant consideration related to breast cancer survivors' overall quality of life. Art therapy is beneficial for examining, exploring, gaining insight, and improving mental health and quality of life by supporting mind, body, and spirit. Therapeutic approaches which involved mind-body connection are presented, including mindfulness-based art therapy, which was the most frequently utilized intervention in both group and individual formats. Goals include mind-body connections, compassionate awareness, and creative expression. The outcomes of the studies included improvements in distress, depression, anxiety, fatigue, pain, and overall quality of life. Quality of life and body image have an interconnected relationship. A treatment approach that influences compassionate awareness and attunement to the felt sense, interconnected facets of body image, and reciprocal relationship with the outer world is beneficial and important for the breast cancer survivor.

In Chapter XIV, Marshall explores how art therapy can address body image issues in *men with cancer*. Sharing his personal and professional background, he models the importance of therapist perspective and clinical approaches for the reader. Marshall dives deeper into the multiple factors associated with body image development, including culture, family, peers, and media. He describes how cancer can affect a man's perception of body image, purpose in life, and sense of well-being. Marshall recommends applying the Expressive Therapies Continuum to guide an art therapist's understanding of a man's way of processing body image and cancer. He advocates for clinical decisions that support men with cancer by building insight and coping skills to enrich their life.

Please note, in some cases, artwork within this book has been recreated by the authors to preserve the anonymity of the client.

There are supplementary materials which can be downloaded from https://digitalhub.jkp.com for personal use with this program, but may not be reproduced for any other purposes without the permission of the publisher. Please use the code RZMSRLG.

CHAPTER I

Mental Freedom and Social Power

Defining Positive Body Image

—— EILEEN MISLUK-GERVASE ——

As a field of clinical and psychometric interest, body image outside the field of eating disorders emerged because of the work of Dr. Thomas Cash, who laid the foundation for how to study, measure, conceptualize, and improve it (Jarry *et al.*, 2019; Tylka, 2019).

> Tom envisions the various ways appearance and body image impact the lives of individuals, which has led him to research topics such as: appearance evaluation, appearance investment, body image quality of life, ways of coping with appearance-related threats, body image cognitive distortions, body image ideals, body image disturbance (dysphoria, dissatisfaction, and dysfunction), state fluctuations in body image, body exposure during sexual activity, appearance stereotypes, and positive body image. He also sought to understand the role various medical conditions, such as androgenetic alopecia, had on body image, as well as how appearance-related discrimination, such as weight stigma and stigma regarding race-related features (e.g., skin tone), impacted body image. (Tylka, 2019, p.191)

Cash's interest in expanding discourse around trait and state body image indicators that impact body image satisfaction and pathology led to a body of work that laid the foundation for future researchers. He implored researchers to explore the complexity of body image in a broader range of populations and diagnoses, for example body image in pregnancy, sexual intimacy, oncology, and chronic illnesses, as well as with the ethnically diverse, and individuals with disabilities. Increased research in the last

20 years has expanded the exploration of body image across a range of groups, but this is still far from creating a deep understanding of the impact of body image (Fuller-Tyszkiewicz, 2019).

Individual differences, cultures, and social groups celebrate beauty and diversity differently. Using an intersectional approach to conceptualizing body image in treatment is necessary for understanding the complex and dynamic nature of positive body image (Tylka & Wood-Barcalow, 2015). Currently, most research on negative and positive body image is on cisgender, white, college-aged females, with a small but growing body of research on a more diverse scope of identities.

DEVELOPING A POSITIVE BODY IMAGE

Body image is often perceived through a singular lens, with the definition landing on how the viewer perceives their body, and a focus on weight and size (Jarry *et al.*, 2019). Poor body image is a negative lens, while positive body image is favorable. This perspective is reductionistic and ignores the complexity of the continuously evolving development of body image: "Body image is a complex, multifaceted construct distinct from low levels of negative body image and extending beyond body satisfaction or appearance evaluation..." (Webb *et al.*, 2015, p.131). It requires exploration into the nuances that compose and support the healthy development of body image. Jarry *et al.* (2019) noted that Cash's influence on the contemporary understanding of body image resulted in a multidimensional construct of body image expanding beyond weight, size, and satisfaction to include attitudes and behaviors that influence the ways that we evaluate and invest in the body, overall appearance, specific body parts, skin tone, hair texture, body functions, and quality of life. Quality of life is negatively impacted by body dissatisfaction, negative body image emotions, and a dysfunctional over-valuation of appearance that determines self-worth (Tylka & Wood-Barcalow, 2015). Positive body image is not the opposite of negative body image. Positive body image requires the development of adaptive body-related attitudes, cognitions, and behaviors.

Presented in treatment, body image may be treated as a single clinical issue, with clinicians lacking the knowledge of the complexity of body image development and neurological implications in developing a consistent body concept. Body image literature and research have focused on pathology to understand the impact of negative body image without considering positive body image (Tylka & Wood-Barcalow, 2015). Fredrickson and Losada (2005) noted that positive characteristics do not represent the absence of negative characteristics and that fostering positive affect is more therapeutically beneficial than lowering negative affect. The absence of pathology does not equate to thriving or high-level well-being; eliminating or reducing negative characteristics without focusing on increasing positive ones merely leads to intermediate mental health (Wood-Barcalow et al., 2010). With this in mind, this chapter aims to understand the benefits of deliberately addressing the individual components of positive body image by adopting Wood-Barcalow et al.'s definition of positive body image:

> An overarching love and respect for the body that allows individuals to (a) appreciate the unique beauty of their body and the functions that it performs for them; (b) accept and even admire their body, including those aspects that are inconsistent with idealized images; (c) feel beautiful, comfortable, confident and happy with their body, which is often reflected as an outer radiance, or a "glow;" (d) emphasize their body's assets rather than dwell on their imperfections; and (f) interpret incoming information in a body-protective manner whereby most positive information is internalized and most negative information is rejected or reframed. (2010, p.112)

Positive body image is a holistic, multidimensional construct where facets are explored in parallel to or simultaneously with varying degrees of success. It requires attunement—the reciprocal and mutual influence of internal and external systems that support regulation and reciprocity between the individual and the environment (Tylka & Wood-Barcalow, 2015). It requires cognitive, affective, perceptual, and behavioral interventions. Furthermore, the holistic model highlights the fluidity between the various components, including developmental level and the use, type, and impact of social media, friendship networks, and level of cultural and spiritual involvement. The developmental level focuses on cognitive development, social experiences such as sexual objectification and intimacy experiences, quality and longevity of relationships, educational and occupational opportunities, and physical and psychological wellness (Wood-Barcalow et al., 2010).

BODY IMAGE INVESTMENT AND STATE AND TRAIT

The interplay between state body image and trait body image lays the foundation for understanding the complexity of treatment. Evaluating the interplay between trait and state interactions includes assessing the average level or frequency (e.g., satisfaction or dissatisfaction) in daily life, the extent to which factors influence body image, and the duration and consequence of these experiences. State body image work attempts to categorize and understand the variability of state body experiences, antecedents, and consequences in daily life. Trait variables may help predict the frequency and severity of state-based experiences. State-based body image assessments focus on the following factors: body (dis)satisfaction, appearance comparisons, body appreciation, appearance-related self-compassion, appearance-related stress, appearance self-consciousness/body surveillance, social physique anxiety, perceived attractiveness, body awareness, internalization, social interactions involving discussion of appearance, and rumination about weight and shape (Fuller-Tyszkiewicz, 2019). State body image experiences can be conceptualized through a sequence:

> (1) Activators of state body image – events or situations that promote a meaningful shift in state body image; (2) Beliefs – affective and evaluative cognitions in that situation about one's body; and (3) Consequences – emotional and behavioral reactions to the immediate body image experience. (Fuller-Tyszkiewicz, 2019, p.266)

This sequence provides a framework for understanding mitigating factors and the resulting traits that perpetuate (dis)satisfaction in body image. For example, individuals with elevated appearance investment are more attentive to their appearance, engage in appearance-related behaviors to maintain or enhance, and are more reactive to appearance-related stressors. An indicator for trait-level disturbances in body image may be the variability in the state body image. This aligns with the stress continuum models of pathology. The increase in severity and duration of trait disturbance negatively impacts the functioning state, and vice versa.

Trait constructs include dissatisfaction, eating disorder pathology, self-evaluation, and coping strategies, appearance-related cognitive distortions, and perfectionism. Fuller-Tyszkiewicz (2019) noted the correlation between body-checking behaviors (e.g., pinching skin, compulsive mirror checking) and increased negative emotions, negative affect, and rumination over food and weight. Researchers have raised awareness of the deleterious impacts of negative body image and the qualities needed to develop a stable and positive view of the self (Fuller-Tyszkiewicz, 2019). Through a review of body image assessments, Webb and colleagues (2015) provide an understanding of the complex factors of body image based on a review of existing body image assessments. The factors include appearance comparison, attunement, functionality, flexibility, rational acceptance and coping, positive and self-accepting talk, acceptance, a broad conceptualization of beauty, appreciation, pride and satisfaction, media literacy, and a protective filter.

Appearance comparison

Appearance comparison has significant negative impacts, including shame, guilt, anxiety, negative mood, ruminating thoughts about dieting and exercise, body checking, binge eating, exercise for weight management, and food restriction. An overemphasis on the importance of weight and shape (body ideal, drive for thinness) is correlated with poor interoceptive awareness and a pervading sense of ineffectiveness (Morrissey *et al.*, 2020). Fardouly *et al.* (2017) found that social media-based comparisons were more harmful than in-person. Fitzsimmons-Craft *et al.* (2016) noted that comparisons in food and exercise influenced body image states and traits. Exposure to weight stigmatization, objectification, and negative appearance comments on social media results in negative affect, body image concerns, and self-objectification.

Additionally, interactions with others who engage in *fat talk*, diet, and appearance-related exercise negatively impact body image. As part of appearance comparison, individuals engage in motivational salience— an attendance to appearance to make it aesthetically pleasing and within the individual's acceptable standard. As a result of the over-valuation of appearance, individuals engage in cognitive investment, which is when appearance is a centrally defining feature of the self. This includes life outcomes, mood, and self-evaluation, leading to the development of an appearance schema for self, others, and the environment and influencing the processing of information (Jarry *et al.*, 2019).

Attunement

Cook-Cottone (2006) defines attunement as the ability to appropriately sense, identify, and respect the body's needs through adaptive behaviors, and it can be assessed through two concepts: body responsiveness, and mindful self-care. Attunement requires trust between mind and body, specifically, so that the bodily cues will be attended to and the body will respond accordingly. Body responsiveness positively correlates with increased body awareness, satisfaction, body image, and decreased self-objectification. Utilizing mindful self-care practices—explained as daily practices of awareness of basic physiological and emotional needs through restructuring the environment, relationships, and routines (Cook-Cottone, 2015)—provides a foundation of self-regulation (Linehan, 1993). This foundation facilitates and maintains a positive body image (Wood-Barcalow *et al.*, 2010). Furthermore, symptom monitoring supports self-awareness and improves attunement (Cash, 2002) while developing a tolerance for subjective affective experiences. This tolerance is part of developing internal representations of body states and a stable body image (Petrucelli, 2016).

Body functionality

Body functionality is the process of recognizing and appreciating the body's functionality. It serves as a proactive resistance to the passive process of self-objectification that prioritizes appearance through socially constructed concepts of beauty (McKinley & Hyde, 1996). This is not wholly dependent on physical ability; this concept embraces the understanding that all bodies have differing ability statuses. Developing a sense of the internal experience of the body in time and space and the evoked cognitions and emotions has been positively correlated with increased body appreciation, satisfaction, acceptance by others, and intuitive eating behaviors (Homan & Tylka, 2014).

Body image flexibility

Psychological flexibility disrupts the relationship between negative thoughts and subsequent behaviors without evading or discrediting negative thoughts (Tan *et al.*, 2019). Body image flexibility is a compassionate response to aversive body-related thoughts and feelings utilizing mindfulness and acceptance skills rather than engaging in avoidance or escape (Webb *et al.*, 2015). It entails an intentional openness to experiencing perceptions, sensations, feelings, thoughts, and beliefs about the body without trying to change the intensity and frequency (Tylka & Wood-Barcalow, 2015). It requires the capacity to deal with the contextual influences that lead to negative body image and negative experiences and reduce the severity and duration when they arise (Fuller-Tyszkiewicz, 2019). For example, if you experience internal criticism of your body (e.g., having a bad body image day), you would engage in self-care activities such as journaling or calling a friend to demonstrate flexibility. It is the act of purposefully evoking self-kindness and compassion. Body image flexibility positively correlates with lower body dissatisfaction, eating attitudes, food preoccupation, and increased overall psychological flexibility (Sandoz et al., 2013; Tan et al., 2019).

Furthermore, body image flexibility correlates with increased self-compassion, self-esteem, distress tolerance, body appreciation, intuitive eating, lower internalization of appearance ideals, disordered eating, weight concerns, and psychological distress (Webb et al., 2015). It is a buffer between body dissatisfaction and disordered eating (Tylka & Wood-Barcalow, 2015). Body image flexibility can expand our understanding of factors influencing positive body image. It encourages mindful awareness of negative experiences that may emerge in triggering or threatening situations, facilitating body acceptance and commitment to positive cognitive and behavioral changes through self-care and coping (Webb et al., 2015).

Positive rational acceptance and coping

Positive rational acceptance is the engagement in "adaptive mental and behavioral activities, such as positive self-care and rational self-talk, that reflect the acceptance of body image-related threats" (Tylka & Wood-Barcalow, 2015, p.119). Cash et al. (2005) identified adaptive coping responses to body image-related stressors: an adaptive response, a positive rational acceptance and coping response, an acceptance that the distressing event occurred, and addressing the cognitive-emotional reactions through self-care and rational self-talk. Additionally, Cash et al. (2005) identified two maladaptive responses to body image threats: avoidance and appearance fixing. Avoidance attempts to avert or escape the body image threat, and appearance fixing attempts to alter appearance through covering, camouflaging, or correcting the perceived flaw. Utilizing an adaptive approach positively correlates to higher subjective well-being and internal and external emotional regulation and has the potential to minimize the adverse effects of body image threats on well-being and inversely correlates with self-objectification.

Positive and self-accepting body talk

Fat talk is a pervasive and harmful communication style where individuals disparage their appearance as a means of social acceptance. *Fat talk* and shaming focus on weight, size, and shape, prompting body dissatisfaction in the discloser and recipient (Corning *et al.*, 2014). *Fat talk* perpetuates body shame, dissatisfaction, and image difficulties and contributes to eating disorder behaviors. It is insidious and ubiquitous (Petrucelli, 2016). Utilizing self-accepting body statements and conversations positively correlates with body satisfaction, self-esteem, and friendship quality. Inversely those who engage in fat talk show higher rates of body-related cognitive distortions (Corning *et al.*, 2014).

Body acceptance and appearance investment

Body acceptance is expressing love and caring for your body, even though you may not be completely satisfied with all aspects. It supports connection to others and accepting unique physical features. Body acceptance is not vanity or narcissism, and it is linked to the perception that others accept your body (Tylka & Wood-Barcalow, 2015). Augustus-Horvath and Tylka (2011) found that self-perceived body acceptance by others was positively related to body appreciation and functionality. Experiencing acceptance of our body directly (verbal statements) or indirectly (not focusing on the body) with family, friends, intimate partners, and society reduces preoccupation with appearance-related expectations and supports a focus on how the body feels and functions (Avalos & Tylka, 2006). For example, a study of college-aged women in the United States found that "unconditional acceptance from family, friends, and partners was central in the formation and maintenance of their positive body image" (Tylka & Wood-Barcalow, 2015, p.126).

Adaptive appearance investment is engaging in appearance-related self-care, including non-invasive grooming and styling behaviors that enhance positive body image. It is not engaging in destructive or harmful behaviors geared towards changing or altering the body to fit into sociocultural body ideals, basing self-worth on appearance, and fixating on appearance (Tylka & Wood-Barcalow, 2015). Cook-Cottone (2015) states that positive body image neither judges nor ignores the body; instead, positive body image is the engagement in adaptive appearance investment and is viewed as self-care and kindness.

Broad conceptualization of beauty

Representing the spectrum of bodies is vital in helping shape acceptance and a broad definition of beauty. A flexible and inclusive definition of beauty appreciates differences in appearance (unchangeable or modifiable) and styles that understand that beauty reflects inner positivity and confidence (Tylka & Wood-Barcalow, 2015; Webb *et al.*, 2015). Broadly conceptualizing beauty employs body appreciation and self-compassion approaches that counter body surveillance, body-ideal internalization, and body comparison. It celebrates the wide range of differences that make individuals unique. Holding a broad conceptualization of beauty adopts the belief that it is acceptable and preferable that bodies differ from societal ideals. It advocates for body diversity, rejecting body hate or shamed-based dialog or actions by challenging weight stigma and physical and psychological health and well-being barriers. Connected embodiment—the experience of engaging the body in the world—supports physical freedom, mental freedom, and social power, leading to resilience and resistance to body image threats (Tylka & Wood-Barcalow, 2015).

Body appreciation

Body appreciation is the act of accepting one's body regardless of size or imperfections, respecting and attending to the body's needs through health-promoting behaviors, and protecting the body by resisting the internalization of the narrow standards of beauty promoted in media (Avalos *et al.*, 2005). It includes praising the body for its functionality, representation, and uniqueness (Tylka & Wood-Barcalow, 2015). Developing body appreciation requires attunement, understanding and attending to needs, rational and flexible thinking, and a broad conceptualization of beauty to develop acceptance for the body and resist the internalizations of body standards. A positive relationship exists between body appreciation, self-esteem, and appearance evaluation. Furthermore, body appreciation is positively linked to eating according to hunger and satiety cues, sexual arousal and satisfaction, and enjoyment-based physical activity. Body appreciation has an inverse relationship with body preoccupation, dissatisfaction, objectification, shame, disordered eating, social physique anxiety, body image avoidance, body checking, body comparison, internalization of societal appearance ideals, and perfectionism (Webb *et al.*, 2015). Additionally, body appreciation can be fostered independently of body satisfaction, with an understanding that individuals may not be entirely satisfied with their bodies but can appreciate them (Tylka & Wood-Barcalow, 2015).

Body pride and body sanctification

According to Webb *et al.*, "Body pride is a strong, positive, self-conscious emotion towards the body that results from engaging in valued behaviors or presenting with positive characteristics" (2015, p.135). Body pride focuses on valuing the body's functionality and connectivity to others and increasing health-promoting behaviors rather than an alignment with social determinants of beauty and has been aligned to increases in health-promoting behaviors. Body pride may be embedded in racial, ethnic, cultural, and religious identities. Incorporating body appreciation by engaging in prideful moments includes allowing oneself to partake in the customs and traditions of one's culture (Tylka & Wood-Barcalow, 2015).

Mahoney *et al.* (2005) noted that the body holds spiritual significance for some individuals. This perspective may be theistic (body as a manifestation of God) or secular (body as imbued with value and purpose), and Wood-Barcalow *et al.* (2010) found that when people sanctify their bodies, they engage in more mindful self-care to protect and preserve them through health-protective behaviors. Body sanctification positively correlates with body and appearance satisfaction (Jacobson *et al.*, 2013). Depending on the client's identity factors, exploring body pride and sanctification may be relevant in developing body image.

Media literacy

Parental, peer, and media pressures to meet body ideals intensify social comparisons, are internalized, and become the personal standard central to self-worth (Vannucci & Ohannessian, 2018). As noted, comparisons on social media cause more distress and body dissatisfaction than those in-person. To address body dissatisfaction, the media promotes dieting because of the pervasive belief that it is an effective strategy. In fact, dieting behaviors lead to greater dissatisfaction and perpetuate the cycle of dissatisfaction and food restriction, resulting in inaccurate identification of internal stimuli (hunger cues) and a reliance on external cues for self-regulation (calories, weight, size) (Morrissey *et al.*, 2020).

Perceived pressures from media (print and digital) to conform to idealized body standards lead to the internalization of unrealistic body standards, upward comparison, and appearance preoccupation (Ahadzadeh *et al.*, 2022). Social media has a more powerful influence than traditional media because of its highly visual and instantaneous nature, targeted-user advertising, self- and commercial-created content, and the continuous feedback loop (Paxton *et al.*, 2022). Media literacy is the "capacity to critically appraise and evaluate media content, and consume and use media accordingly" (Paxton *et al.*, 2022, p.159). Engaging in critical scrutiny includes 1) identifying who created the content, whom it is targeting, and the purpose and content; 2) identifying the values and points of view of the content with an understanding that they impact attitudes and behaviors; and 3) identifying the extent to which that content is distorted or truthfully represents reality (Paxton *et al.*, 2022). Developing media literacy includes offering opportunities to protest, alter, and communicate alternative messages to disrupt social and cultural messaging to promote body dissatisfaction (Piran *et al.*, 2000). Piran *et al.* found that those who engaged in media literacy demonstrated greater self- and body acceptance, increased self-confidence, and empowerment (2000).

Protective filter

Filtering information to protect the body requires the ability to accept information consistent with positive body image views and beliefs and reject messaging aimed at increasing negative body image (Tylka & Wood-Barcalow, 2015). This filter is a way of engaging in the world to maintain a positive body image even under continuous sociocultural and public health pressures of body ideals and the capitalistic practice of body shaming to sell products. This is not a foolproof process. It requires the development of many of the skills above, including acceptance, a broad conceptualization of beauty, attunement, flexibility, media literacy, and positive self-talk skills. Increasing state self-esteem and self-compassion supports positive state body image, lower drive for thinness, and development of coping skills to alleviate momentary negative body image and reduce disordered eating behaviors. Incorporating movement or exercise for health-enhancing reasons positively influences body image, and the inverse is true when engaging in these activities for appearance or weight-related reasons (Fuller-Tyszkiewicz, 2019). A protective filter requires the development of interpersonal capacities, including regulating affect, maintaining body image stability, positive self-worth, and connections to others (Petrucelli, 2016). Furthermore, modifying interoceptive deficits to develop greater interoceptive awareness is a protective factor and is more effective than focusing on challenging body ideal beliefs (Morrissey *et al.*, 2020).

Utilizing a protective filter leads to increased inner positivity. Inner positivity connects positive body image, positive feelings, and adaptive behaviors. Engagement in regular pleasurable exercise, adaptive stress relief, prevention care (e.g., dental and doctor visits), intuitive eating, body pampering (e.g., manicure, massage), and cultural or community activities support inner positivity. Developing and maintaining a positive body image requires individuals to consciously change and mold their behaviors and environments in growth-enhancing ways, including seeking others with positive body image, rejecting fat and body-related talk, seeking friends and partners with body acceptance mindsets, engaging in self-care, and avoiding potentially harmful body image threats such as appearance-focused social media. Positive body image is malleable and stable, requires maintenance, and protects psychological and physical well-being (Tylka & Wood-Barcalow, 2015).

CONCLUSION

Developing positive body image adopts a non-pathological approach to addressing normative discontent present for many within society. Normative discontent creates significant psychological distress and restricts the ability to live fully in the world. Exploring the components of positive body image to develop a protective filter in therapy can surpass social campaigns of liking or loving the body. Positive body-image development supports a holistic, multidimensional relationship between mind, body, self, and others, leading to physical and mental freedom and social power.

REFERENCES

Ahadzadeh, A.S., Wu, S.L., Ong, F.S., Deng, R., & Lee, K. F. A. (2022). Moderated mediation model of perceived effect of fitspiration images on self: The influence of media literacy and BMI. *International Journal of Environmental Research and Public Health, 19,* 5077. https://doi.org/10.3390/ijerph19095077

Augustus-Horvath, C. L. & Tylka, T. L. (2011). The acceptance model of intuitive eating: A comparison of women in emerging adulthood, early adulthood, and middle adulthood. *Journal of Counseling Psychology, 58,* 110–125. http://dx.doi.org/10.1037/a0022129

Avalos, L. C. & Tylka, T. L. (2006). Exploring a model of intuitive eating with college women. *Journal of Counseling Psychology, 53,* 486–497. https://doi.org/10.1037/0022-0167.53.4.486

Avalos, L. C., Tylka, T. L., & Wood-Barcalow, N. (2005). The Body Appreciation Scale: Development and psychometric evaluation. *Body Image, 2,* 285–297. http://dx.doi.org/10.1016/j.bodyim.2005.06.002

Cash, T. F. (2002). Cognitive-Behavioral Perspectives on Body Image. In T. F. Cash & T. Pruzinsky (eds), *Body Image: A Handbook of Theory, Research, and Clinical Practice* (pp.38–46). Guilford Press.

Cash, T. L., Santos, M. T., & Williams, E. F. (2005). Coping with body-image threats and challenges: Validation of the Body Image Coping Strategies Inventory. *Journal of Psychosomatic Research, 58,* 190–199. http://dx.doi.org/10.1016/j.jpsychores.2004.07.008

Cook-Cottone, C. (2006). The attuned representation model for the primary prevention of eating disorders: An overview for school psychologists. *Psychology in the Schools, 43,* 223–230. http://dx.doi.org/10.1002/pits.20139

Cook-Cottone, C. P. (2015). Incorporating positive body image into the treatment of eating disorders: A model for attunement and mindful self-care. *Body Image, 14,* 158–167. http://dx.doi.org/10.1016/j.bodyim.2015.03.004

Corning, A. F., Bucchianeri, M. M., & Pick, C. M. (2014). Thin or overweight women's fat talk: Which is worse for other women's body satisfaction? *Eating Disorders, 22,* 121–135. http://dx.doi.org/10.1080/10640266.2013.860850

Fardouly, J., Pinkus, R. T., & Vartanian, L. R. (2017). The impact of appearance comparisons made through social media, traditional media, and in person in women's everyday lives. *Body Image, 20,* 31–39. http://dx.doi.org/10.1016/j.bodyim.2016.11.002

Fitzsimmons-Craft, E. E., Bardone-Cone, A. M., Crosby, R. D., Engel, S. G., Wonderlich, S. A., & Bulik, C. M. (2016). Mediators of the relationship between thin-ideal internalization and body dissatisfaction in the natural environment. *Body Image, 18,* 113–122. http://dx.doi.org/10.1016/j.bodyim.2016.06.006

Fredrickson, B. L. & Losada, M. F. (2005). Positive affect and the complex dynamics of human flourishing. *American Psychologist, 60,* 678–686. http://dx.doi.org/10.1037/0003-066X.60.7.678

Fuller-Tyszkiewicz, M. (2019). Body image states in everyday life: Evidence from ecological momentary assessment methodology. *Body Image, 31,* 245–272. https://doi.org/10.1016/j.bodyim.2019.02.010

Homan, K. J. & Tylka, T. L. (2014). Appearance-based exercise motivation moderates the relationship between exercise frequency and positive body image. *Body Image, 11,* 101–108. http://dx.doi.org/10.1016/j.bodyim.2014.01.003

Jacobson, H. L., Hall, E. L., & Anderson, T. L. (2013). Theology and the body: Sanctification and bodily experiences. *Psychology of Religion and Spirituality, 5,* 41–50. http://dx.doi.org/10.1037/a0028042

Jarry, J. L., Dignard, N. A. L., & O'Driscoll, L. M. (2019). Appearance investment: The construct that changed the field of body image. *Body Image, 31,* 221–224. https://doi.org/10.1016/j.bodyim.2019.09.001

Linehan, M. (1993). *Cognitive-Behavioral Treatment of Borderline Personality Disorder.* Guilford Press.

Mahoney, A., Carels, R. A., Pargament, K. I., Wachholtz, A., *et al.* (2005). The sanctification of the body and behavioral health patterns of college students. *International Journal for the Psychology of Religion, 15,* 221–238. http://dx.doi.org/10.1207/s15327582ijpr1503_3

McKinley, N. M. & Hyde, J. S. (1996). The Objectified Body Consciousness Scale: Development and validation. *Psychology of Women Quarterly, 20,* 181–215. http://dx.doi.org/10.1111/j.1471-6402.1996.tb00467.x

Morrissey, R. A., Gondoli, D. M., & Corning, A. F. (2020). Reexamining the restraint pathway as a conditional process among adolescent girls: When does dieting link body dissatisfaction to bulimia? *Development and Psychopathology, 32,* 1031–1043. https://doi.org/10.1017/S0954579419001287

Paxton, S. J., McLean, S. A, & Rodgers, R. F. (2022). "My critical filter buffers your app filter": Social media literacy as a protective factor for body image. *Body Image, 40,* 158–164. https://doi.org/10.1016/j.bodyim.2021.12.009

Petrucelli, J. (2016). Body-states, body image and dissociation: When not-me is "not body." *Clinical Social Work, 44,* 18–26. https://doi.org/10.1007/s10615-015-0539-0

Piran, N., Levine, M. P., & Irvin, L. M. (2000). GO GIRLS! Media literacy, activism, and advocacy project. *Healthy Weight Journal, 14*(6), 89–91.

Sandoz, E. K., Wilson, K. G., Merwin, R. M., & Kellum, K. K. (2013). Assessment of body image flexibility: The Body Image-Acceptance and Action Questionnaire. *Journal of Contextual and Behavioral Science, 2*, 39–48. http://dx.doi.org/10.1016/j.jcbs.2013.03.002

Tan, W., Holt, N., Krug, I., Ling, M., *et al.* (2019). Trait body image flexibility as a predictor of body image states in everyday life of young Australian women. *Body Image, 30*, 212–220. https://doi.org/10.1016/j.bodyim.2019.07.006

Tylka, T. L. (2019). Beyond "truly exceptional": A tribute to Thomas F. Cash, an innovative leader in the body image field. *Body Image, 31*, 191–197. https://doi.org/10.1016/j.bodyim.2019.10.011

Tylka, T. L. & Wood-Barcalow, N. L. (2015). What is and what is not positive body image? Conceptual foundations and construct definition. *Body Image, 14*, 118–129. http://dx.doi.org/10.1016/j.bodyim.2015.04.001

Vannucci, A. & Ohannessian, C. M. (2018). Body image dissatisfaction and anxiety trajectories during adolescence. *Journal of Clinical Child and Adolescent Psychology, 47*(5), 785–795. https://doi.org/10.1080/15374416.2017.1390755

Webb, J. B., Wood-Barcalow, N. L., & Tylka, T. L. (2015). Assessing positive body image: Contemporary approaches and future directions. *Body Image, 14*, 130–145. http://dx.doi.org/10.1016/j.bodyim.2015.03.010

Wood-Barcalow, N. L., Tylka, T. L., & Augustus-Horvath, C. L. (2010). "But I like my body": Positive body image characteristics and a holistic model for young adult women. *Body Image, 7*, 106–116. http://dx.doi.org/10.1016/j.bodyim.2010.01.001

PART 1

BODY IMAGE AND EATING DISORDERS

CHAPTER II

Body Image in Clients with Eating Disorders

An Overview

— TAYLOR MCLANE —

Body image is a crucial dimension in the understanding of the development, maintenance, and treatment of eating disorders. Commonly, body image concerns precipitate and perpetuate eating disorders (Makin, 2000). Totenbier (1995) likened body image to personality as "a multi-layered feature of humanness, not an experience which can be quantified or measured comprehensively" (p.193). Body image is as much a physical experience as it is a psychological one: a collection of unique philosophies, thoughts, interpersonal experiences, and emotions as they filter through biological and external factors that travel beyond weight and size. Because of its enormous complexity, body image cannot be narrowed into a singular dimension of identity as mental health professionals attend to the needs of clients.

To further its comprehension, tripartite models of body image recognize biological, sociological, and psychological domains (Gaete & Fuchs, 2016; Pylvanainen, 2003; Schneider *et al.*, 1990; Totenbier, 1995). Biologically, genetic factors may contribute to one's body shape and weight in addition to co-occurring physical health conditions. Sociologically, surrounding cultural factors, such as body norms, can dictate personal attitudes towards the body. Comorbid conditions, self-perceptions, cognitions, and affectual components contribute to the psychological domain of body image. Identity can become cognitively frozen within a one-dimensional understanding of body image.

An individual's internal sense of self relies on sensations from the external world. The foundations of body identity begin as soon as individuals start to integrate internal and external stimuli as it contributes to self-image. Self-image is "one's view or concept of oneself and is a crucial aspect of an individual's personality that can determine the success of relationships and a sense of general well-being" (American Psychiatric Association, 2022). Body identity informs awareness of self and the physical actions of the body (Rabin, 2003). The alignment of the external body to the internal sense of self can be essential to a cohesive and authentic sense of self.

THE BIOLOGICAL DOMAIN

From a developmental and cognitive level, life begins with bodily stimuli and sensations at the sensorimotor level (Piaget, 1923/1929). Fundamental to developing body identity is the safe exploration and attendance to internal body sensations and stimuli. As early as infancy, humans gain a sense of body boundaries by navigating hunger signals as one of the first lived bodily experiences. The sense of self begins with body sensations, signaling the start of body boundaries and self-image (Schilder, 1950; Schneider *et al.*, 1990). Bodily sensations are fundamental instincts that inform how individuals feel their bodies move through space and interact with the physical world. Body image continues to develop through somatic and emotional experiences.

When the brain is malnourished, the sensitivity required to cognitively attend to internal body cues can dull, including interoceptive responsiveness (Herbert, 2020). The mind and body function to regulate what the body experiences. Starving and purging affect blood flow to the brain and deplete nutrients from other important organ systems. Disordered eating behaviors threaten a state of homeostasis by affecting how the brain interprets and integrates sociological and psychological factors. Alterations in important brain systems can create imbalances in perceptive and cognitive functions. Prolonged failure to attend to physical needs of the body by clients with eating disorders can worsen body image disturbances, distortions, and dissatisfaction.

The neurobiological body

Hunger and thirst are evolutionary bodily sensations, key to daily functioning. Food restriction, bingeing, purging, and excessive exercising can affect reward circuitry and brain structures important to cognitive functioning, motivation, and perceptions (Arnold, 2012; Frank *et al.*, 2019; Herbert, 2020). When these domains are negatively impacted, this can perpetuate a cycle of disordered eating and further patterns of compensatory behaviors. Important brain structures that influence the perceptual, affective, and behavioral domains of body image have likely begun to shift or have been functioning from an altered state by the time individuals seek professional help.

The brain requires a certain number of calories to function properly (Arnold, 2012). Within the insula, the process of interoception monitors the internal state of the body, like feelings of hunger, thirst, body temperature, pain, and disgust (Arnold, 2012). The insula is an important connector between almost all other structures of the brain as it integrates outside somatic information into one's inner world. Interoceptive awareness informs how the mind and body relate and respond to the surrounding environment (Arnold, 2012; Herbert, 2020). Restricting, bingeing, and purging can therefore deplete the brain of nutrients for the mind to practice resiliency and cognitive flexibility as individuals organize personal meanings of body image.

THE SOCIAL DOMAIN

According to the American Psychiatric Association (2013), eating disorders are typically diagnosed by adolescence or early adulthood. Adolescents and young adults are normally transitioning into a peak of biological development, elevated awareness in social settings, emotional fluctuations, and identity formation, which can leave their body image susceptible to distortions or disturbances. Disordered eating behaviors may develop as a means to reconcile personal and social expectations of the body. Perceived pressure for belonging and acceptance at the height of social comparison can motivate compliant behaviors and thought patterns to meet peer ideals of beauty (Verschueren *et al.*, 2018). As individuals mature, body image becomes a visible mode of social relatedness to peers. When the body is rejected by peers, this can feel like a rejection of the self.

Pylvanainen (2003), a psychologist who studied dance/movement therapy, explained that body image develops partly through social interactions. Part of a positive body image requires navigating whether self-perceptions of body image align to how others see the body. The body can become the object of peer scrutiny or acceptance, and the object of risky or impulsive behaviors (Verschueren *et al.*, 2018). Attitudes and thoughts of what the body *should* look like can lead to disordered eating or excessive exercising. Successes or failures may be measured in the ability, or lack thereof, to implement strict eating patterns or weight control behaviors in order to manipulate the body to match sociocultural body ideals.

The body of society and culture

Lived social and cultural experiences impact thoughts and feelings towards one's body. People tend to mirror and internalize the body image ideals of the society they operate in day-to-day life (Franko *et al.*, 2012; Webb *et al.*, 2015). Social body norms affect perceptions of body sizes and what body shapes are attractive, and promote specific body features as highly desirable. When bodies fall outside these standards, the likelihood of developing a poor mind-body connection can increase. In Cook-Cottone's Attuned Representational Model of Self (2015), community and culture are labeled as outer aspects of the self. When the self cannot regulate the needs of the inner self with the body attitudes and norms of external systems, misattunement can occur. A stable sense of self-image may be lost in this process as the body becomes a tangible object for sociocultural acceptance or rejection.

The ability to align body appearance with societal and cultural norms can contribute to feelings of belongingness. It is possible that individuals with multiple cultural identities are notably vulnerable. To be clear, being a member of a minority group does not lead to the development of an eating disorder. However, given its occurrence is not isolated to any one race/ethnicity, religion, gender, sexuality, or age, it is important to consider how the intersectionality of a person alters personal body attitudes and impacts the presentation of symptoms from diagnosis and through treatment. Those with cross-cultural identities likely face unique challenges related to body weight and shape as they reconcile body ideals of different cultures.

Body image has a fluid quality in the way the ideals spread from one audience to another. Perceptions and attitudes towards food and bodies oscillate as individuals strive to attain the beauty standards dictated by the dominant culture and within their immediate surroundings. Through qualitative research studies, Davids and Green (2011) found that some individuals developed disordered eating to cope with the distress of marginalization or discrimination. Discriminatory stress within marginalized groups can influence the report of eating disorders and the emergence of symptoms, and hinder the treatment process. Symptoms could blunt the pain and fear of rejection in the face of social groups that may devalue and discriminate against non-normative bodies.

The body of social media

Webb *et al.* (2015) cited the role of social media cross-culturally in the marketing of body ideals, furthering attitudes about what body sizes, parts, and shapes are desirable. Social media poses a long-standing topic of interest in the role of body image in persons with eating disorders. The media does not hesitate to spotlight and praise bodies and body parts that reflect the beauty ideals of the current culture. Certain body shapes and attributes become trendy and praised across various social media platforms. Moreover, those bodies are usually of a particular skin tone, age, fit into specific sizes of clothing, or maintain curves "in all the right places" that signals features of a person are acceptable, but perhaps not the person in totality.

Sociocultural systems declare that certain bodies are acceptable (Taylor, 2018), leaving bodies of multiple cultural identities without visibility. The harm of selective body representation in the media further isolates marginalized bodies and reinforces damaging attitudes pointed at bodies outside the majority culture. This may be further compounded by unfiltered, body critical remarks left in comment sections and direct messages. In a study of Twitter (now known as X) profiles, Arseniev-Koehler *et al.* (2016) found pro-eating disorder content in online forums and hashtags may now overlap *fitsporation (fit inspiration)* posts. This may further blur the lines of fitness-related content and pro-eating disorder content. There are certainly benefits to online communities, but it is important that clinicians remain sensitive to the ways social media disseminates ideas of what bodies are labeled as acceptable or incite public criticism, and what bodies receive visibility versus bodies that lack representation. Greater emotional distress could result as individuals navigate media input and integrate this into individual meanings of body image.

THE PSYCHOLOGICAL DOMAIN

Historically, the term body image originated as a neuropsychological concept (Schneider *et al.*, 1990). The body is a vessel, holding attitudes and emotions towards the self. Disordered eating affects the brain at neurological levels, influencing perceptual, affectual, and behavioral domains of body image. Clients may over-identify with their disorder, relying heavily on maladaptive eating behaviors to draw focus from unresolved, neglected, or negative body experiences (Verschueren *et al.*, 2018). Psychological distress is expressed directly through the physical body. When challenging feelings are perceived as overwhelming or threatening to the self, disordered eating and compensatory behaviors can draw attention away from those.

Progressively ignoring body cues can dull sensitivity and further deteriorate the mind-body relationship. Gaete and Fuchs (2016) posited that managing the body through restrictive eating, purging, and bingeing can redirect the identity into the most visible component of the self instead of working through complex, potentially threatening emotions. Cook-Cottone (2015) identified the inner aspects of the self in physiological, feeling, and thinking domains. Failed integration interaction of these domains can result in a misalignment within their authentic self. How individuals perceive the appearance of their body and interpret sensory experiences informs the mental structure of body image.

The body of emotional coping

Ignoring the agony or discomfort from hunger and thirst signals can divert attention away from processing complex, painful emotions. Emotions such as sadness, anger, and emptiness may be interpreted as perilous to the self, and disordered eating serves as immediate relief. In case examples Channa *et al.* (2019) and Churruca *et al.* (2020), researchers noticed that food became a means to self-soothe as a form of protection from perceived emotional threats. Body image becomes dangerously intertwined with a portion of a person's self-worth. Unsurprisingly, their self-esteem lowers as their perceptions of body image fall.

In cases of co-occurring trauma, the person can subconsciously detach their mind from the body, and the body becomes the object to withstand pain (Gaete & Fuchs, 2016; Martin, 2019). Traumatic experiences can turn the body into an enemy, displacing negative body emotions and memories. Leonidas and Santos (2017) explained that uncomfortable feelings can be swallowed and ejected or avoided entirely. A lack of control over the body during trauma can heighten feelings of shame after the event, prompting the person to feel that the body is unsafe. Dissociation in various forms of trauma and in disordered eating turns the overwhelming into something less overwhelming (Martin, 2019).

The body of controllable identity

Personal accounts of individuals with eating disorders demonstrate a powerful dynamic of control and no control. Disordered eating and compensatory behaviors can reduce big feelings and concentrate them in forms that are tangible and manageable. Body boundaries inform where the self ends and the other begins. For those with eating disorders, body and emotional boundaries may be at an elevated risk of being violated by self and others, leaving body identity highly vulnerable. Social relationships, cultural standards of beauty, strained family relationships, bullying, and trauma can induce feelings of little to no control. Monitoring caloric intake or engaging in weight-control behaviors can give the impression that the person has reinstated control over their body.

Through longitudinal studies, Conti (2018) and Grilo *et al.* (2019a) noticed that clients with anorexia nervosa felt a sense of competence and autonomy when they were able to strictly adhere to eating rules and extreme exercise regimens. Concurrently, Churruca *et al.* (2020) recorded a similar feeling, where the client described her commitment to grueling bingeing and purging behaviors as exemplification of mental fortitude and elicited a sense of pride, asking, "Without my body, who am I?" (Churruca *et al.*, 2020, p.292). During binge eating episodes, there can be temporary relief from hyperarousal, and binge eating can activate reward systems in times of stress or depression (Franko *et al.*, 2012; Verschueren *et al.*, 2018). Somatic body reactions when the limbic system is activated can render a feeling of helplessness, but the knowledge that food can soothe can revitalize an impression of control or comfort.

The body of shame and guilt

Moments of dissociation or a loss of control are commonly reported during binge eating episodes and moderated feelings of guilt and shame (American Psychiatric Association, 2013; Grilo *et al.*, 2019b; Vanderlinden & Palmisano, 2018). Body image is used against its owner to induce feelings of shame and guilt by the self and others. Any of these factors could degrade an individual's resiliency to uphold stability of the self in the face of shame-related experiences, such as perfectionism, bullying, and trauma. The American Psychiatric Association (2013) lists that individuals may attempt to conceal their disordered eating. Cook-Cottone (2015) attributed this to a concern to appear functional. This could underlie a people-pleasing nature and general feelings of guilt that often accompany eating disorders.

Body and emotional boundaries can decrease as the body is used as an object to negotiate the needs of other people, leading to further disembodiment. The body morphs into an object of disdain as it fails to fit into predetermined body image expectations. Vanderlinden and Palmisano (2018) proposed that exposure to negative comments pertaining to shape, weight, and eating could be considered risk factors in the development of eating disorders. In longitudinal studies by Dahlenburg *et al.* (2019) and Dawson and Thornberry (2018), individuals used disordered eating behaviors to reconcile the high expectations of themselves, peers, and family, leading to rigid thinking and perceived failures to meet standards, and to greater feelings of shame.

THE ROLE OF BODY IMAGE IN ANOREXIA NERVOSA

The *Diagnostic and Statistical Manual of Mental Disorders* (DSM-5) recognizes two subtypes of anorexia nervosa: restriction type, indicative of a person who loses weight primarily through self-starvation, excessive exercising, and dieting, and bingeing/purging type, in which the person employs intermittent patterns of bingeing and/or purging (Guarda, 2021). Psychologically, distorted body image perceptions lead to frequent weighing, measuring, and over-evaluation. The physical symptoms may indicate a strong desire for control over the environment, restrictive emotional control, and/or rigid thinking that foster body image distortions. Individuals with anorexia nervosa show a greater preoccupation with a fear of gaining weight and body image distortions (Grilo *et al.*, 2019a). Rituals surrounding food and eating commonly appear and it is not unusual for obsessive-compulsive features and depressive symptoms to emerge.

Undernourishment can magnify negative psychosocial functioning, and the individual's self-worth and self-esteem become dependent on controlling the physical body. Arnold (2012) presented a case in which

Rachel, a British woman diagnosed with anorexia nervosa, used self-starvation and excessive exercise to calm her anxieties. Her weight continued to drop until it was dangerously low. Her perceived need for emotional control overruled the consequences of severe malnutrition. Gaete and Fuchs (2016) explained that there is a difference between physical bodily sensations and emotional bodily sensations. Both are crucial to how the body reacts to worldly experiences and how they build body image, but they can become muddled.

Perfectionism

Perfectionism appears frequently as a psychological trait in cases of anorexia nervosa. However, perfectionism in itself is not necessarily a risk factor "as long as the acceptance of imperfection is part of the equation" (Hinz, 2006, p.125). Setting high expectations and a desire to surpass limitations can be functional, even motivational. However, socially prescribed perfectionism, other-oriented perfectionism, and self-oriented perfectionism can result in maladaptive body schemas (Dahlenburg *et al.*, 2019; Dawson & Thornberry, 2018). Perfectionistic thinking and behaviors can become performance-related coping mechanisms to quell negative emotions related to the body. To the person with anorexia nervosa, perfectionism represents a powerful cognitive component of control (Herbert, 2020).

Control over the body to be perfect delineates a desire for control over the self (Arnold, 2012). Such unrelenting standards can disturb a stable sense of identity (Leonidas & Santos, 2017). Self-esteem in those with anorexia nervosa can become dependent on the commitment devoted to the strict internal rules over the body. Control over the body and restricting bodily emotions can feel like self-efficacy. In a series of interviews, Conti (2018) documented former patients deemed recovered, who felt successful by adhering to restrictive eating, purging, and compulsive exercising routines. Perfectionism acted as a key source of identity.

Perfectionism shifts into a personal narrative, signifying a core belief in cases of anorexia nervosa. Even following recovery, maladaptive perfectionism and bodily shame can persist (Boone *et al.*, 2013). Treatment classifies symptoms as traits that need to be viewed as bad, challenging the self-perceptions that have previously guided how individuals once centered themselves. Attempts to address the perfect body image of a person with anorexia nervosa can feel like cruelly stripping away identity, and injecting a greater separation of the self from the body. Vende *et al.* (2016) explained that achieving the perfect body can function as an existential project, providing direction and life meaning.

THE ROLE OF BODY IMAGE IN BULIMIA NERVOSA

Recurrent episodes of binge eating followed by compensatory behaviors to prevent weight gain are the essential diagnostic criteria of bulimia nervosa (American Psychiatric Association, 2013). Compensatory behaviors include self-induced vomiting, misuse of laxatives, diuretics, fasting, or excessive physical activity. In some cases, individuals reported dissociative experiences during and after binge eating episodes (Grilo *et al.*, 2019a). Bingeing and purging may arbitrate the disdain for the physical body. Studies discovered higher levels of body dissatisfaction and body image preoccupation in clients with bulimia nervosa (Grilo *et al.*, 2019a; Grilo *et al.*, 2019b).

Individuals with bulimia nervosa may address negative self-devaluation and affectivity preceding and following binge episodes with compensatory behaviors. These persons may feel overwhelmed by emotional body experiences (Gaete & Fuchs, 2016). Purging behaviors may serve as a physical ejection of the overwhelming feelings. Compensatory behaviors can reinvigorate a sense of control by manipulating the body. The body is the vessel where the input and output of physical conditions, mental and emotional states live. Ideas of self-worth fluctuate as body image distortions and disturbances surface. The physical body becomes a collateral casualty of inner or unresolved conflict related to unstable body schema and self-image.

Interpersonal stressors

Negative affectivity from interpersonal stressors, and over-evaluation of body weight and shape, normally precede episodes of bingeing and purging. Individuals with bulimia nervosa usually keep their eating behaviors secret from peers and family, out of embarrassment and shame associated with bingeing and purging. Early negative experiences, such as abusive environments or trauma, can be hard to process. Bingeing and purging become a way to manage terrifying body memories and emotions tied to those events (Boone *et al.*, 2013). In abusive or traumatic experiences, the body may not be viewed as belonging to that person. Ticen (1987) described the process of bingeing and purging to purify the body following trauma. Restriction and making the body small can also signal a means to find safety and control within the body. Cleansing and purification of the body may be attempts to emotionally regulate unresolved feelings from devastating life events.

Strained family dynamics are often cited as negative interpersonal stressor related to body image in cases of bulimia nervosa (Churruca et al., 2020; Leonidas & Santos, 2017). Allen et al. (2015) specified that family and primary caregivers transmit cultural ideals, including weight shape comments or concerns. Internalizing such comments can moderate bingeing and purging behaviors. Leonidas and Santos (2017) and Churruca et al. (2020) found that bullying within the family system increased body image concerns and weight stigma. Cycles of compensatory behaviors may offset feelings of shame and guilt related to self and compensate for hard-to-manage feelings from social relationships.

THE ROLE OF BODY IMAGE IN BINGE EATING DISORDER

Some individuals describe their episodes as uncontrollable eating: a total abandonment of efforts to refrain or stop themselves from eating (American Psychiatric Association, 2013). Individuals tend to ignore body cues until feeling physically ill or uncomfortable, or eat in the absence of hunger (American Psychiatric Association, 2013; Buchholz, 2017; Cook-Cottone, 2015). A self-reported dissociative state during episodes is prevalent. Understanding how the body is sensed in binge eating disorder remains an important contextual domain. Individuals with binge eating disorder tend to ignore fullness cues and report a loss of control during episodes (American Psychiatric Association, 2013). In a collaborative study of semi-structured interviews, Grilo et al. (2019b) found that individuals showed concerns for body dissatisfaction, over-valuation, preoccupation with weight and shape, and a fear of weight gain.

Depression and anxiety are among the most common co-occurring mental conditions in binge eating disorders (American Psychiatric Association, 2013; Grilo et al., 2019b). Negative affect is a key feature in the maintenance of symptoms (American Psychiatric Association, 2013; Duarte & Pinto-Gouveia, 2017). Binge eating could act as an attempt to avoid emotions that can threaten individual sense of self (Duarte et al., 2017). Intense feelings of sadness, emptiness, and anger can be temporarily forgotten during the dissociative qualities of bingeing episodes. Food may replace internal self-soothing methods as an external method of comfort (Channa *et al.*, 2019; Churruca *et al.*, 2020). A cycle ensues, as the immediate gratification of self-soothing through binge eating prolongs difficult feelings or thoughts, suggesting an ongoing inner conflict.

Weight stigma

Weight-stigmatizing, sociocultural attitudes can increase feelings of guilt, embarrassment, and low self-esteem in individuals with binge eating disorder. Pylvanainen (2003) asserted body image is used to undermine personal value and worth. Terms such as obese and overweight carry as much shame as the word fat (Saguy & Ward, 2011). Weight stigma can compound vulnerability, risk factors, and comorbid mental conditions. Internalization of prejudice or discrimination against being overweight or obese can increase body shame (Brownstone *et al.*, 2021; Grilo *et al.*, 2019b). People are inclined to view body weight and shape as manifestations of physical health, giving zero credence to the biological, sociological, and psychological domains of body image. Yet there is no one universal standard of health for everybody, and "bodies are diverse in size, race, ethnicity, sexual orientation, gender, physical ability and mental health" (Taylor, 2018, p.22).

Meanwhile, size privilege grants safety from public criticism. Harsh judgments that overweight individuals should avoid eating fast food or sweets incite self and peer scrutiny (Brownstone *et al.*, 2021). The public is quick to make assumptions about the appearance of those with binge eating disorder, with little consideration of an individual's intersectionality. Rumination over negative comments and weight discrimination can induce feelings of embarrassment for the physical body (Brownstone *et al.*, 2021). The resulting weight gain from binge eating is usually associated with laziness, denoting that the individual is culpable for their eating pathology (Doley *et al.*, 2017). Weight stigmatizing and sociocultural attitudes can increase feelings of guilt, embarrassment, and low self-esteem, furthering symptoms and degrading the mind-body connection.

ART THERAPY IN THE TREATMENT OF BODY IMAGE IN CLIENTS WITH EATING DISORDERS

Body-oriented interventions in art therapy can transform body image and experiences into externalized representations. Participants can learn to convey their emotions through creative processes, surpassing restrictions of the spoken word. Given that weight stabilization techniques and other medical treatments can increase psychological and physical distress (Misluk-Gervase, 2021), art therapy can redirect the psychological pain of clients with eating disorders into creative release and offer a reprieve from stress during recovery. Individuals with eating disorders work through a body image and symptoms that once gave them a sense of identity, control, or purpose, and confront potentially scary changes to their bodies in treatment. The creative environment serves a less threatening arena to confront the disembodied self, deconstruct the layers of personal body image, and embody the self wholly.

Art therapies can bring the bodily experiences of those with eating disorders into the three-dimensional realm in a way that can be disarming. Hinz (2006) and Misluk-Gervase (2021) examined somatic experiences of the body and introduced interventions that allowed for sensory exploration, decreased body discomfort, and increased their tolerance for stress. Cognitive behavioral methods confronted body image distortions and self-perceptions by documenting them externally through art (Hinz, 2006). Directives can address conceptual, sociocultural influences on body image and present them in external forms. Client examples of Hinz (2006) and Misluk-Gervase (2021) displayed how art interventions can confront perfectionistic cognitions and increase self-soothing.

Art therapies can connect somatic experiences of the body and provide safe, reflective distance to address body image disturbances and explore the feelings underneath symptoms. Control within the artmaking process could diminish the perceived need for control over body identity, thus reducing behaviors. Art therapy can provide a safe medium to explore body boundaries and increase emotional expression, teaching body presence through techniques such as guided imagery, mindfulness-based art therapy, and incorporating somatic experiences in directives. Increasing presence within the body during times of emotional vulnerability may help clients with eating disorders who are prone to interpret their feelings as threats, and strengthen the mind-body connection. The treatment of body image in art therapy in eating disorders can build resiliency and esteem as individuals integrate all domains of body image.

CONCLUSION

The research indicates that body image contains biological and sociocultural influences with intricate, personal subtleties in the intrapersonal and interpersonal domains. People constantly navigate internal and external experiences through the body. Body image is a collection of biological, mental, and emotional experiences that transforms among different environments and groups of people. It demonstrates the powerful link of the mind-body connection that organizes layers of the self. Taylor (2018) clarified that investing in one's body identity is not antithetical to self-love, but helps to question and increase awareness of political and societal systems that tie a person's worth to the external self.

Art therapy interventions can explore the layers of body image, inclusive of body sensations, boundaries, and disturbances in tangible mediums. Participants are free to explore body boundaries through creative means rather than through disordered eating and compensatory behaviors. Body image is one facet of identity but seeps into other realms of the self, which are prominent in cases of eating disorders. Embodiment in art therapy treatment relates to self-image, self-perception, and self-concept: conceptions that likely affect a good portion of the population. Art therapy interventions can give safe, reflective distance to process emotions once perceived as threatening to the bodily self. Clients with eating disorders can connect to their authentic selves, enhancing embodiment, and reducing symptoms.

REFERENCES

Allen, K. L., Byrne, S. M., & Crosby, R. D. (2015). Distinguishing between risk factors for bulimia nervosa, binge eating disorder, and purging disorder. *Journal of Youth and Adolescence,* 44(8), 1580–1591. https://doi.org/10.1007/s10964-014-0186-8

American Psychiatric Association (2013). *Diagnostic and Statistical Manual of Mental Disorders* (5th ed.). https://doi.org/10.1176/appi.books.9780890425596

American Psychiatric Association (2022). *Self-image.* https://dictionary.apa.org/self-image

Arnold, C. (2012). *Decoding Anorexia: How Breakthroughs in Science Offer Hope for Eating Disorders.* Routledge.

Arseniev-Koehler, A., Lee, H., McCormick, T., & Moreno, M. A. (2016). #proana: Pro-eating disorder socialization on Twitter. *Journal of Adolescent Health,* 58(6), 659–664. https://doi.org/10.1016/j.jadohealth.2016.02.012

Boone, L., Braet, C., Vandereycken, W., & Claes, L. (2013). Are maladaptive schema domains and perfectionism related to body image concerns in eating disorder patients?: Perfectionism, schemas, and eating disorders. *European Eating Disorders Review, 21*(1), 45–51. https://doi.org/10.1002/erv.2175

Brownstone, L. M., Kelly, D. A., Ko, S.-J. "Stella," Jasper, M. L., *et al.* (2021). Dismantling weight stigma: A group intervention in a partial hospitalization and intensive outpatient eating disorder treatment program. *Psychotherapy, 58*(2), 282–287. https://doi.org/10.1037/pst0000358

Buchholz, L. J., King, P. R., & Wray, L. O. (2017). Identification and management of eating disorders in integrated primary care: Recommendations for psychologists in integrated care settings. *Journal of Clinical Psychology in Medical Settings, 24*(2), 163–177. https://doi.org/10.1007/s10880-017-9497-8

Channa, S., Lavis, A., Connor, C., Palmer, C., Leung, N., & Birchwood, M. (2019). Overlaps and disjunctures: A cultural case study of a British Indian young woman's experiences of bulimia nervosa. *Culture, Medicine, and Psychiatry, 43*(3), 361–386. https://doi.org/10.1007/s11013-019-09625-w

Churruca, K., Ussher, J. M., Perz, J., & Rapport, F. (2020). "It's always about the eating disorder": Finding the person through recovery-oriented practice for bulimia. *Culture, Medicine, and Psychiatry, 44*(2), 286–303. https://doi.org/10.1007/s11013-019-09654-5

Conti, J. E. (2018). Recovering identity from anorexia nervosa: Women's constructions of their experiences of recovery from anorexia nervosa over 10 years. *Journal of Constructivist Psychology, 31*(1), 72–94. https://doi.org/10.1080/10720537.2016.1251366

Cook-Cottone, C. P. (2015). Incorporating positive body image into the treatment of eating disorders: A model for attunement and mindful self-care. *Body Image, 14*, 158–167. https://doi.org/10.1016/j.bodyim.2015.03.004

Dahlenburg, S. C., Gleaves, D. H., & Hutchinson, A. D. (2019). Anorexia nervosa and perfectionism: A meta-analysis. *International Journal of Eating Disorders, 52*(3), 219–229. https://doi.org/10.1002/eat.23009

Davids, C. M. & Green, M. A. (2011). A preliminary investigation of body dissatisfaction and eating disorder symptomatology with bisexual individuals. *Sex Roles, 65*(7–8), 533–547. https://doi.org/10.1007/s11199-011-9963-y

Dawson, N. & Thornberry, T. (2018). The perfect body: A potential pathway of anorexic symptom development in women. *Psi Chi Journal of Psychological Research, 23*(1), 28–39. https://doi.org/10.24839/2325-7342.JN23.1.28

Doley, J. R., Hart, L. M., Stukas, A. A., Petrovic, K., Bouguettaya, A., & Paxton, S. J. (2017). Interventions to reduce the stigma of eating disorders: A systematic review and metaanalysis. *International Journal of Eating Disorders, 50*(3), 210–230. https://doi.org/10.1002/eat.22691

Duarte, C. & Pinto-Gouveia, J. (2017). Self-defining memories of body image shame and binge eating in men and women: Body image shame and self-criticism in adulthood as mediating mechanisms. *Sex Roles, 77*(5–6), 338–351. https://doi.org/10.1007/s11199-016-0728-5

Duarte, C., Pinto-Gouveia, J., & Ferreira, C. (2017). Ashamed and fused with body image and eating: Binge eating as an avoidance strategy. *Clinical Psychology & Psychotherapy, 24*(1), 195–202. https://doi.org/10.1002/cpp.1996

Frank, G. K., Shott, M. E., & DeGuzman, M. C. (2019). The neurobiology of eating disorders. *Child and Adolescent Psychiatry Clinics of North America, 28*(4), 629–640. https://doi.org/10.1016/j.chc.2019.05.007

Franko, D. L., Thompson-Brenner, H., Thompson, D. R., Boisseau, C. L., *et al.* (2012). Racial/ethnic differences in adults in randomized clinical trials of binge eating disorder. *Journal of Consulting and Clinical Psychology, 80*(2), 186–195. https://doi.org/10.1037/a0026700

Gaete, M. I. & Fuchs, T. (2016). From body image to emotional bodily experience in eating disorders. *Journal of Phenomenological Psychology, 47*(1), 17–40. https://doi.org/10.1163/15691624-12341303

Grilo, C. M., Crosby, R. D., & Machado, P. P. P. (2019a). Examining the distinctiveness of body image concerns in patients with anorexia nervosa and bulimia nervosa. *International Journal of Eating Disorders, 52*(11), 1229–1236. https://doi.org/10.1002/eat.23161

Grilo, C. M., Ivezaj, V., Lydecker, J. A., & White, M. A. (2019b). Toward an understanding of the distinctiveness of body-image constructs in persons categorized with overweight/obesity, bulimia nervosa, and binge-eating disorder. *Journal of Psychosomatic Research, 126*, 109757. https://doi.org/10.1016/j.jpsychores.2019.109757

Guarda, M. (2021). *What are eating disorders?* American Psychiatric Association. www.psychiatry.org/patients-families/eating-disorders/what-are-eating-disorders

Herbert, B. M. (2020). Interoception and its role for eating, obesity and eating disorders: Empirical findings and conceptual conclusions. *European Journal of Health Psychology, 27*(4), 188–205. https://doi.org/10.1027/2512-8442/a000062

Hinz, L. D. (2006). *Drawing from Within Using Art to Treat Eating Disorders*. Jessica Kingsley Publishers.

Leonidas, C. & Santos, M. A. (2017). Emotional meanings assigned to eating disorders: Narratives of women with anorexia and bulimia nervosa. *Universitas Psychologica, 16*(4), 1. https://doi.org/10.11144/Javeriana.upsy16-4.emae

Makin, S. (2000). *More than Just a Meal: The Art of Eating Disorders*. Jessica Kingsley Publishers.

Martin, K. M. (2019). Structural Dissociation in the Treatment of Trauma and Eating Disorders. In A. Seubert & P. Virdi (eds), *Trauma-Informed Approaches to Eating Disorders* (pp.231–234). Springer Publishing.

Misluk-Gervase, E. (2021). Art therapy and the malnourished brain: The development of the nourishment framework. *Art Therapy, 38*(2), 87–97. https://doi.org/10.1080/07421656.2020.173959

Piaget, J. (1923/1929). *The Child's Conception of the World*. Kegan Paul, Trench & Trubner.

Pylvanainen, P. (2003). Body image: A tripartite model for use in dance/movement therapy. *American Journal of Dance Therapy, 25*(1), 39–55. https://doi.org/10.1023/A:1025517232383

Rabin, M. (2003). *Art Therapy and Eating Disorders: The Self as Significant Form*. Colombia University.

Saguy, A.C. & Ward, A. (2011). Coming out as fat: Rethinking stigma. *Social Psychology Quarterly, 74*(1), 53–75. https://doi.org/10.1177/0190272511398190

Schilder, P. (1950). *The Image and Appearance of the Human Body*. International Universities Press.

Schneider, S., Ostroff, S., & Legow, N. (1990). Enhancement of body-image: A structured art therapy group with adolescents. *Art Therapy, 7*(3), 134–138. https://doi.org/10.1080/07421656.1990.10758908

Taylor, S. R. (2018). *The Body Is Not an Apology: The Power of Radical Self-Love*. Berrett-Koehler.

Ticen, S. (1987). Feed me ... cleanse me ... sexual trauma projected in the art of bulimics. *Art Therapy, 7*(1), 17–21. https://doi.org/10.1080/07421656.1990.10758885

Totenbier, S. L. (1995). A New Way of Working with Body Image in Therapy, Incorporating Dance/Movement Therapy Methodology. In D. Dokter (ed.), *Art Therapies and Clients with Eating Disorders Fragile Board* (pp.139–207). Jessica Kingsley Publishers.

Vanderlinden, J. & Palmisano, G. (2018). Trauma and Eating Disorders: The Stat of the Art. In Seubert, A. & Virdi, P. (eds). *Trauma-Informed Approaches to Eating Disorders* (pp.15–32). Springer Publishing Company.

Vende, K., Orinska, S., Majore-Dusele, I., & Upmale, A. (2016). Dance and Movement Therapy for Patients with Eating Disorders: Model of Expressive Therapies Continuum. In A. Heiderscheit (ed.), *Creative Arts Therapies and Clients with Eating Disorders* (pp.241–262). Jessica Kingsley Publishers.

Verschueren, M., Claes, L., Bogaerts, A., Palmeroni, N., *et al.* (2018). Eating disorder symptomology and identity formation in adolescence: A crosslagged longitudinal approach. *Frontiers in Psychology, 9*, 816. https://doi.org/10.3389/fpsyg.2018.00816

Webb, J. B., Wood-Barclow, N. L., & Tylka, T. L. (2015). Assessing positive body image: Contemporary approaches and future directions. *Body Image, 14*, 130–145. https://doi.org/10.1016/j.bodyim.2015.03.010

CHAPTER III

Neuroscience-Informed Art Therapy for Clients with Eating Disorders

—— EILEEN MISLUK-GERVASE ——

Body image disturbance, a diagnostic criterion in anorexia nervosa (AN) and a clinical concern in bulimia nervosa (BN), binge eating disorder (BED), and otherwise specified feeding and eating disorder (OSFED) (American Psychiatric Association, 2013), causes significant psychological distress long after the behavioral aspects are treated. After more than a decade of specializing in eating disorder work, I find that body image disturbance is the most challenging aspect because of the many internal and external factors that can solicit a relapse. It is anticipated in eating disorder treatment that once food's behavioral aspects are addressed, body image disturbance increases, including body-checking behaviors, self-objectification, body comparison, intrusive thoughts, and compulsory urges. Early in treatment, addressing body image concerns as they pertain to the body's appearance is a primary concern for clients, although given the impacts of the eating disorder on the brain and body, time is needed before homeostasis can be restored, so focusing early treatment on meal compliance, increasing cognitive flexibility, and developing distress tolerance skills is most important. The psychological distress around weight restoration, weight maintenance, and mind-body connectedness negatively impacts the individual long after their behavioral aspects around food have subsided. Body image issues remain a constant impacting potential for relapse.

Eating disorders often begin during adolescence, when underlying traits are acted on and supported by hormonal, developmental, and environmental pressures. The disorder is sustained by intrinsic and environmental states that are hardwired and difficult to change. As a normal part of brain development, adolescents experience neural imbalances leading to sensitivity to perceived threats and immature cognitive control. Adolescents have a limited capacity to regulate emotions, and experience negative self-evaluations, cognitive vulnerabilities and biases, and safety behaviors (Vannucci & Ohannessian, 2018). Treatment must address state-dependent factors for adolescents and adults and then work on alternate coping mechanisms to minimize long-term risks of the individual factors that led to and perpetuated the illness. Recovery does not mean *fixed*. Due to the strong genetic, neurological, and metabolic underpinnings of the disorder, recovery focuses on addressing the traits that are reacting to the underlying states. In more simplistic terms, genetics loads the gun, and the environment pulls the trigger.

Traits of individuals with eating disorders include higher negative body image experiences, higher body dissatisfaction, intrusive thoughts, frequent body checking (e.g., pinching, mirror checking), weight monitoring, appearance comparison, guilt and shame associated with eating, bingeing and restricted food patterns, and compensatory exercise. Body checking increases negative emotions, leading to negative affect and rumination over food and weight (Fuller-Tyszkiewicz, 2019). The trust between mind and body has been severed in individuals with eating disorders due to behavioral patterns of avoiding psychological and physiological cues limiting distress tolerance. Conversely, body responsiveness has shown an increase in body awareness and satisfaction and a decrease in self-objectification.

THE NEUROSCIENCE OF BODY IMAGE
The role of the brain in body image development

The neuroscience research on body image is still in its infancy, and further advances in the field will enhance our understanding of the complex interactions of the brain. The following information serves as an overview of the brain systems—with a focus on the insula—involved in body image development. The insula integrates and evaluates interoceptive (taste, pains, touch, and visceral sensations) and exteroceptive sensory stimuli (sight, smell, hearing, touch, and taste) to anticipate and process sensations, maintain homeostasis, and guide behaviors (Avery *et al.*, 2017; Bischoff-Grethe *et al.*, 2018; Koeppel *et al.*, 2020; Simmons *et al.*, 2013; Wierenga *et al.*, 2020). Furthermore, due to its connectivity with the anterior cingulate cortex, amygdala, nucleus accumbens, thalamus, and the ventral tegmental area, it helps form the Salience Network, aiding in affective and sensory processing, reward, and emotional responses (Bischoff-Grethe *et al.*, 2018; Esposito *et al.*, 2018; Koeppel *et al.*, 2020). The insula supports social-emotional and sensorimotor information processing—the mechanism for integrating interoceptive stimuli and emotional responses that facilitate an action or decision (Bischoff-Grethe *et al.*, 2018; Wierenga *et al.*, 2020). The insula is activated in sympathetic and parasympathetic responses to interoceptive information focused on energy acquisition and enrichment (Simmons *et al.*, 2013).

The insula plays a significant role in our ability to nourish our bodies. It is the hub for afferent gustatory and interoceptive signals from the intestinal tract, including integrating orosensory (oral senses) information used to regulate the detection of and behavioral responses to nutrients based on interceptive signals (Avery *et al.*, 2017). To demonstrate the complex system of nourishment in the brain, for example, just viewing food activates the bilateral anterior insula along with the orbitofrontal cortex, dorsolateral prefrontal cortex, caudate, cuneus, fusiform gyrus, amygdala, ventral striatum, and the thalamus (Simmons *et al.*, 2013). Additionally, the left insula responds to gustatory sensations. In contrast, the right mid-insula responds to taste (Simmons *et al.*, 2013), and the mid-insula integrates visual, auditory, and vestibular feedback (Avery *et al.*, 2017). Also, the rostral insula maintains stable conceptual representations of food categories, while the mid insula allows for conceptual flexibility, depending on body states (Simmons *et al.*, 2013).

In addition to the insula, numerous areas of the brain interact in developing body image by receiving, interpreting, and communicating internal and external stimuli. For example, Esposito *et al.* (2018) identified the brain areas implicated in body image and the functions they perform. The parietal cortex integrates proprioceptive (ability to sense movement, action, and location) and visual information of the body to construct body image. It is suggested that the precuneus integrates emotional, physical, and visual inputs into a view of self, supports self-referential processes, and increases self-focus, rumination, and cognitive control. The prefrontal cortex (PFC) integrates information about food (odor, flavor, texture) and updates learning to promote or inhibit food-seeking behaviors such as feeding motivation and foraging (Reyes-Haro, 2022). The medial prefrontal cortex (MPFC) supports self-referential mental processes, monitors psychological states, and is the area of convergence for internal (bodily sensations, proprioceptive) and external (visual, auditory) stimuli to integrate and process body image. The amygdala mediates visceromotor aspects connected to emotions, supports the convergence of external and internal stimuli, and serves as a pre-conscious process that becomes conscious through modulations of other brain regions (Press *et al.*, 2022). The co-activation of the anterior cingulate cortex (ACC) and the insula is essential in establishing a sense of self. The brain network between the thalamus and the insula supports the balance of body sensations between real and perceived body states and integrates visuospatial and homeostatic signals. The hypothalamus integrates somatosensory signals and adaptive responses involved in the homeostatic regulation of eating.

In addition to these individual neurological processes, Gao *et al.* (2016) identified the brain regions that process self-reflection, perspective, and affective components of body image, including the inferior parietal lobe (IPL), extrastriate body area (EBA), and the fusiform body area (FBA). This network is activated when viewing images of bodies (self, other, and renderings), appearance-related comparisons, and self-reflection. Specifically, the EBA encodes body representation and body perception disturbances related to the body shape and size in space taken from external stimuli, including touch, action, and motion of both body parts and the whole (Moayedi *et al.*, 2020). A body schema emerges with the integration of interoception, exteroceptive, proprioceptive, and nociceptive stimuli in the insula with the IPL, FBA, and EBA network processing self-reflective and affective experiences. A body schema is a subjective experience of the body's position—parts and whole—within physical constraints. Body schema informs body image, which is the subjective experience of the body with conscious experiences into a dynamic and plastic representation that is "free of physical constraints, as the shape and size of the body need not be realistic in order for perception and ownership to occur" (Moayedi *et al.*, 2020, p.3616).

For this chapter, interoception is used inclusively as an umbrella term for phenomenological experiences of body states. The current conceptualization of interoceptive awareness includes visceral signals, heartbeat, breathing rate, body temperature, visceral and somatic pain (Ceunen *et al.*, 2016), itch, and affective touch (Wierenga *et al.*, 2020). Interoception is the ability to sense, process, and integrate internal sensations and body-state signals, determining the overall psychological condition of the body and organizing behaviors to meet physiological needs (Ceunen *et al.*, 2016; Wierenga *et al.*, 2020). The interpretation of these sensations helps establish emotions and guides behaviors. This awareness supports affective functioning and a stable concept of the body (Bischoff-Grethe *et al.*, 2018). Interoception relies on learned associations, memories, and emotions and integrates these into a holistic experience and a subjective body representation (Ceunen *et al.*, 2016). Interoceptive awareness is critical for self-awareness because it connects cognitive and affective processes. Impairment in interoceptive processing supports body image disturbances, increased avoidance of affective and social stimuli, and difficulty with accurate self-assessment of one's body (Bischoff-Grethe *et al.*, 2018).

In conclusion, the insula is the hub for processing internal and external stimuli and, most important, sensory information. This processing involves brain regions that decode this information into a body schema. Interoceptive awareness supports attunement, self-awareness, learning, and self-assessment to form body image.

Eating disorders

Press *et al.* (2022) noted that "women with eating disorders have altered responses to body images in body-processing areas (such as EBA and FBA) and emotion-processing areas (such as insula and amygdala) compared to healthy control subjects" (p.351). Furthermore, processing in this network demonstrates altered activation in those with anorexia nervosa (Gao *et al.*, 2016). Grey matter density in the EBA negatively correlated to body size misjudgment (Moayedi *et al.*, 2020). Individuals with AN showed an altered response to physiological sensations (taste, hunger, stomach distention, heartbeat, gut attention, aversive breathing load, and pain)—supporting interoception deficits. "Poor prediction, coupled with elevated response to receipt, likely leads to the perception of a more intense experience" (Bischoff-Grethe *et al.*, 2018, p.10). Bischoff-Grethe *et al.* (2018) and Groves *et al.* (2020) found that individuals with AN—both recovered and ill—experience elevated intensity to perceived somatosensory stimuli, with increased experiences of arousal and aversion.

In malnourishment, the insula becomes immobilized, and information is not properly channeled to the correct brain areas (Arnold, 2012). The brain cannot prioritize information, concentration deteriorates, and a limited concept of self and environment develops. In AN, insular dysfunctionality may result from early developmental damage, genetics, sociocultural factors related to body weight, and non-specific stressors such as puberty and diet (Esposito *et al.*, 2018).

The pervasiveness of eating disorders

Esposito *et al.* (2018) report that only 50% of individuals with an eating disorder diagnosis will fully recover, with only 30% experiencing partial remission, meaning that they still experience a disordered relationship with food and body and utilize eating disorder-related coping skills to address psychological and physiological distress. Furthermore, they found that perfectionism, distorted body image, and obsessive-compulsive personality disorder are predisposing factors and persist after recovery. Franzoni *et al.* (2013) reported that individuals with an eating disorder diagnosis fluctuated over time and met the criteria for AN, BN, and BED, demonstrating the pervasiveness of this broader diagnosis. They found that alexithymia— difficulty in identifying feelings and failure to integrate perceptions and emotions into conscience experiences—continues after food-related behaviors are in remission and has long-term negative impacts.

Morrissey *et al.* (2020) stated that individuals with eating disorders overemphasize the importance of weight and shape (e.g., body type ideal, high drive for thinness) and exhibit ego deficits (e.g., poor interoceptive awareness, a pervading sense of ineffectiveness). They perceive pressure from parents, peers, and media to meet ideal body types, leading to body dissatisfaction. Societally, elevated body dissatisfaction is considered "normative discontent," and leads to negative affect and dieting which has become synonymous with "normal eating" (Morrissey *et al.*, 2020, p.1032).

Dieting behavior promotes a false identification of internal stimuli and a reliance on external cues and sources for self-regulation, resulting in ineffective results that are often arbitrary or based on short-term consequences and a strong predictor of an eating disorder.

ART THERAPY

Body representations arise from multimodal sensory inputs—visual, tactile, proprioceptive, interoceptive, nociceptive, and motor. Moayedi *et al.* (2020) suggest that integrating tactile and visual information supports multisensory processing and binding at several levels of the nervous system that are all implicated in developing body image. LeFranc *et al.* (2020) found that engaging the senses (i.e., sight, hearing, smell, taste, touch) helps interpret external stimuli essential in determining the human experience. The ability of art materials to engage multiple senses at one time makes them uniquely capable of addressing body image dissatisfaction on a neurological level. By intentionally focusing on external stimuli and the resulting internal stimulations of art materials, art therapists can use materials to explore body image, from sensations to representations. Morrissey *et al.* (2020) noted that modifying interoceptive deficits may be more effective in addressing body image disturbances than challenging rigid thought processes around body ideals. When exploring body image with individuals with eating disorders, it is important to remember that it has nothing and everything to do with the body.

Intentional body image work happens once individuals are medically stable, consistently meet nutritional goals, and can identify eating disorder thoughts and cognitive rigidity from health-affirming thoughts and behaviors. Before this, addressing body image may lead to therapeutic battles that often have little to do with body image and more with eating disorder pathology and cognitive rigidity. Also, addressing body image too early in treatment, prior to establishing investment and trust in the therapeutic process, can lead to triggering body-based trauma responses and hinder future treatment. Using a step approach to body image helps scaffold skills to increase positive body image traits and, in turn, develop states of less distress and dissatisfaction (Cash, 1997). By addressing state body image through developing traits that directly target positive body image, clients will experience an increase in positive state body image. This cyclical process requires clients to work simultaneously on internal exploration and behavioral changes.

BODY IMAGE DIRECTIVES

The following directives are organized in a step approach, from developing cognitive flexibility and coping skills through dialoguing with the body to rebuilding a relationship between the two. The directives then focus on interoceptive processes to increase awareness, attunement, and appreciation. These are offered as a guide, and materials are adapted when working with clients based on their needs and preferences.

Dialoguing with the body

Rationale

Using a compassion-focused therapy approach, letter writing supports self-compassion and understanding rather than judgment and can reduce shame and eating disorder pathology. Furthermore, it was noted that self-compassionate letter writing improved treatment readiness (Kelly & Waring, 2018).

Directives

These are examples of letter-writing prompts that can promote self-compassion and insight:

- Write a letter from your mind to your body and your body to your mind.

- Narrate the story of your body.

- How does your body feel about your eating disorder?

Materials

Visual journaling materials include an unlined sketchbook or journal, two-dimensional art materials, and writing tools.

Altered books as metaphor

Rationale

Altered books are excellent for exploring and assessing cognitive flexibility and risk-taking. They serve as a container for self-expression, feelings, and growth. Also, they can serve as transitional objects outside the therapeutic setting (Williams, 2018). The ability to change and adapt an existing object becomes the metaphor for the therapeutic process.

Directive

Black-out poetry—identify a page and, using this black marker, mark out words you do not want to create a poem or story about your body.

Materials

A book and a wide range of two-dimensional materials, including found objects and non-traditional materials.

CLIENT EXAMPLE: Ellie

Ellie is a white woman in her mid-thirties in outpatient art therapy for anorexia nervosa and post-traumatic stress disorder. Utilizing an altered book, Ellie explored black-out poetry, journaling, and collage as a means of self-reflection and a tool to use outside art therapy to contain and self-soothe. As a result, a narrative of familial trauma and neglect moved towards compassionate self-talk and cognitive flexibility.

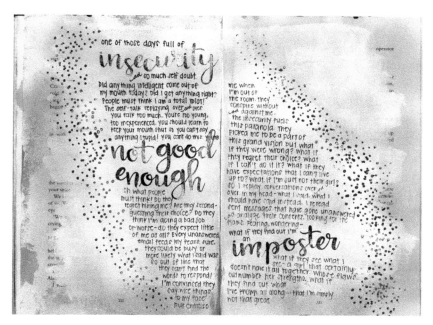

FIGURE 3.1: ALTERED BOOK PAGE

FIGURE 3.2: BLACK-OUT POETRY

Media literacy

Rationale

The wide range of imagery that the internet offers can benefit clients in art therapy. However, the art therapist must engage in media literacy with clients to critically review content that may promote body ideals, fitspiration, and thinspiration content masked as wellness and diet-based content. Then, utilizing content that supports a broad conceptualization of beauty allows for a greater representation of intersectional identities and images that clients can use in developing their definition of body image and beauty.

Directives

- Who has profited from your body discomfort?
- What messages have you received from media (social media, social/cultural/religious groups) about your body?
- What do you find beautiful in others and yourself?

- Find images of bodies that you think are similar or different from yours.

- What do you value? How does the eating disorder influence these values?

Materials

Collage directives help clients develop media and cultural literacy on eating disorders. Collage is an effective approach to media because it empowers clients to interact directly with harmful messaging in a supportive environment.

Personal definition of body image

Rationale

Therapists must not assume that their definition of positive body image is the same as their clients'. Prior to this step, we are setting the groundwork for developing a complex multidimensional definition of body image. Before starting in-depth body image work, the initial question is, "What does body image mean to you?" As an eating disorder art therapist, I do not prescribe to the "love your body campaign" or the "positive body image movement" because they place significant importance on the body's appearance and unnecessary pressure. Also, it can lead to questions like, "What if I do not love my body? Does that mean I cannot live fully?" "If I do not love my body, does that mean I am not good enough?" Starting body image work with clients through their definition is imperative. What happens if a client says, "Body image means that I am skinny and that I weigh less than 110 lbs"? If that is the response, they may not be ready to dive into intensive body image work and focus on cognitive reframing and flexibility. Values exploration may be a more appropriate approach prior to moving forward.

Directive

Use these materials to represent what body image means to you visually.

Materials

A wide range of two-dimensional materials and varying paper sizes.

Identifying smells

Rationale

Aligning with exposure therapy approaches, spice paintings engage the olfactory sense, triggering the body's process of food-seeking behaviors (Koeppel *et al.*, 2020). Experiencing hunger cues can be overwhelming, so exploring senses in therapy can support nutritional goals such as eating fear foods (i.e., foods that are avoided because they create distress and perpetuate eating disorder behaviors) or new tastes and textures and tolerating the body's reaction to new foods. Engaging in smelling the spices and dialoguing with the client about the different smells engages the client in shared storytelling.

Directive

Use these spices to create an image.

Materials

There are many recipes to make spice paints; I use powdered spices and water to create thin watercolor paint and Yupo Paper™.

CLIENT EXAMPLE: Christina

FIGURE 3.3: CHRISTINA: SPICE PAINTING

Christina, a white female in her late teens in outpatient art therapy for anorexia nervosa and generalized anxiety disorder, was working on diversifying food options. We each brought a variety of spices from home that we introduced to one another. We proceeded to smell each spice and create the paint. The client used the paint to create a free-form image while she talked about different food experiences. This allowed her to create connections between food, smells, and bodily sensations that emerge within the therapeutic space while also talking about her fear foods through an arts-based exposure experience.

EXPLORING INTERNAL SENSATIONS DIRECTIVES

Recognizing internal experiences without judgment or change promotes psychological flexibility and self-compassion (Tylka & Wood-Barcalow, 2015). With this approach, threats to body image are understood as time-limited, and not absolute truth. The individual can choose the direction to proceed, which does not have to be rumination, body shaming, or self-harm. Self-compassion promotes body compassion and an understanding that internal distress is a universal experience. Utilizing mindfulness-based approaches in art therapy supports the externalization of internal processes, allowing clients a visual representation of a conceptual experience, and provides a tangible tool to use while engaging in this process outside therapy (Williams, 2018). Using art materials helps to *close the loop* when working on mindfulness by creating a closing ritual. These approaches increase "self-related processes (interoceptive awareness, self-efficacy, self-critical rumination and self-monitoring)...emotional regulation (emotional differentiation, decentering) and attentional/cognitive control (volitional orienting, alerting, conflicting monitoring and inhibitory control)" (Warschburger *et al.*, 2022, p.6).

The following processes are scaffolded to engage the client in interoceptive activities slowly. Being present in the body is not a singular action. It must be consistently repeated to build distress tolerance, attune to the body's needs, and strengthen the relationship between mind and body (Sandoz & DuFrene, 2013). For all body-based interventions, I ask the client to find a comfortable position and I offer pillows and blankets. I have found that offering comforting items helps to provide external containment because this process can be difficult and overwhelming. Clients are invited to close their eyes, soften their gaze, or find a place to rest their gaze. Due to the high rate of trauma within my client population, it is essential to offer modifications and suggestions during this process. When I bring the client out of the mindfulness activity, they are asked to wiggle their toes and fingers, open their eyes, and reorient to the space. The materials remain consistent with medium-sized drawing paper (e.g., 12" x 18") with a pre-drawn circle, gingerbread form, or left blank, and two-dimensional materials (e.g., markers, colored pencils, oil pastels). After the guided practice, I ask them to use these materials to represent the sensations they experienced. This allows the clients to create a tangible representation to be used in the future to visually and verbally process this experience. Over time, the materials offered can expand to three-dimensional materials based on clinical needs and client preferences.

Heartbeat identification
Rationale
Researchers use heartbeat awareness tests to assess levels of interoceptive awareness. Individuals with low interoceptive awareness struggle to find and remain connected to their heartbeat, especially clients with AN (Bischoff-Grethe *et al.*, 2018).

Directive
Bring your awareness to your heart, and when you can feel your heartbeat, let me know. (This may take several minutes, or you may repeat this activity multiple times until the individual can identify it.) Now that you have identified your heartbeat, stay focused on it. See if you can find the rhythm. When you are ready, open your eyes. (Note how long it took the client to identify their heartbeat and how long they could stay focused. The goal is to decrease the time to recognize and increase the time spent focusing.) Using these materials represents the sensations and heartbeat pattern.

Body attention scan
Rationale
I utilize a body scan as the starting point to assess the client's ability to tolerate bodily sensations (Warschburger *et al.*, 2022). It requires clients to be aware of sensations at the moment and remain present.

Directive

Start by bringing your attention to your toes (slowly moving through the body, pausing for three to five seconds per body part), and notice any sensations or feelings that arise. Just notice and allow the feeling to be. (It is likely that early on in body image work, you will not get through the entire body. Depending on the level of body safety, you may only start with feet, arms, and head. Moreover, in each subsequent scan, you add another body area, ranging from two to 20 minutes.)

Awareness of breath scan

Rationale

Similar to heartbeat identification, this process aims to connect clients to their breath. This is particularly challenging for clients with an eating disorder, specifically AN because it requires relaxation and distention of the belly, which can mirror the feeling of fullness and vulnerability. Repeating this intervention will help develop in-the-moment coping skills to help tolerate uncomfortable or body image-threatening situations, ultimately supporting a protective filter (Tylka & Wood-Barcalow, 2015). For this exercise, if a client is lying down, I offer a lightly weighted object (small book, pillow, pack of crayons) for them to place on their belly. This gentle pressure helps clients to focus on this area.

Directive

Become aware of your breath and where you feel it. Is it in your throat or maybe the top of your chest? Do not do anything else besides feel it (pause for one to two minutes). Deepen your breath by increasing the inhale and allowing your chest to expand and contract when you breathe out. Stay here for a minute. Deepen your breath further and allow the belly to expand (lifting the book/pillow/crayons) and contract as you exhale. Stay here for several breaths.

Identifying emotions within the body

Rationale

It engages clients in interoceptive experiences that allow them to connect internal sensations and emotions and develop a tolerance for pleasurable, benign, and painful body experiences without engaging in avoidance or aversion. This tolerance is imperative in developing attunement and flexibility (Ceunen *et al.*, 2016).

Directive

Identify a time when you felt [insert feeling] in your body. This can mean a lot of different things. What does it mean to you? Connect to the feelings and sensations in your body when you think about this time.

CLIENT EXAMPLE: Ellie

Using this circle (16" x 16", raw canvas) and these acrylic paints, fill this circle. Ellie stated, "You are not going to want to hear what I have to say. It was when I was deep in the eating disorder. I went shopping at this little boutique in town to buy a pink dress for an upcoming wedding. I was at my smallest, and I could go shopping and knew that anything would fit me. I still had all of my pain, but it didn't seem as bad. At this time, I would get compliments from people about how good I looked, even though I was so sick."

Ellie continued to share this moment as she painted the long straight line starting with red and adding white. She moved to the curved line with the same paint pattern. She added black to the edges and continued to add red, white, and pink. At one point, she stated, "I want to add black, shocking. I don't know what I am doing, but I am sure you will tell me."

I reflected her statements, "I fit. I was seen and complimented. I still hurt. It was tolerable." As we closed the session, her homework was to fill in this circle over the next two weeks, focusing on times when she felt good in her body. I reminded her of previous sessions when she told me she felt strong, powerful, and respected during recent life events.

CLIENT EXAMPLE: Ellie

Due to chronic medical pain, Ellie found interoceptive awareness work difficult. "It doesn't feel good to go into my body. And not just because of the eating disorder but because I am always in pain." Ellie was provided with needle-felting tools and a 6" x 6" felt square with the directive of noticing the pain while creating an image. Working simultaneously with the pain, the kinesthetic and sensory properties of the materials aimed to reduce the distress around the pain. Ellie noted that while the pain didn't go away, sitting in it while working helped her to tolerate it. Once she finished the needle-felting process, she noted that her piece looked like a brain. She felt that was fitting because she tended to be cognitive and avoid feelings.

FIGURE 3.4: FELTED BRAIN

Breath and compassion body scan
Rationale
Breath and compassion body scans focus on attunement, acceptance, coping, positive and self-accepting talk, and appreciation. They integrate breathing skills, body scanning, and compassionate self-talk to develop traits necessary for developing a protective filter (Heiderscheit, 2016). If needed, before this activity, select the body areas that will be focused on and have the client write down what they appreciate about this part. This helps to reduce the anxiety of an in-the-moment response; it may also be read by the therapist first, and then the client can repeat it to themselves or aloud.

Directive
Today you will use your breath to connect to the various parts of the body. As you inhale, you will focus on an area of the body and thank it for how it supports you. As you exhale, you will release any negative or judgmental statements. (Start at the toes and move up the entire body, pausing at body areas such as feet, legs, pelvis, spine, arms, hands, digestive organs, heart, face, brain. Before this process, the client may pre-select body parts to reduce anxiety or unanticipated distress.)

Materials

This directive lends itself to a wide range of materials, and I prefer offering materials that support creating a transitional object. For example, artist trading cards or beads for a bracelet can serve as reminders outside the therapy room (Garrett, 2015) to increase positive body states; utilizing the cards during distress encourages adaptive traits.

CLIENT EXAMPLE: Jackie

Jackie, a white adolescent female in early treatment, expressed body image concerns because of weight restoration. She created a list of each body part and its function using cognitive reframing strategies. Next, she used polymer clay to create a bead for each body part and its function. A hole was made in each bead and baked. The beads were strung into a bracelet and served as a reminder and a self-soothing tool for addressing body threats outside therapy.

SPECIAL CONSIDERATIONS AND FUTURE IMPLICATIONS

A therapist's awareness of the relationship between the body, nutrition, and exercise is imperative to ethical treatment. Many well-intended therapists not trained in eating disorders offer advice about diets and exercise that exacerbate the disorder. Due to minimal education opportunities about eating disorders for medical and mental health providers, many individuals with eating disorders go improperly treated. Due to limited opportunities, some clinicians utilize outdated sources addressing body image, such as body tracings and other body-challenging directives (Breiner, 2003; Cash, 1997). These directives do not align with current neurological research on the deleterious impact eating disorders have on the brain and the subsequent impact on body image. They promote a focus on how the body appears and try to demonstrate to the client that their perception of the body is wrong. This ineffective approach creates a power struggle, inciting shame and frustration and perpetuating a negative experience in the body (Williams *et al.*, 2014). Being critical consumers of research, questioning outdated practices, and aligning therapeutic interventions with current neuroscience research leads to better treatment outcomes.

I believe expressive therapies are integral to the interdisciplinary eating disorder treatment team. By collaborating with psychologists, psychiatrists, physicians, and nutritionists, we support brain-based approaches to therapy, with an active therapeutic process that aims to uncover, explore, and process emotional and behavioral content that supports healing. Furthermore, documenting and sharing this work will offer guidance and guidelines for non-eating disorder art therapists in their practice.

REFERENCES

American Psychiatric Association (2013). *Diagnostic and Statistical Manual of Mental Disorders* (5th ed.). https://doi.org/10.1176/appi.books.9780890425596

Arnold, C. (2012). *Decoding Anorexia: How Breakthroughs in Science Offer Hope for Eating Disorders*. Routledge.

Avery, J. A., Gotts, S. J., Kerr, K. L., Burrows, K., *et al.* (2017). Convergent gustatory and viscerosensory processing in the human dorsal mid-insula. *Human Brain Mapping, 38*, 2150–2164. https://doi.org/10.1002/hbm.23510

Bischoff-Grethe, A., Wierenga, C. E., Berner, L. A., Simmons, A. N., *et al.* (2018). Neural hypersensitivity to pleasant touch in women remitted from anorexia nervosa. *Translational Psychiatry, 8*, 161. https://doi.org/10.1038.s41398-018-0218-3

Breiner, S. (2003). An evidence-based eating disorder program. *Journal of Pediatric Nursing, 18*(1), 75–80. https://doi.org/10.1053/jpdn.2003.14

Cash, T. (1997). *The Body Image Workbook: An 8-Step Program for Learning to Like Your Looks.* New Harbinger Publications.

Ceunen, E., Vlaeyen, J. W. S., & Van Diest, I. (2016). On the origin of interoception. *Frontiers in Psychology, 7*(743), 1–17. https://dx.doi.org/10.3389/fpsyg.2016.00743

Esposito, R., Cieri, F., di Giannantonio, M., & Tartaro, A. (2018). The role of body image and self-perception in anorexia nervosa: The neuroimaging perspective. *Journal of Neuropsychology, 12*, 41–52. https://doi:10.1111jnp.12106

Franzoni, E., Gualandi, S., Caretti, V., Schimmenti, A. *et al.* (2013). The relationship between alexithymia, shame, trauma, and body image disorders: Investigation over a large clinical sample. *Neuropsychiatric Disease and Treatment, 9*, 185–193. doi:10.2147/NDT.S34822

Fuller-Tyszkiewicz, M. (2019). Body image states in everyday life: Evidence from ecological momentary assessment methodology. *Body Image, 31*, 245–272. https://doi.org/10.1016/j.bodyim.2019.02.010

Gao, X., Deng, X., Wen, X., She. Y., Vinke, P. C., & Chen, H. (2016). My body looks like that girl's: Body mass index modulates brain activity during body image self-reflection among young women. *PLoS ONE, 11*(10), e0164450. https://doi.10.1371/journal.pone.0164450

Garrett, M. (2015). Using artist trading cards as an expressive arts intervention in counseling. *Journal of Creativity in Mental Health, 10*(1), 77–88. https://doi:10.1080/15401383.2014.914455

Groves, K., Kennett, S., & Gillmeister, H. (2020). Evidence for altered configural body processing in women at risk of disorders characterized by body image disturbance. *British Journal of Psychology, 111*, 508–535. https://doi.org/10.1111/bjop.12412

Heiderscheit, A. (2016). *Creative Arts Therapies and Clients with Eating Disorders.* Jessica Kingsley Publishers.

Kelly, A. C. & Waring, S. V. (2018). A feasibility study of a 2-week self-compassionate letter-writing intervention for nontreatment seeking individuals with typical and atypical anorexia nervosa. *International Journal of Eating Disorders, 51*(8), 1005–1009. https://doi.org/10.1002/eat.22930

Koeppel, C. J., Ruser, P., Kitzler, H., Hummel, T., & Croy, I. (2020). Interoceptive accuracy and its impact on neuronal responses to olfactory stimulation in the insular cortex. *Human Brain Mapping, 41*, 2898-2908. https://doi.org/10.1002/hbm.24985

LeFranc, B., Martin-Krumm, C., Aufauvre-Poupon, Berthail, B., & Trousselard, M. (2020). Mindfulness, interoception, and olfaction: A network approach. *Brain Sciences, 10*(12), 921. https://doi.org/10.3390/brainsci10120921

Moayedi, M., Noroozbahari, N., Hadjis, G., Themelis, K., *et al.* (2020). The structural and functional connectivity neural underpinnings of body image. *Human Brain Mapping, 42*, 3608-3619. https://doi.org/10.1002/hbm.25457

Morrissey, R. A., Gondoli, D. M., & Corning, A. F. (2020). Reexamining the restraint pathway as a conditional process among adolescent girls: When does dieting link body dissatisfaction to bulimia? *Development and Psychopathology, 32*(3), 1031-1043. https://doi.org/10.1017/S0954579419001287

Press, S. A., Biehl, S. C., Vatheuer, C. C., Domes, G., & Svaldi, J. (2022). Neural correlates of body image processing in binge eating disorder. *Journal of Psychopathology and Clinical Science, 131*(4), 350-364. https://doi.org/10.1037/abn0000750

Reyes-Haro, D. (2022). Glial cells in anorexia. *Frontiers in Cellular Neuroscience, 16*, 1-8. https://doi.org/10.3389/fncel.2022.983577

Sandoz, E. & DuFrene, T. (2013). *Living with Your Body & Other Things You Hate: How to Let Go of Your Struggle with Body Image Using Acceptance & Commitment Therapy*. New Harbinger Publications.

Simmons, W. K., Rapuano, K. M., Kallman, S. J., Ingeholm, J. E., *et al.* (2013). Category-specific integration of homeostatic signals in caudal, but not rostral, human insula. *Nature Neuroscience, 16*(11), 1551-1552. https://doi.org/10.1038/nn.3535

Tylka, T. L. & Wood-Barcalow, N. L. (2015). What is and what is not positive body image? Conceptual foundations and construct definition. *Body Image, 14*, 118-129. http://dx.doi.org/10.1016/j.bodyim.2015.04.001

Vannucci, A. & Ohannessian, C. M. (2018). Body image dissatisfaction and anxiety trajectories during adolescence. *Journal of Clinical Child and Adolescent Psychology, 47*(5), 785-795. https://doi.org/10.1080/15374416.2017.1390755

Warschburger, P., Wortmann, H. R., Gisch, U. A., Baer, N., *et al.* (2022). An experimental approach to training interoceptive sensitivity: Study protocol for a pilot randomized controlled trial. *Nutrition Journal, 21*(74), 1-16. https://doi.org/10.1186/s12937-022-00827-4

Wierenga, C. E., Bischoff-Grethe, A., Berner, L. A., Simmons, A. N., *et al.* (2020). Increased anticipatory brain response to pleasant touch in women remitted from bulimia nervosa. *Translational Psychiatry, 10*, 236. https://doi.org/10.1038/s41398-020-00916-0

Williams, G. A., Hudson, D. L., Whisenhunt, B. L., & Crowther, J. H. (2014). An examination of body tracing among women with high body dissatisfaction. *Body Image, 11*(4), 346-349. https://doi.org/10.1016/j.bodyim.2014.05.005

Williams, L. (2018). *Exploring the Use of Altered Books as a Tool for Self-Care with Adolescent Girls Diagnosed with Eating Disorders in a Residential Treatment Facility* [Master's thesis, Lesley University]. DigitalCommons@Lesley. https://digitalcommons.lesley.edu/expressive_theses/60

CHAPTER IV

Returning the Body to Safety

Somatic, Nature-Attuned Art Therapy with Eating
Disordered Adult Trauma Survivors

—— LIZA HYATT ——

This chapter describes trauma-informed, somatically focused, art-based treatment approaches that help those with eating disorders reduce how they objectify and dissociate from their bodies while enhancing their felt sense of embodied safety. While the philosophy and techniques described here also inform the facilitation of individual outpatient therapy sessions, this chapter focuses on how this approach is utilized within outpatient group therapy for adults aged 18–60+. These adults attend a weekly one-and-a-half-hour art therapy group at an eating disorder clinic in addition to other treatments, including individual therapy and dietician support. All group members have histories of previous trauma and attachment injury. Participants are diagnosed with some form of an eating disorder, including anorexia nervosa, bulimia nervosa, and binge eating disorder, as well as depression, anxiety, and/or post-traumatic stress disorder.

HOW BODY IMAGE IS UNDERSTOOD IN THE POPULATION

Many people with eating disorders have experienced trauma and/or attachment injury in childhood. Both attachment ruptures and trauma are all experienced bodily. In other words, the body directly experiences all physical harm and relational lack of emotional safety that occurs. The trauma survivor's perception of their body is negatively tied to this trauma, linking the body to lack of safety. Recent literature identifies that between 20% and 50% of people with eating disorders report a history of childhood trauma and abuse (Groth *et al.*, 2019; Guillaume *et al.*, 2016; Tasca *et al.*, 2013). Thus, those who encounter a traumatic experience in their childhood may be more vulnerable to developing an eating disorder than those who do not.

Traumatic experiences in childhood are rarely a single incident and often include a recurring lack of safe connection and repeated exposure to dysregulated adults. This repeated exposure prevents those living in such environments from forming secure attachments with others and developing a stable sense of self. Thus, due to this ongoing lack of safety, these clients begin to perceive their body as the cause of their distress and as the space that stores their traumatic pain (Caldwell, 2018). Trauma and attachment injury prevent a person from forming a regulated and connected relationship with their body. Instead, these survivors of harmful relationships detach from their bodies, which they experience as unsafe.

An attachment and trauma-informed approach recognizes that patients with eating disorders will likely feel high levels of anxiety, lack of safety, distrust of their bodies, and shame when presented with any directives involving re-establishing connection to their bodies. Those living amid recurring childhood abuse try to find relief from the harm their bodies are undergoing by dissociating and disconnecting from their body. Detachment from their bodies begins before these children are old enough to cognitively understand that the various abuses which they experience are not their fault. When inadequate help to address attachment injury and trauma is available, disordered eating behaviors can seem to offer some control over their bodies and help to numb the traumatic pain (Finlay, 2019).

At some point, almost all children are exposed to societal messages about body perfection. Through this exposure, children begin to compare their bodies to others, and feel pressure to strive to attain external, often misogynistic and hypermasculine societal standards of perfect bodies. These external messages about body appearance add additional injury to the trauma survivor's experience of their body. They perceive that their body is not safe in familiar home environments and in society at large. For the child and adolescent trauma survivor, dissociation from the body was already a needed coping mechanism. As they experience recurring harmful and attacking societal messages about the body, their body shame from the underlying trauma is reinforced. This double onslaught of harmful societal messaging and personal experiences of trauma and attachment injury leads the trauma survivor to rely more heavily on somatic disconnection and punishing behaviors towards their bodies. If neither home nor society is safe, the constantly threatened body cannot regulate back to connection and safety.

These clients grow up internalizing their ongoing lack of safety and insecure attachment as their fault. Bodies that are not adequately reassured or comforted after harmful experiences carry implicit memories of being unsafe, put in danger, blamed, ridiculed, ignored, demeaned, shunned, left too alone, and other attachment failures. These implicit memories resurface as negative beliefs and shame, such as: I am not good enough; I am bad; I am unlovable. Such beliefs insist that the trauma survivor's primal need for safety was not met because there was something wrong with them (Fay, 2021). The eating disorder is an attempt to find some relief from these beliefs.

Abusive, critical, or stressful and misattuned relationships have, from an early age, conditioned these clients to comply with the expectations and demands of others with more power. These clients come to expect that their own needs will not be met or considered. Once exposure to societal body perfection messages is added to these clients' trauma and attachment injuries, comparing their body to external expectations, and trying to comply, becomes another strategy seeking to achieve the connection and safety they have not yet known. The eating disorder enacts shame-based beliefs, such as: If I lose weight and become skinny, people will accept me; if I become small and take up less space, I will be safe; I need to look a certain way to be loved. These beliefs are evidence of the body having become objectified, now both critiqued negatively by societal standards and distrusted as a separate, unsafe entity by the disembodied client (Cook-Cottone, 2020).

This deeply ingrained shame is therefore reinforced by manipulative messages from societal systems that promote body shame, fat phobia, beauty industry profiteering, hierarchical attitudes that value certain bodies more than others, misogyny, hyper masculinity, and repeated diet culture directives for attaining body perfection based on impossible standards. Because those who grow up with unmet attachment needs are conditioned to comply in neglectful and abusive relationships, they are prone to also comply with these systemic forms of *body terrorism* (Taylor, 2018) by striving to appease societal dictations for perfecting the body. The trauma survivor internalizes this pervasive societal attack on the body. Failing to attain radical changes in physical appearance to meet impossible external standards increases shame beliefs and reinforces self-loathing. As a result, the trauma survivor's internalized lack of safety increases. The eating disorder itself feels like the only safe thing left to which they might form an attachment (Cook-Cottone, 2020).

Therefore, when working with this population, the focus is on helping such clients shift their attachment away from the eating disorder while learning to connect instead to experiences of embodied safety and connection. This embodied approach differs from more cognitive concepts of body image, which mostly consider a person's perception of how they believe others see them, or how they see themselves in the context of external standards. Instead, a trauma-informed somatic treatment approach helps clients with eating disorders regain trust that their body is a resource for healing. They learn that their body can give them states of calm, connection, stability, support, and well-being (Cook-Cottone, 2020).

ART THERAPY GOALS UNIQUE TO POPULATION

Art therapy offers many ways to help this population regain feelings of safety, connection, and embodied awareness. Group members utilize this group as a long-term support in their ongoing recovery process. New members are asked to attend the group for a minimum of eight weeks to establish trust with group members and art therapy experiential processes. Many group members continue attending for a year or longer.

In this group, members are provided with psychoeducation to learn to track nervous system arousal states of fight, flight, freeze, and shutdown. Group members also begin to identify specific resources, practices, and behaviors that help them access the ventral vagal component of the nervous system, which enables them to establish safety, connection, and states of attunement (Dana, 2020). Through these polyvagal approaches to regulating the nervous system, group participants begin to discover that their bodies are resources to help them heal.

In the group, guidelines about bringing a non-judgmental stance towards art products and one's creative process are discussed. Guided meditations that incorporate felt experiences of nature's creative vitality encourage the client to view their body as an animate presence held within and connected to Earth's body in healing ways (Sidorova, 2022).

Directives for art processes linked to the guided meditation are offered to the entire group. Given the long-term participation of some group members, all participants are encouraged to incorporate a self-directed approach whenever this feels appropriate.

An overall goal of this group is to help clients feel how eating disordered behaviors and thoughts perpetuate their lack of safety. They learn to recognize self-critical thoughts and perfectionism as forms of self-aggression as opposed to self-compassion. They learn to recognize these hurtful stances towards their imperfect artworks and their bodies. They are encouraged to let go of striving for external and impossible standards of perfection in art and in life. As this awareness increases, group participants also experience moments of present safety while making art and engaging in guided meditation. They learn to observe their body shifting from aroused states to increased calm. They begin finding that they can feel safe inside their bodies by learning to creatively self-regulate within their bodies.

Making art in a group evokes fear of being seen as not as good as other participants. This fear reveals how group members habitually judge their art creations in the same way they judge their bodies, comparing both, as objects, to external standards of perfection. Group members are encouraged to observe the difference between objectifying and comparing versus staying present to their own internal embodied experience during the creative process. They begin to notice that objectifying and comparing do not feel safe. They discover that habitually comparing causes them to contract, shrink, take fewer creative risks, be less playful, and focus instead on external approval, while expecting criticism. Through cultivating this awareness, clients learn to approach their artmaking and recovery as processes full of opportunities to recognize and break free from old, disembodied patterns. These patterns include contracting and diminishing their self-energy, conforming, basing self-worth on external criteria, seeking approval by people-pleasing, ignoring their own needs, and complying with shame-based internalized beliefs that they are both too much and yet never enough.

Those recovering from eating disorders need ample opportunities in which they can experience freedom from these habitual disembodied patterns and gain increased access to felt experience. Simply put, they need moments of feeling vitally alive. Through artmaking and nature awareness, these clients can safely yet pleasurably connect their physical bodies to the physical sensations of art materials and the living world. As they practice staying present to this felt experience, they notice shifts towards safety and connection within their somatic states. They feel a rekindling of their own body's ability to regulate nervous system arousal. They increase their ability to encounter nature with authentic connection, and they engage in the creative process with more curiosity and openness. Over time, group members begin to shift from the above patterns of disembodied, diminished existence and to experience new internal states of embodied safety and connection. These new embodied states include allowing their self-energy to open and expand, becoming freer to be more authentic, basing self-worth on personal values, validating their own deep, undeniable needs, increasing self-compassion, and aligning more fully with new internal messages of being *so much and still growing*.

In all these ways, within every group session, all offered nature meditations and art directives are focused around helping group participants decenter from old diminishing and conforming patterns, enter the liminal space of creativity, listen to the body as guide during the artmaking, and find some degree of increased connection to their authentic self. In other words, these group processes are all invitations for group members to experience poiesis, which is the process of learning about self and world through making things. Through poiesis, the person is changed and healed by the process of creating (Levine, 2019).

APPROACHES, INTERVENTIONS, AND DIRECTIVES

Group sessions are conducted as an integration of nervous system regulation, attunement to nature, and somatic and kinesthetic/sensory aspects of the artmaking processes. Group interventions are not scripted or mapped out as a fixed curriculum. Instead, the group facilitator witnesses group members' bodies, nervous system arousal, attachment needs, and present moment levels of safety. From this witnessing, the facilitator responds as a supportive presence. The facilitator focuses on creating a safe, playful space so that nervous system regulation can be fostered. The facilitator recognizes the many resources the art therapy group offers to help clients access embodied safety and brings these resources to the attention of group members. These resources include the embodied process of artmaking itself, the way making art can utilize and release nervous system energy, the state shifts felt within the guided nature meditation, the co-regulating experience of making art together with others in the same space, and the opportunity to help each other through empathic sharing and feedback.

Each group session begins with a verbal check-in that offers every group member an opportunity to share a short update on issues that they bring from the past week. The facilitator listens for metaphors, images, and somatic states offered in each participant's check-in. Group members also identify their levels of nervous system arousal, anxiety, and current states of safety or self-negation. Drawing from this check-in, the facilitator then leads the group through a guided meditation that intentionally focuses on somatic awareness of support, stability, and present moment safety. The meditation might also incorporate relaxing movement and breathing techniques. Through these grounding meditations, participants practice accessing resources within both the natural world and their embodied self. These meditations help group members regulate, settle, and more deeply connect with internal experience before entering the artmaking process. To respond empathically to group members' present states, the grounding meditation must be improvisational, not scripted. It follows basic grounding practices of connecting feet to the floor, feeling the support and stability of the earth and the chair, and attuning to the breath. In addition, other elements of the meditation are spontaneous, attuned responses to the group members' check-ins. These improvised responses offer soothing possibilities for the release of nervous system arousal states and personal struggles that group members described in the check-in.

While participants are still connected to the meditative state, suggested paths to enter the artmaking process are offered. Again, to respond empathically to participant present needs, the art directives are not pre-planned and are offered in an impromptu way in indirect response to the participant check-ins. To counter patterns of overly restricting, diminished playfulness, following directions perfectly, and people-pleasing, more than one suggestion for where to begin is generally offered. The improvised art directives are linked to nature imagery and offer invitations to seek increased capacity for embodied safety and connection. The art directives also invite participants to illustrate somatic shifts towards embodied safety that were sensed during the grounding practice. Art directives are described poetically with open-ended possibilities.

Clients are encouraged to interpret directives in their own ways and to ask for help if they become overly critical while creating. Participants are even encouraged to completely ignore the directive and trust whatever creative process they find themselves pulled toward. Patients move from meditation directly into making art. Very often, the art that is created is influenced by the imagery and embodied sensations that group participants accessed during the meditation. The artmaking portion of the group is allotted at least 45 minutes, during which connecting to internal imagery, sensation, and creative flow is fostered by limiting chit-chat. To help encourage inward focus, relaxing music and/or nature sounds are streamed in the background. Speaking mindfully in support of the creative process is allowed. The group concludes with verbal processing and sharing of what was experienced during the artmaking.

These approaches are informed by current neuroscience understanding of the impact of trauma upon the body. Using the Expressive Therapies Continuum (ETC), group members are taught to move more fluently into kinesthetic, sensory, and affective levels within their creative process and to shift out of their more habitual, disembodied reliance on thinking. A primary eating disorder behavior is the compulsive need to know what is going to happen next and to control what might be taken in or released. In the creative process, group participants often transfer this controlling into a need to know what they will make before they begin. Focus on the kinesthetic, sensory, and affective components of artmaking helps clients shift from over-reliance on cognition. They learn to recognize how relying on thought-driven planning keeps them detached and dissociated from felt experience. This use of the Expressive Therapies Continuum through a trauma-informed approach also understands that the kinesthetic, sensory, and affective levels of creativity invite somatic awareness and release, which can empower patients to safely express their current states of arousal, release needed fight-flight responses, and shift towards more regulated states of safety and connection (Lusebrink & Hinz, 2016).

Improvisation comes from the body, not the intellect. It flows out of how one lives and engages with others in the moment. The only way to fluently improvise as the group facilitator is to personally live the practices until they feel natural and encoded in body memory. Then what is being facilitated flows out organically and with heartfelt presence through the group leader's regulated and ever-healing relationship with their own body. To facilitate in this way, the author/facilitator leading this group cultivates embodied presence, connection to nature, and creative poiesis in their own life through a variety of practices. These practices include meditation, self-care focused on nervous system regulation, yoga and mindful movement, earth literacy studies, hiking, and contemplative artmaking.

The implementation of group interventions and directives is best illustrated by describing a group session as it unfolds. This description offers as examples two specific group members' verbalizations and art expressions. To protect confidentiality, fictitious names are assigned to these participants.

EXAMPLE PARTICIPANTS

Amy was a middle-aged woman with a history of complex childhood trauma, including assault. Through this trauma, she learned to hate her body for being weak. To avoid any relationship with her body, she turned to alcohol, drugs, and eating disordered behaviors. She was active in substance abuse recovery, but continued using eating disordered behaviors compulsively, restricting food intake daily, then bingeing on sugary foods. After years of being overweight, she stopped eating almost entirely, and lost almost 100 lbs before being referred by her doctor to treatment for her eating disorder. She had brief periods of full compliance with the recommended meal plan but returned to restriction and bingeing frequently.

She hated her body for regaining the weight she lost when severely restricting her food intake. Both her hatred of her body and her reliance on eating disordered behaviors became especially problematic during times of high stress and seasonal triggers. Due to the impact of recurring childhood trauma on her body, she had multiple autoimmune health issues. These health problems made it harder for her to find compassion for her body, which she described as "turning against itself" when long-term health issues worsened.

Clarissa was a 39-year-old woman who was actively engaged in recovery from anorexia nervosa mixed with binge-purge behaviors. She participated in the group for over a year during an earlier stage of treatment and left the group when she felt a strong recovery foundation had been established. She returned to the group when a combination of destabilizing situations triggered a relapse of eating disordered behaviors. She also had a trauma history involving sexual molestation from a family member, and being a caregiver to a relative (a stabilizing adult in her life) who later died.

Media

An art studio with an ample supply of diverse art materials was available to in-person participants in the group. The art studio was well stocked to provide a generous feast of materials instead of restricting supplies and thereby mirroring anorexia. The patients named the art studio *The Room of Requirement*—a magical room from Harry Potter's Hogwarts in which a person finds exactly what they most require at that precise moment (Rowling, 2000). The natural landscape surrounding the suburban office complex in which the treatment center was located was also considered a vital resource to patients, offering access to old trees, ponds, and prairie wildflowers along accessible paths.

Virtual attendance was possible for those participants who could not access the group otherwise. Clarissa attended the group in person, while Amy attended virtually. Virtual participants were given a list of easily affordable art materials, recycled objects, and basic supplies. In some cases, if needed, virtual participants could also take supplies home from the treatment center.

Initial check-in

At the beginning of the group session, during the initial check-in, Amy shared that she had been triggered by seeing her body in a full-length mirror earlier in the week. She stated, "I want to go crawl under a rock" and described feeling frozen with almost no sense of safety in her body, along with high anxiety about making art and sharing it with the group. She said she did not expect group members would be overly critical of her, but said, "I don't feel safe, and I want everything to be perfect." She said to other group members, "Even if you don't judge me, I will judge myself." She insisted that when body acceptance and self-compassion were encouraged, she heard the part of her that relied on eating disorder behaviors yelling, "Bullshit! I would feel better if I weighed less!"

Clarissa described feeling disconnected and not in control. She said, "I want to hide. I spent the day lying in bed, unable to get out of it." She identified being in a mixed nervous system state of flight and freeze. Yet, she described feeling safe about making art and sharing with the group. She stated, "I feel safe here. I compare sometimes, but more about my process than the product."

Grounding guided meditation

During the check-in, I observed that most group members described states of freeze and low levels of embodied safety. Many members experienced recent triggers and were actively engaged in eating disordered restriction and body shaming. The images of hiding in bed, and crawling under a rock were noted as was the critical need for perfection and control. In response, I began the grounding meditation with basic elements of breathing, settling into the chair, and feeling feet on the ground. After establishing this foundation, additional elements were improvised, including flowing water, trees, and a supportive rock to sit up on or lean against. Through this imagery, participants were invited to take in the soothing sensory contact of being in an imagined place where their bodies were safe out in the world, receiving support from the rock instead of hiding under it. Participants were invited to feel the sun on their face, the gentle breeze, the warmth of the rock and to imagine putting bare feet or a hand into the flowing water of a stream or a pond. They were invited to explore how it would feel to allow their body to let go of the nervous system's defensive tension and soften. They were invited to recall what they love in the world, and to feel connected to animals and plants in their imagined safe natural environment.

Art process

Following this meditation, group members were offered three possible directions. In addition to the ongoing permission to engage in their own improvisational process, without direction, they could:

- respond to what they imagined and experienced in the guided meditation

- create an illustration or an abstract representation of how it would feel to be an animal resting, in a relaxed state, in a place where it knows it is safe (a pet or wild animal), and then reflect on when they were recently most able to feel like this in any way

- create something that expressed being able to let the body feel connected to the world around them and a contrasting piece expressing how a body hiding under a rock would feel, and then to write, in the voice of both images, a dialogue between the two states.

Examples of art response

Amy responded to the third prompt, connecting the state of hiding under a rock to the autumn trauma triggers she was experiencing that evening. She described wanting to experience feeling safe in autumn and to find healing ways her body could enjoy the pleasures of the season. She worked with a handful of leaves that she had gathered, creating two art responses. In the first, she crushed one leaf and glued it to paper, splattering paint on the pieces. Next to this she glued a whole leaf and wrote underneath it, "What power do leaves have over me? It's just nature. Not good or bad..." (Figure 4.1).

In the second, she traced leaves then crushed them and scattered the pieces around the tracings. Inside the tracings she wrote a poem in which she described the leaves in the present, recognizing they were no longer sticking to her as they had in the past (Figure 4.2). She described seeing them now as "simply leaves falling from the strong, sturdy trees."

Clarissa also responded to the third prompt, using a variety of textile materials and tissue paper to create a three-dimensional body shape (Figure 4.3). She did not write a dialogue. She described feeling the body shape "was too big" and that she "wanted it to be more constricted" so she wrapped it with twine and found herself tightening the twine repeatedly. When she looked at the finished piece, she stated, "I liked it better when it was loose. It was prettier, more flowy, and softer. Now it is more rigid and doesn't move or dance." She recognized that her own body could shift from rigid to flowy, or flowy to rigid, depending on how safe she felt. She stated that wrapping and tightening the twine helped her gain a sense of control by enacting her urge to hide. She recognized it as "an old familiar record with well-worn grooves" played by "the trickster" eating disorder. She attached a fox image to the body to symbolize this trickster.

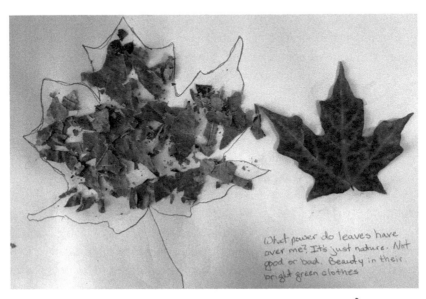

FIGURE 4.1: WHAT POWER DO LEAVES HAVE OVER ME?

FIGURE 4.2: SIMPLY LEAVES FALLING FROM THE STRONG, STURDY TREES

FIGURE 4.3: THREE-DIMENSIONAL BODY SHAPE

Outcomes

Both Amy and Clarissa described and demonstrated significant shifts towards safety. They began the group in states of trauma-related nervous system arousal and shutdown. They acknowledged ways in which the art helped them regulate towards more embodied safety. Amy stated that after making the art she felt "less frozen" because she was "taking away from the leaves some of their power" to automatically trigger her. She observed that she was still often critical of her art products yet had become more spontaneous and curious within her creative process. She stated that she felt more able to express her felt experience through a variety of art media. She also described the feeling that the evening's artmaking helped her feel calmer and kinder to her body. Clarissa stated that she no longer wanted to stay in the constricted, shutdown state of rigid and hiding. As she described her art to the group, she appeared visibly more present and open to connection than at the start of the group. She laughed as she spoke and made playful dance gestures with the group's encouragement. She acknowledged feeling safer and "glad to be back" from shutdown.

SPECIAL CONSIDERATIONS

When facilitating nature-based therapy practices, it is important to include an awareness of ways in which natural elements might be triggering, such as deep water (that might evoke drowning), or certain plants and animals (that might feel threatening). As seen with Amy's case, it could be potentially triggering to assume that all group members would perceive autumn leaves as beautiful and pleasurable. Therefore, when facilitating guided meditations for the group, I did not include autumn scenery in the nature imagery provided. However, because Amy had established safety and trust with both the group facilitator and group members, she chose times to incorporate autumn leaves into her artwork to address her nervous system arousal and reclaim her ability to experience autumn's beauty on her own terms.

It is also important to discuss with group members the difference between absolute safety and relative safety. Many people with eating disorders and trauma will insist that they never feel safe in their bodies. Their trauma has taught them that there are real dangers in the world and that no one can ever be safe all the time. It is important to validate that as living beings we are vulnerable; no one is absolutely safe. However, we can experience relative safety in some way almost every day. It is important to help group members orient to the present moment, using their senses and their bodies to perceive that the current environment is threat-free and most likely will stay that way for the duration of the group. This teaches them an essential polyvagal-informed skill for accessing a more relaxed, connected state.

The significant impact of the Covid-19 pandemic, which required me to develop virtual practices that continued to incorporate connection to nature experiences and somatic awareness, is worth mentioning. During the first two years of the pandemic, the art therapy group described in this chapter met in an entirely virtual format. Much to my surprise, having to shift from in-person to virtual sessions did not result in abandoning these favored nature-based and somatic approaches. Instead, working virtually inspired me to creatively help patients access connection to nature and experiences of connection with each other while making art in separate locations and dialoguing over Zoom. The need of all bodies to belong to the living world and to feel safe was felt even more clearly amid the isolation and challenges of the pandemic.

During this time of isolation, group members expressed feelings of loss about not being able to walk to a nearby tree we call "the grandmother oak," or sit around the table creating together in *The Room of Requirement*. Because we no longer met in a shared physical space, it became extremely important that we imagined being together in a natural setting in our grounding meditations. We also experienced the support given by group members' home environments as well as the impacts of any changes to that environment, such as when two group members moved. The group's focus on safety and connection helped these group members re-establish a sense of stability in their new environment, which the group was able to enter and visit virtually.

In addition, new ways of accessing nature over telehealth were cultivated. Participants looked out of the windows to see what nature was available to them, and when possible, went outside for sensory contact with plants, sun, wind and so on, either during the grounding meditation or the artmaking portion of the group. Group members' pets also became important natural resources for safety and connection. We needed the soft animal bodies of each other's cats and dogs to visit during each group session. Rather than proving to be an entirely limiting situation, the pandemic motivated me to more fully integrate an ecotherapy, somatic, and polyvagal approach into art therapy group facilitation.

FUTURE PLANNING

Future program development is under way at my worksite to bring this approach into a new adult Partial Hospitalization Program (PHP). Compared to the outpatient participants described here, who have a longer commitment to the recovery process, many people entering a PHP treatment process will be in the early stages of separating from eating disordered behaviors, and others will be attempting to leave a severe relapse experience. In both cases, the PHP participant enters treatment more physically unstable than those in outpatient treatment, therefore experiencing higher levels of pain, emotional and physical discomfort, body dysmorphia, brain malnourishment, as well as difficulty calming their nervous system and focusing mentally. I anticipate that the art therapy approach described in this chapter will help these PHP patients establish greater hope. As they let go of relying on the eating disorder, these approaches will help them experience real, tangible moments in which their body feels safer. Therefore, future discussion of how this approach is best adapted to assist people at these early stages of recovery will be of value.

REFERENCES

Caldwell, C. (2018). *Bodyfulness: Somatic Practices for Presence, Empowerment, and Waking Up in This Life*. Shambala.

Cook-Cottone, C. (2020). *Embodiment and the Treatment of Eating Disorders: The Body as a Resource in Recovery*. W. W. Norton.

Dana, D. (2020). *Polyvagal Exercises for Safety and Connection: 50 Client-Centered Practices*. W. W. Norton.

Fay, D. (2021). *Becoming Safely Embodied: A Guide to Organize your Mind, Body, and Heart to Feel Secure in the World*. Morgan James Publishing.

Finlay, H. (2019). Recognizing the Territory: The Interaction between Trauma, Attachment Injury, and Dissociation in Treating Eating Disorders. In A. Seubert & P. Virdi (eds), *Trauma Informed Approaches to Eating Disorders* (pp.35–44). Springer Publishing.

Groth, T., Hilsenroth, M., Boccio, D., & Gold, J. (2019). Relationship between trauma history and eating disorders in adolescents. *Journal of Child and Adolescent Trauma, 13*(4), 443–453. https://doi.org/10.1007/s40653-019-00275-z

Guillaume, S., Jaussent, L., Maimoun, L., Ryst, A., *et al.* (2016). Associations between adverse childhood experiences and clinical characteristics of eating disorders. *Scientific Reports, 6*, 35761. https://doi.org/10.1038/srep35761

Levine, S. (2019). *Philosophy of Expressive Arts Therapy: Poiesis and the Therapeutic Imagination*. Jessica Kingsley Publishers.

Lusebrink, V. & Hinz, L. (2016). The Expressive Therapies Continuum as a Framework in the Treatment of Trauma. In J. King (ed.), *Art Therapy, Trauma, and Neuroscience: Theoretical and Practical Perspectives* (pp.42–63). Routledge.

Rowling, J. K. (2000). *Harry Potter and the Goblet of Fire* (1st American ed.). Arthur A. Levine Books.

Sidorova, V. (2022). Culture and Nature: The Play of Ecopoiesis. In S. Levine & A. Kopytin (eds), *Ecopoiesis: A New Perspective for the Expressive and Creative Arts Therapies in the 21st Century* (p.97). Jessica Kingsley Publishers.

Tasca, G. A., Richie, K., Zachariades, F., Proulx, G., *et al.* (2013). Attachment insecurity mediates the relationship between childhood trauma and eating disorder psychopathology in a clinical sample: A structural equation model. *Child Abuse and Neglect, 37*(11), 926–933. https://doi.org/10.1016/j.chiabu.2013.03.004

Taylor, S. (2018). *The Body Is Not an Apology: The Power of Radical Self-Love.* Berrett-Koehler.

PART 2

BODY IMAGE AND TRAUMA

CHAPTER V

Trauma and the Body

Relationships between Art and Experience

—— RACHEL PAIGE FELDWISCH AND EILEEN MISLUK-GERVASE ——

Imagine watching a scary movie. One favorite was *Halloween*, with the terrifying Michael Myers, who stalks Laurie the teenage babysitter played by Jamie Lee Curtis (Carpenter & Hill, 1978). What happens to our bodies when we watch a scary movie? Our eyes widen, our pulses quicken, and we might even jump as the antagonist comes around the corner in pursuit of the terrified heroine. Recalling our body-based reactions to anxiety and fear gives us a glimpse of what happens to people in a moment of trauma. The sympathetic nervous system (SNS) releases cortisol and adrenaline, hormones that defend us against a potential threat. Stress hormones prepare us for the most common reactions to a dangerous situation: fight, flight, or freeze. Our bodies cannot remain in this hyper-aroused state in perpetuity; thus, the parasympathetic nervous system (PSNS) restores homeostasis by releasing acetylcholine (Cleveland Clinic, 2022). Within minutes of watching a scary movie, most people return to feeling like they did before pressing play, because the PSNS has facilitated our return to feeling normal.

People who have experienced traumas may feel that their sense of normality is distorted by their past experiences. They cannot simply turn off the scary movie that appears in sudden flashbacks, distorts their views of reality, and haunts their dreams. The American Psychological Association (2023) defines trauma as "an emotional response to a terrible event like an accident, rape, or natural disaster" (para. 1). Ogden explained, "For traumatized individuals, the debilitating, repetitive cycle of interaction between mind and body keeps past trauma 'alive,' disrupting the sense of self and maintaining trauma-related disorders" (Ogden *et al.*, 2006, p.3). Understanding how trauma affects the body, and more specifically body image, helps art therapists to design interventions that meet the complex needs of clients who have experienced traumatic circumstances and life events.

HISTORICAL PERSPECTIVES ON TRAUMA AND THE BODY

Documented exploration of connections between trauma, mind, and body dates to the second millennium BCE when hysteria was observed to be a condition impacting people who identified as female (Tasca *et al.*, 2012). Hippocrates used the term hysteria to describe a feeling of suffocation, intense anxiety, convulsions, and paralysis exhibited by women. Ancient Egyptians used perfumes and tonics placed around the body to facilitate movement of the uterus, which they believed would facilitate healing. In the late 1800s, physicians including Charcot, Freud, Breuer, and Janet exhibited renewed interest in the study of hysteria, which they identified as a medical disorder with psychological symptoms (Bogousslavsky & Dieguez, 2014). Charcot described symptoms of hysteria including convulsions, sensory loss, motor paralysis, and amnesia (Herman, 2022). However, the etiology of the cluster of symptoms known as hysteria had not yet been connected to traumatic experiences and was believed to be rooted in the uterus.

Towards the end of the 19th century, Sigmund Freud was inspired by Charcot and began his study of hysteria (Herman, 2022). Freud gathered his findings on hysteria in a paper titled "The aetiology of hysteria," which included 18 case studies linking the physical and psychological symptoms of hysteria to childhood sexual abuse (Freud, 1962). The article was met with harsh criticism because it acknowledged the widespread sexual abuse of children, and Freud's patients were mostly women from families with wealth and social stature (Herman, 2022). Professional and public backlash stalled the exploration of connections between trauma and the body.

While sociopolitical pressure ultimately led Freud and his colleagues to abandon their study of hysteria (Herman, 2022), their investigation of connections between the body and trauma had a lasting impact on the fields of psychiatry, psychology, and art therapy. For example, Margaret Naumburg (1944) explored connections between art therapy, traumatic experiences, and conversion disorder, a condition where a person experiences mind-body distortions that do not have a physiological cause.

ADVERSE CHILDHOOD EXPERIENCES: THE IMPACT OF DIFFICULT EXPERIENCES ON THE BODY

Kaiser Permanente's Adverse Childhood Experiences (ACEs) study led by Dr. Vincent Felitti (Centers for Disease Control and Prevention, 2021) contributed to our knowledge of the prevalence and long-term impact of trauma on the body. Felitti worked in an obesity clinic, frustrated by a patient dropout rate that exceeded 50%. He conducted a study to better understand the common characteristics of people within his patient group, and subsequently discovered that 55% of patients experienced sexual abuse during childhood (Centers for Disease Control and Prevention, 2021). As the study expanded, so did Felitti's understanding of the complex relationship between ACEs and the body.

The ACEs study included over 17,000 middle-class adults and assessed for history of physical, psychological, and sexual abuse; domestic violence; people in the childhood home who had substance abuse concerns, were mentally ill, and/or were suicidal; and a household member being incarcerated (Felitti & Anda, 2010; Felitti *et al.*, 1998). The number of ACEs was compared to each person's health and disease status, and their adult risk behaviors. Results identified that more than half of the participants endorsed at least one category of ACEs, and more than 25% of participants reported two or more ACEs. As the number of participants grew during the longitudinal study, the results remained clear; 28% of the total sample had been physically abused as children, and 28% of female participants had been sexually abused as children (Felitti & Anda, 2010). Statistically significant relationships were found between adult risk behaviors, poor health, and the number of ACEs. Felitti *et al.* (1998) found that "The number of categories of adverse childhood exposures showed a graded relationship to the presence of adult diseases including ischemic heart disease, cancer, chronic lung disease, skeletal fractures, and liver disease" (p.245).

In a recent study, positive associations were found between ACEs and body dysmorphic disorder (BDD), a condition that involves distortion of body image (Longobardi *et al.*, 2022). In addition, a moderate to large association (95%) was found between BDD and a history of being teased during childhood. For participants in the ACEs studies, childhood trauma negatively influenced general health and increased body image concerns.

PREVALENCE OF TRAUMA AND ASSOCIATED DISORDERS

Traumatic experiences are prevalent in the United States and worldwide. In 2017, Kessler and colleagues performed a review of World Health Organization (WHO) Mental Health Surveys within 24 countries (n = 68,894) to understand the impact of trauma around the world. A total of 29 trauma types were assessed within seven broad categories, including war, physical violence, intimate partner or sexual violence, accidents, unexpected or traumatic death of a loved one, traumas to other people, and a residual category of other traumas. They found that 70.4% of respondents experienced lifetime traumas, with a rate of 3.2 exposures per capita. The greatest prevalence of a post-traumatic stress disorder (PTSD) diagnosis was from intimate partner violence, rape, stalking, and lower rates from the unexpected death of a loved one. Kessler *et al.* (2017) concluded that trauma exposure is common throughout the world and unequally distributed with insufficient treatment outcomes.

The astounding prevalence of trauma shifts the question from "What is wrong with you?" to, "What happened to you?" (Sweeney *et al.*, 2018).

However, given that many art therapists and other mental health professionals work in managed care settings, workplaces may necessitate providing a specific diagnosis. The *Diagnostic and Statistical Manual of Mental Disorders* (DSM-5-TR) (American Psychiatric Association, 2022) provided two diagnostic codes most commonly associated with a specific traumatic event: acute stress disorder and post-traumatic stress disorder. The *International Classification of Diseases* (ICD-11) (World Health Organization, 2019a) also included post-traumatic stress disorder and added complex post-traumatic stress disorder (World Health Organization, 2019b). These diagnoses include somatic responses to trauma-like changes in arousal, affect regulation, and dissociation. Dissociation is defined as "a variation in normal consciousness that arises from reduced or altered access to one's thoughts, feelings, perceptions, and/or memories, often in response to a traumatic event, that is not attributable to an underlying medical disorder" (Briere & Scott, 2014, p.46). Dissociation could include distorted perceptions of body image, feeling detached from their bodies, and feeling as though they are looking at themselves through the eyes of another person or from a different vantage point, and may cause people to feel disrupted or disconnected both cognitively and physically. For example, they may feel as though they are viewing the world through a fog or haze, or experience temporary difficulty with their vision. Also, they may experience an alternate sense of reality, time appearing to speed up or slow down. Dissociative symptoms impact the connections between mind and body, altering the way that people view themselves in relation to the world around them. When something terrible happens to a person, their bodies react at that moment and are often impacted over time.

RESILIENCE AND RISK FACTORS

An important consideration for all mental health clinicians, including art therapists, is that experiencing a traumatic event does not always lead to a diagnosis like acute stress disorder, PTSD, or complex PTSD. Less than 10% of people who experience a significant traumatic event subsequently develop PTSD (American Psychiatric Association, 2022; Kilpatrick *et al.*, 2013). We might hear people's trauma narratives and see them illustrated on paper, then wonder how it could be possible that they have not developed a psychological disorder. The answer to this question lies somewhere between risk factors and resilience. Risk factors increase the likelihood that someone who experiences a traumatic event or series of events will develop a disorder. The National Institute of Mental Health (NIMH) (2022) identified risk factors for PTSD, including: experiencing extreme horror, fear, and/or helplessness during the event; physical injury; witnessing the physical injury of another person (including seeing a dead body); trauma occurring during childhood; lack of social support; post-event stressors (e.g., loss of a loved one, loss of a home); and a history of substance abuse or other mental health diagnoses.

Conversely, the NIMH (2022) identified factors that promote resilience, including social support from family and friends; support from a structured group (e.g., a veterans' support group) after a traumatic event; and positive coping strategies. Outcomes were also more positive for people who developed a positive mindset regarding their own actions during the trauma and those who were able to respond actively and effectively during a traumatic event. This is further detailed in the work of Wood-Barcalow and colleagues regarding the factors embedded in body image development and resilience using protective filters that help mitigate triggers (Fuller-Tyszkiewicz, 2019; Tylka & Wood-Barcalow, 2015; Webb *et al.*, 2015; Wood-Barcalow *et al.*, 2010). Keeping risk and resilience factors in mind can bring perspective to our interactions with people who have faced traumatic events and difficult life circumstances, and support the development of positive body image.

TRAUMA AND BODY IMAGE

Trauma impacts state and trait body image and disrupts the development of body image throughout life. During or after a traumatic experience, thoughts and feelings about the body are altered, resulting in emotional and behavioral reactions to this immediate body image experience (Fuller-Tyszkiewicz, 2019). Activated states create a narrative for body image by categorizing variabilities, antecedents, and consequences. Coupled with body image traits (e.g., negative self-evaluation, limited coping skills, cognitive distortions) these states vary in duration and severity of disturbance (Fuller-Tyszkiewicz, 2019). Enough of these body image state experiences can exacerbate negative body image traits and thought processes, and in turn, increase vulnerability to triggers. McDonald clarifies that:

> traumatic memories are retrieved as sensory and affective elements, not alongside sensory and affective elements. The implication here is that the traumatic memory is primarily (and sometimes only) sensory and affective and not necessarily available as the subject of conscious thought. (2018, p.85)

In addition, the sensory and affective elements of these memories are distressing and intrusive, seizing the present and manipulating thoughts and behaviors (McDonald, 2018). The impact of trauma—somatic responses, affect regulation, and dissociation—on body image development throughout life directly impacts the individual's ability to fully engage in life-enhancing experiences.

DEVELOPMENTAL TRAUMA AND BODY IMAGE

A history of the self is a history of the body. A history that includes developmental trauma is a history of pain in the body, distorted images, and a body-self that has been disrupted by trauma (Goodwin & Attias, 1999).

The body plays a special role in developing reality testing and cohesive identity formation, relying on tangible experiences of the body's boundaries. Trauma during childhood and adolescence can increase body image dissatisfaction and emotional dysregulation (Wu *et al.*, 2023), and negatively impact sexual development, intimacy, and a sense of self (Hanna, 1996). In trauma, and specifically body-based trauma (such as physical and sexual abuse), experiences disrupt typical developmental processes (Armstrong *et al.*, 1999). Young (1992) states that:

> The experience of trauma also calls into question our relation to "having a body" and "living in a body" and makes profoundly troubling the centrality of the body in human experience and the body's claim upon us... And, yet it is undeniable that severe trauma is inscribed in and often on the bodies of survivors, leaving a mark that can perhaps be explained but never effaced. (p.92)

Abuse of the body may lead to disruptions in connections with self and others, negative body image and self-perceptions, insecurities in bodily functions, and lower awareness of bodily cues, sensations, and processes. Unresolved trauma causes stress hormones to circulate throughout the body long after the traumatic event has ended, causing emotional and physical responses to continue in the present. When the body does not serve as a container, it becomes the regulator, and externalizing behaviors like self-injurious behaviors, bingeing, and purging serve to control internal states (Armstrong *et al.*, 1999; van der Kolk, 2014).

Body image has been identified as one of the most salient issues affecting adolescents and young adults (Ricciardelli & Yager, 2016). The rapid developmental changes that occur during early adolescence may intensify body image concerns. In addition, adolescence is the average age of onset for eating disorders, which often include distorted body image and body dissatisfaction (Volpe *et al.*, 2016). A recent study of older adolescents and young adults revealed connections between trauma and eating disorders. When a sample of young women (n = 143) from an outpatient eating disorder clinic was given the Trauma Symptom Inventory Alternate Version (TSI-A), Franzoni *et al.* (2013) found that the participants had significantly higher TSI-A scores compared to the general population. Franzoni and colleagues' results are not surprising given the findings from the ACEs studies (Felitti & Anda, 2010; Felitti *et al.*, 1998). Given the intersectionality of body image concerns and trauma, many teenage trauma clients have body-based concerns, including distorted body image and eating disorders.

Clients of all ages benefit from developmentally appropriate psychoeducation that helps them make sense of what is occurring in their bodies post-trauma (Briere & Scott, 2014). Psychoeducation may include information about biological, psychological, and social impacts of trauma using visual aids, demonstrations, and verbal explanation. Providing psychoeducation regarding the effects of trauma is a fundamental component of trauma therapy because it helps people understand what is happening to their minds and bodies (Briere & Scott, 2014), thus it should also be included as part of a comprehensive art therapy treatment plan.

TRAUMA, BODY IMAGE, AND ART THERAPY

Art therapists' incorporation of body movement and images of the body dates to the beginning of the profession (Hill, 1951; Kramer, 1958; Cane, 1951; Naumburg, 1947) and has continued into the present. During the past several decades, prominent art therapists such as Savneet Talwar (2007), Cathy Malchiodi (2008, 2012, 2020), Noah Hass-Cohen (Hass-Cohen & Finlay, 2015, 2019; Hass-Cohen *et al.*, 2014), and Amy Backos (2021) created trauma-informed models of art therapy that incorporate processing body-based trauma, engaging the body in movement along with artmaking, and creating images of the body. Several contributors to King's (2016) book on trauma, art therapy, and neuroscience incorporated directives and imagery that included images of the body and/or body-based work. A review of the literature revealed that body image and trauma is not a new line of inquiry in art therapy, nor would it be typical for an art therapist to focus only on body image during their work with trauma survivors. Furthermore, due to the neurological impact of trauma, it is imperative to understand how this may impact the creative process and the resulting product.

Many areas of the brain are impacted by trauma, and art therapists and mental health clinicians should familiarize themselves with this aspect. For example, the hippocampus is located near the amygdala and plays a major role in memory and learning as well as spatial navigation (Anand & Dhikav, 2012). Trauma alters the connections between the hippocampus and other structures of the brain, including the amygdala (Malivoire *et al.*, 2018), and may modify an individual's ability to make connections between what happened in the past (their memories) and what is happening in the present. Prolonged exposure to trauma may atrophy the hippocampus, resulting in shrinking and impaired performance on reality tasks, scene construction, including disproportionate scenes, and less detailed and vivid memories (Marlatte *et al.*, 2022). Examples of this may be seen in the artwork and corresponding verbal processing of people who have PTSD, as differences in their abilities may relate directly to their neurological functioning and are not necessarily reflective of defense mechanisms.

Artmaking as a means of communicating experiences is functionally beneficial and cognitively necessary because of the disruption in the encoding of traumatic memories and their retrievability. "Art provides a schema-based process by which severely traumatized clients can render these inner experiences visible isomorphically" (Cohen & Mills, 1999, p.203). The directives below are influenced by the work of Herman (2022), Backos (2021), and van der Kolk (2014). They are organized into three stages outlined by Herman (2022): from early treatment where the therapeutic goal is establishing "safety" (p.155), to mid-treatment exploring "remembrance and mourning" (p.175), and end-of-treatment "reconnection" (p.196). The art therapy interventions were designed with an understanding that the impact of trauma on the brain and the body can leave individuals feeling out of control, vulnerable, and powerless. In turn, offering a variety of materials that can be used with specific directives is intended to support control, decision-making, and autonomy. The resulting product can serve as a transitional object that aids in integrating the body through rhythms and shapes into a tangible image of the body (Goodwin & Attias, 1999).

SAFETY
A safe place

This directive is used early in trauma treatment because it is both an assessment tool and a therapeutic intervention to elicit information about the client's world outside therapy. Once it is completed, it provides the client with a tangible image that can be used during distressing times. This supports developing attunement with the body and working towards regulation (Cook-Cottone, 2015).

Directive

Picture yourself in a safe place. What does this place look like? Where are you located within your safe place?

Materials

Tripp and colleagues (2019) utilized collage for this directive, but a variety of two- and three-dimensional materials can empower the client to utilize materials they prefer. Material choice and use can provide the clinician with additional information regarding the person's current psychological state and safety needs.

Comfort collage

Wadeson (2000) explained that collage is a good first choice in art therapy because it is non-threatening and easy for people of all ages to master; for this reason, it may reduce resistance. This directive supports the introduction of grounding exercises and calming techniques while focusing on attunement and identifying self-soothing techniques that can be used in self-regulation (Warschburger, 2022).

Directive

Think about what brings you comfort. Select pictures and words from the magazine images that bring you comfort.

Materials

Pre-cut images and words minimize distraction and maximize time for artmaking and processing. Offering a wide variety of paper sizes, or a box that holds the comfort objects, empowers the client to make decisions within the therapy space.

Symptoms collage

The symptoms collage aims to depict the inner and outer world of the trauma survivor. The intention is to externalize symptoms, provide an image of these emotional and physical experiences, and hold them within a container. This externalizing helps to gain therapeutic distance (Warschburger, 2022); however, this process may reveal a disorganized or fragmented experience of sensations, emotions, and internal processes (Goodwin & Attias, 1999).

Directive
Select some pictures and words from the magazine images to depict what it feels like to have PTSD/symptoms of trauma.

Materials
Pre-cut collage and drawing materials provide instant imagery and containment. Allowing the client to select the container continues the theme of empowerment and decision-making as it pertains to their symptomology. Containers can include paper (e.g., creating a dyad drawing with one side depicting internal reactions, and the other, external reactions) a mask (e.g., the inside depicting internal experiences and the outside depicting what the world sees), or a box (e.g., depicting internal and external experiences).

Symptom-focused body images
Body images can be depicted in a number of ways, ranging from a simple body outline to a complex, realistic rendering. Using a pre-printed body form as a pre-, mid-, and post-assessment provides insight into the experience of the body throughout treatment. In being offered the pre-printed and self-drawn options for exploring symptomology, the client makes a choice based on their level of comfort and safety.

If a client decides to use a body tracing for this exercise, it is imperative that the therapist discusses body autonomy and touch before proceeding. Individuals with body-based trauma, especially childhood sexual abuse, may not be aware of or confident in setting clear body expectations or boundaries with others. Body tracings have the potential to be re-traumatizing, thus the circumstances of the individual client should be considered carefully before proceeding.

The purpose of this directive is to identify the client's connection to the body and target areas of the body most impacted by trauma in order to develop attunement and flexibility (Ceunen *et al.*, 2016; Warschburger, 2022). Symptom-focused body images can help identify areas of the body that are activated or unavailable in times of calm and distress and may provide an understanding of the developing relationship with the body over time.

Directive

I would like to know more about where you feel your symptoms within your body. We can use a printed body outline, or you can create your own. What would you prefer? How can I support you?

Materials

Printed gender-neutral body forms (e.g., gingerbread body), blank drawing paper, or large sheets of butcher paper (for body tracing), and drawing materials.

REMEMBRANCE AND MOURNING
Self before and self after

Exploration of the trauma narrative is something that takes time and should be prompted following the establishment of safety and rapport (Backos, 2021; Herman, 2022). However, it is typically safe and appropriate to explore a person's sense of self before and after a traumatic event during the early and middle phases of treatment. The purpose of this directive is to explore body images before and after trauma, including what has changed or been lost due to a traumatic event. Exploring how loss and change have impacted the body enhances attunement and autonomy and helps the client to develop insight into current reactions and interactions that are impacting their sense of self in the present (Ceunen et al., 2016).

Directive

Create two versions of the self, one before the traumatic event and one after the traumatic event.

Materials

This directive can be approached with a wide variety of materials; for example, using dyad drawings or three-dimensional sculptures that can be viewed side by side.

The self in the moment of trauma

Images of traumatic events could be viewed as illustrations of the trauma narrative (Malchiodi, 2020). Depictions of the self in the moment of trauma should only be undertaken when the person expresses feeling ready, and the therapist agrees based on their professional assessment. The use of metaphor may buffer against potential negative effects (such as flashbacks) that may occur when someone draws a literal illustration of their trauma. For example, using the tree as a metaphor allows for the projection of the experience onto the body, limbs, trunk, or crown. Introducing a metaphoric element that parallels the human body offers a gentle confrontation of the experience of trauma on the body (Cohen & Mills, 1999).

Directive
Draw a tree before, during, and after a storm.

Materials
A 12" x 18" piece of multi-media paper folded into thirds and a range of two-dimensional drawing materials.

Self-portrait

Self-portraits are another commonly used directive in art therapy with trauma survivors (Hass-Cohen & Findlay, 2015, 2019; Klorer, 2016); however, the idea of drawn portraits may feel intimidating to clients if photo-realism is their expectation. The therapist may need to clarify that self-portraits can be represented in a variety of styles and media to render abstract or realistic portrayals of the self. Unlike the before and after drawing, the self-portrait intervention focuses on the here and now. In addition to creating images of the self in the present, furthering this directive to create a future self helps clients to experience hope, set goals, and envision who they want to be months or years into the future.

Directive
Create a piece of artwork that shows who you are today.

Alternative directive
Create a piece of artwork that shows who you want to be in the future.

Materials
Offer a variety of materials, including two-dimensional drawing materials, paint, found objects, collage, and so on, based on the client's comfort within the creative process and their interpretation of a self-portrait.

RECONNECTION

"Reconnection" occurs because, "relationships have been tested and forever changed by the trauma; now she must develop new relationships" (Herman, 2022, p.196).

Circles of closeness

Exploring the word *closeness* with the client is important, especially if their trauma is related to individuals who were supposed to be protective. For example, closeness could depict both physical proximity (e.g., who do I allow to touch me?) and emotional closeness (e.g., who do I feel most emotionally connected to?). The circles of closeness directive explores relational support systems and identifies areas of growth in connection with others (Burns, 1991).

Directive

Draw an image of the self in the center of a paper, and then draw several circles around with at least an inch or two in between the circles. Write names or draw images of people according to their closeness to you.

Materials

Offering a wide variety of paper sizes allows the client to select a size that helps to explore the space between self and others. Providing drawing materials like colored pencils, markers, crayons, and writing tools supports the cognitive process of this directive.

Images of self with others

Building on the previous directive, clients can be prompted to reflect on relational patterns, both supportive and potentially harmful, as they continue to explore the impact of their trauma on their physical and emotional self. Due to the relational aspects of trauma, the process of exploring self in relation to others through a variety of materials and modalities supports the development of interpersonal control, autonomy, and decision-making. Ultimately, this also translates to healing within the body and developing a more attuned connection (Tylka & Wood-Barcalow, 2015).

Directive

Explore your relationship with someone in your life (e.g., family, co-workers, partner, friend).

Materials

Offering a variety of two- and three-dimensional materials supports the exploration of relationships through a variety of kinesthetic processes from small mark-making to large expansive movements, pounding clay to smoothing cracks, or crafting dolls and figurines.

BODY IMAGE AND TRAUMA IN SPECIFIC CONTEXTS

The body is always in space, and it is imperative to bring it into session. "Talking directly about the body combats depersonalization, clarifies traumatic regression and challenges fears that the body is too damaged to be included in the recovery process" (Goodwin & Attias, 1999, p.170). Unfortunately, many trained therapists lack experience and knowledge surrounding connections between trauma, bodily sensations, and body image development. Clinicians may not have reflected on their own relationships with their bodies, leaving them unprepared to guide others in this work (Goodwin & Attias, 1999). Engaging clients in artmaking can help them access bodily experiences that were previously unattainable, frightening, or physically painful, in a contained and supportive space to develop autonomy, control, and trust.

The authors of subsequent chapters of this book explore the complex relationship between trauma and the body within specific contexts and with people from specific backgrounds: Linda Adeniyi on intimate partner violence; Mary Kometiani and Cynthia Wilson on sex trafficking; Deborah Elkis-Abuhoff and Morgan Gaydos on military trauma; and Chelsea Leeds on trauma in the LGTBQIA population.

REFERENCES

American Psychiatric Association (2022). *Diagnostic and Statistical Manual of Mental Disorders* (5th ed., text rev.). https://doi.org/10.1176/appi.books.9780890425787

American Psychological Association (2023). *Psychology Topics: Trauma.* www.apa.org/topics/trauma

Anand, K. S. & Dhikav, V. (2012). Hippocampus in health and disease: An overview. *Annals of Indian Academy of Neurology, 15*(4), 239–246. https://doi.org/10.4103/0972-2327.104323

Armstrong, M. T., Stronck, K., & Carlson, C. D. (1999). Body Image and Self-Perception in Women with Histories of Incest. In J. Goodwin & R. Attias (eds), *Splintered Reflections: Images of the Body in Trauma* (pp.137–153). Basic Books.

Backos, A. (2021). *Post-Traumatic Stress Disorder and Art Therapy*. Jessica Kingsley Publishers.

Bogousslavsky, J. & Dieguez, S. (2014). Sigmund Freud and hysteria: The etiology of psychoanalysis? *Frontiers of Neurology and Neuroscience, 35*, 109–125. https://doi.org/10.1159/000360244

Briere, J. N. & Scott, C. (2014). *Principles of Trauma Therapy: A Guide to Symptoms, Evaluation, and Treatment (DSM-5 update)*. Sage Publications.

Burns, R. C. (1991). *A Guide to Family-Centered Circle Drawings (F-C-C-D): With Symbol Probes and Visual Free Association*. Routledge.

Cane, F. (1951). *The Artist in Each of Us*. Thames and Hudson.

Carpenter, J. (Director) & Hill, D. (Producer) (1978). *Halloween* [Motion Picture]. Compass International Pictures.

Centers for Disease Control and Prevention (2021). *About the CDC-Kaiser ACE Study*. www.cdc.gov/violenceprevention/aces/about.html

Ceunen, E., Vlaeyen, J. W. S., & Van Diest, I. (2016). On the origin of interoception. *Frontiers in Psychology, 7*(743), 1–17. https://dx.doi.org/10.3389/fpsyg.2016.00743

Cleveland Clinic (2022). *Parasympathetic Nervous System (PSNS)*. https://my.clevelandclinic.org/health/body/23266-parasympathetic-nervous-system-psns#:~:text=A%20note%20from%20Cleveland%20Clinic,body's%20short%2Dterm%20survival%20responses

Cohen, B. M. & Mills, A. (1999). Skin/Paper/Bark: Body Image, Trauma and the Diagnostic Drawing Series. In J. Goodwin & R. Attias (eds), *Splintered Reflections: Images of the Body in Trauma* (pp.203–221). Basic Books.

Cook-Cottone, C. P. (2015). Incorporating positive body image into the treatment of eating disorders: A model for attunement and mindful self-care. *Body Image, 14*, 158–167. http://dx.doi.org/10.1016/j.bodyim.2015.03.004

Felitti, V. J. & Anda, R. F. (2010). The Relationship of Adverse Childhood Experiences to Adult Medical Disease, Psychiatric Disorders, and Sexual Behavior. In R. A. Lanius, E. Vermetten, & C. Pain (eds), *Implications for Healthcare. The Impact of Early Life Trauma on Health and Disease: The Hidden Epidemic*. www.theannainstitute.org/LV%20FINAL%202-7-09.pdf

Felitti, V. J., Anda, R. F., Nordenberg, D., Williamson, D. F., *et al.* (1998). Relationship of childhood abuse and household dysfunction to many of the leading causes of death in adults: The Adverse Childhood Experiences (ACE) Study. *American Journal of Preventive Medicine, 14*(4), 245–258. https://doi.org/10.1016/S0749-3797(98)00017-8

Franzoni, E., Gualandi, S., Caretti, V., Schimmenti, A., *et al.* (2013). The relationship between alexithymia, shame, trauma, and body image disorders: Investigation over a large clinical sample. *Neuropsychiatric Disease and Treatment, 9*, 185–193. https://doi.org/10.2147/NDT.S34822

Freud, S. (1962). The Aetiology of Hysteria. In J. Strachey, *The Standard Edition of the Complete Psychological Works of Sigmund Freud* (vol. 3; pp.187–221). Hogarth Press (Original work published 1896).

Fuller-Tyszkiewicz, M. (2019). Body image states in everyday life: Evidence from ecological momentary assessment methodology. *Body Image, 31*, 245–272. https://doi.org/10.1016/j.bodyim.2019.02.010

Goodwin, J. & Attias, R. (1999). Conversations with the Body. In J. Goodwin & R. Attias (eds), *Splintered Reflections: Images of the Body in Trauma* (pp.167–182). Basic Books.

Hanna, B. (1996). Sexuality, body image, and self-esteem: The future after trauma. *Journal of Trauma Nursing, 3*(1), 13–20. doi:10.1097/00043860-199601000-00009

Hass-Cohen, N. & Findlay, J. C. (2015). *Art Therapy and the Neuroscience of Relationships, Creativity, and Resiliency: Skills and Practices* (Norton series on interpersonal neurobiology). W. W. Norton & Company.

Hass-Cohen, N. & Findlay, J. M. C. (2019). The art therapy relational neuroscience and memory reconsolidation four drawing protocol. *The Arts in Psychotherapy, 63*, 51–59. https://doi.org/10.1016/j.aip.2019.03.002

Hass-Cohen, N., Findlay, J. C., Carr, R., & Vanderlan, J. (2014). "Check, change what you need to change and/or keep what you want": An art therapy neurobiological-based trauma protocol. *Art Therapy, 31*(2), 69–78. https://doi.org/10.1080/07421656.2014.903825

Herman, J. L. (2022). *Trauma and Recovery: The Aftermath of Violence—From Domestic Abuse to Political Terror*. Basic Books.

Hill, A. (1951). *Painting Out Illness*. William and Norgate.

Kessler, R. C., Aguilar-Gaxiola, S., Alonso, J., Benjet, C., *et al.* (2017). Trauma and PTSD in the WHO World Mental Health Surveys. *European Journal of Psychotraumatology, 8*(5), 1353383. doi:10.1080/20008198.2017.1353383

Kilpatrick, D. G., Resnick, H. S., Milanak, M. E., Miller, M. W., Keyes, K. M., & Friedman, M. J. (2013). National estimates of exposure to traumatic events and PTSD prevalence using DSM-IV and DSM-5 criteria. *Journal of Trauma Stress, 26*(5), 537–547. doi:10.1002/jts.21848

King, J. L. (ed.) (2016). *Art Therapy, Trauma, and Neuroscience: Theoretical and Practical Perspectives*. Routledge.

Klorer, P. G. (2016). Neuroscience and Art Therapy with Severely Traumatized Children: The Art is the Evidence. In J. King (ed.). *Art Therapy, Trauma, and Neuroscience: Theoretical and Practical Perspectives* (pp.139–156). Routledge.

Kramer, E. (1958). *Art Therapy in a Children's Community: A Study of the Function of Art Therapy in the Treatment Program of Wiltwyck School for Boys*. Charles C. Thomas Publisher. https://doi.org/10.1037/13175-000

Longobardi, C., Badenes-Ribera, L., & Fabris, M. A. (2022). Adverse childhood experiences and body dysmorphic symptoms: A meta-analysis. *Body Image, 40*, 267–284. https://doi.org/10.1016/j.bodyim.2022.01.003

Malchiodi, C. A. (2008). Creative Interventions and Childhood Trauma. In C. A. Malchiodi (ed.), *Creative Interventions with Traumatized Children* (pp.3–21). Guilford Press.

Malchiodi, C. (2012). Trauma Informed Art Therapy and Sexual Abuse in Children. In P. Goodyear-Brown (ed.), *Handbook of Child Sexual Abuse: Identification, Assessment, and Treatment* (pp.341–354). John Wiley & Sons.

Malchiodi, C. A. (2020). *Trauma and Expressive Arts Therapy: Brain, Body, and Imagination in the Healing Process*. Guilford Press.

Malivoire, B. L., Girard, T. A., Patel, R., & Monson, C. M. (2018). Functional connectivity of hippocampal subregions in PTSD: Relations with symptoms. *BioMed Central Psychiatry, 18*(1), 1–9. https://bmcpsychiatry.biomedcentral.com/articles/10.1186/s12888-018-1716-9

Marlatte, H., Beaton, D., Adler-Luzon, S., Abo-Ahmad, L., & Gilboa, A. (2022). Scene construction and spatial processing in post-traumatic stress disorder. *Frontiers in Behavioral Neuroscience, 16*, 888358. https://doi.org/10.3389/fnbeh.2022.888358

McDonald, M. C. (2018). A prismatic account: Body, thought, action in trauma. *Teorema, 37*(3), 83–99.

National Institute of Mental Health (2022). *Post-Traumatic Stress Disorder: Why do some people develop PTSD and other people do not?* www.nimh.nih.gov/health/topics/post-traumatic-stress-disorder-ptsd

Naumburg, M. (1947). *Studies of the "Free" Art Expression of Behavior Problem Children and Adolescents as a Means of Diagnosis and Therapy*. Nervous & Mental Disorders Monograph Series. Grune & Stratton.

Naumburg, M. (1944). The drawings of an adolescent girl suffering from conversion hysteria with amnesia. *The Psychiatric Quarterly, 18*, 197–224.

Ogden, P., Minton, K., & Pain, C. (2006). *Trauma and the Body: A Sensorimotor Approach to Psychotherapy* (Norton series on interpersonal neurobiology). W. W. Norton & Company.

Ricciardelli, L. A. & Yager, Z. (2016). *Adolescence and Body Image: From Development to Preventing Dissatisfaction*. Routledge/Taylor & Francis.

Sweeney, A., Filson, B., Kennedy, A., Collinson, L., & Gillard, S. (2018). A paradigm shift: Relationships in trauma-informed mental health services. *BJPsych Advances, 24*(5), 319–333. https://doi.org/10.1192/bja.2018.29

Talwar, S. (2007). Accessing traumatic memory through art making: An art therapy trauma protocol (ATTP). *The Arts in Psychotherapy, 34*(1), 22–35. https://doi.org/10.1016/j.aip.2006.09.001

Tasca, C., Rapetti, M., Carta, M. G., & Fadda, B. (2012). Women and hysteria in the history of mental health. *Clinical Practice and Epidemiology in Mental Health, 8*, 110–119. https://doi.org/10.2174/1745017901208010110

Tripp, T., Potash, J. S., & Brancheau, D. (2019). Safe Place collage protocol: Art making for managing traumatic stress. *Journal of Trauma & Dissociation, 20*(5), 511–525. https://doi.org/10.1080/15299732.2019.1597813

Tylka, T. L. & Wood-Barcalow, N. L. (2015). What is and what is not positive body image? Conceptual foundations and construct definition. *Body Image, 14*, 118–129. http://dx.doi.org/10.1016/j.bodyim.2015.04.001

van der Kolk, B. (2014). *The Body Keeps the Score: Brain, Mind, and Body in the Healing of Trauma*. Penguin.

Volpe, U., Tortorella, A., Manchia, M., Monteleone, A. M., Albert, U., & Monteleone, P. (2016). Eating disorders: What age at onset? *Psychiatry Research, 238*, 225–227. https://doi.org/10.1016/j.psychres.2016.02.048

Wadeson, H. (2000). *Art Therapy Practice: Innovative Approaches with Diverse Populations*. John Wiley & Sons.

Warschburger, P., Wortmann, H. R., Gisch, U. A., Baer, N., *et al.* (2022). An experimental approach to training interoceptive sensitivity: Study protocol for a pilot randomized controlled trial. *Nutrition Journal, 21*(74), 1–16. https://doi.org/10.1186/s12937-022-00827-4

Webb, J. B., Wood-Barcalow, N. L., & Tylka, T. L. (2015). Assessing positive body image: Contemporary approaches and future directions. *Body Image, 14*, 130–145. http://dx.doi.org/10.1016/j.bodyim.2015.03.010

Wood-Barcalow, N. L., Tylka, T. L., & Augustus-Horvath, C. L. (2010). "But I like my body": Positive body image characteristics and a holistic model for young adult women. *Body Image, 7*, 106–116. http://dx.doi.org/10.1016/j.bodyim.2010.01.001

World Health Organization (2019a). QE84 Acute Stress Reaction. In *International Classification of Diseases* (11th ed.). https://icd.who.int/browse/2024-01/mms/en#505909942

World Health Organization (2019b). 6B41 Complex Post Traumatic Stress Disorder. In *International Classification of Diseases* (11th ed.). https://icd.who.int/browse/2024-01/mms/en#585833559

Wu, S., Liu, J., Xue, Z., Xu. J., *et al.* (2023). Association between childhood trauma and affective lability among adolescents: A moderated mediation model. *Journal of Affective Disorders, 3*(38), 21–31. https://doi.org/10.1016/j.jad.2023.05.092

Young, L. (1992). Sexual abuse and the problem with embodiment. *Child Abuse & Neglect, 16*(1), 89–100.

CHAPTER VI

Treating Body-Based Trauma of Sex Trafficking through Art Therapy

—— MARY K. KOMETIANI AND CYNTHIA WILSON ——

INTRODUCTION TO SEX TRAFFICKING

Sex trafficking (ST) has no geographic limits. Prevailing all over the world (International Labour Organization *et al.*, 2022), ST occurs in each of the states in the United States (National Human Trafficking Hotline, 2021). ST is enlisting, arranging, acquiring, concealing, or moving an individual for the intent of commercial sexual exploitation (Victims of Trafficking and Violence Prevention Act of 2000), which is defined as a sex act in exchange for anything of value (U.S. Department of Health and Human Services, 2017). When individuals under the age of 18 are sexually exploited, they are legally considered trafficked. Violating basic human rights and opposing the natural progression of physical and developmental growth, sex traffickers oppress individuals through the following tactics:

- Forceful harm to acquire and/or sustain control.

- Fraudulent promises of love, employment, or a better life.

- Coercion as manipulation, expropriation of identification, and blackmail (U.S. Department of Health and Human Services, 2017).

Although any gender variant person can be targeted, most reported cases are females. The International Labour Organization *et al.* (2022) reported that of the 6.3 million adults and 1.7 million children forced into commercial sex exploitation, four out of five survivors were women/girls. In addition to gender, victims are of any age, race, nationality, or ethnicity. Not targeting one type of person, ST occurs in countless forms of exploitation. Individuals can be trafficked through their own family, intimate partner violence, organized crime, abduction, or false offers of employment (Gerassi & Nichols, 2018). It is also important to note that the majority of ST survivors have survived childhood abuse, sexual assault, community violence, or natural disaster (U.S. Department of Health and Human Services, 2017). Compounded trauma often burdens survivors of ST, requiring more complex treatment and an extended time to reintegrate back into society.

RAMIFICATIONS OF SEX TRAFFICKING

While each survivor has their own story, many struggle with physical, psychological, emotional, and spiritual ramifications; traffickers force individuals into ST and control them through violence, entrapment, forced drug addiction, abuse, and threats or harm to loved ones and pets. Traffickers violate and manipulate their victims' innate personal rights, identity, and morals. Physically, survivors suffer from problems such as pain, wounds, burns, fractures, ignored (or dissociated from) chronic conditions, dental problems, malnutrition, sexually transmitted infections (STIs), internal and external vaginal and anal tearing, fertility issues, pregnancy, and complications resulting from abortions (Williamson *et al.*, 2012). Severe repercussions from being trafficked include disease, drug addiction, and early death (U.S. Department of State, 2017).

In addition to physical devastation, there is a grievous psychological toll. While symptoms of severe depression, anxiety, and post-traumatic stress disorder (PTSD) have a substantial impact, the multiple traumas occurring from trafficking exploitation may lead to comorbid diagnoses, including complex trauma, anxiety (Abas *et al.*, 2013; Courtois & Ford, 2013; Oram *et al.*, 2012; Tsutsumi *et al.*, 2008) and dissociation (Wilson & Coleman, 2020). Furthermore, chronic conditions from the continued release of stress hormones and heightened constant pain receptors can continue decades after the abuse has stopped due to PTSD and complex-PTSD (C-PTSD). While C-PTSD is not currently a diagnosis in the *Diagnostic and Statistical Manual of Mental Disorders* (American Psychiatric Association, 2022), it is defined by the *International Classification of Diseases* (World Health Organization, 2019) and was first used to explain the experience of surviving severe abuse and violence, cults, and sexual exploitation (Herman, 1992). Highly recognized by mental health practitioners as an aftermath of trauma, C-PTSD is a form of PTSD with a conglomerate of layered abuse caused by the severity and prolonged nature of the abuse (Scarce & Wilson, 2022). The relational aspect that is common with C-PTSD adds convolution to the trauma effects on the mind and body of the survivor.

Psychological diagnoses are complicated by the emotional burden of being trafficked with a loss of control, isolation, terrorization, feeling numb, damaged, despairing, distressed, saddened, and worthless. Trafficking also impacts the social aspect as individuals feel untrusting and disconnected from self, others, and the community (Wilson & Coleman, 2020), and individuals experience injury to their integrity due to lack of protection from society, system corruption, severe betrayal, and dehumanizing treatment (Bloom, 2018). ST is devastating to the survivors' identity (Davidtz *et al.*, 2022), and because of this loss of self and connection to the future, suicidal ideation is common in sex trafficked survivors (Zimmerman *et al.*, 2008).

The exploited person suffers in every aspect of their life. The survivor endures ongoing physical effects from rape, abuse, neglect, and infections; various mental health diagnoses of anxiety, depression, and dissociation; emotional discord; social disconnection and isolation; and spiritual distress that diminishes one's sense of meaning. Sexually exploited victims may die young because their lives often end in illness, murder, suicide, or overdose. If the victims can escape and survive, they often endure complicated, comorbid, and lifelong issues that demand proper help and support.

Body image and quality of life

In addition to the other disconcerting impacts, ST can also mutate survivors' perceptions of their own physical image, self-worth, and personal outlook, causing dissociation, resentment, and shame in their bodies. The quality of life diminishes for sexual abuse survivors due to body image disturbances affecting their emotions and cognitions regarding the body, perception of appearance, and body functions (Fallon & Ackard, 2002). Sexual violence contributes to personalizing feelings of disrespect, disgust, weakness, and detachment, resulting in body dissatisfaction and negative body image (Smolak, 2011; Spring, 1993).

Sexual objectification, a component of sexual violence, consists of the treatment that a body's value is primarily a mere tool to be used by the perpetrator (Fredrickson & Roberts, 1997). ST survivors are objectified as sexual objects and believe that they are inferior to other people, unworthy of a better life and that their only worth is sexual (Sukach *et al.*, 2018). A sexual abuse survivor may believe that their needs do not matter and that they will not be respected (Fallon & Ackard, 2002). Sexual objectification leads survivors to experience body-based shame, anxiety about their appearance and safety, and body discord (Fredrickson & Roberts, 1997). In addition to affecting the survivor's quality of life, body betrayal may occur with an experience of arousal during the abuse (Fallon & Ackard, 2002). ST survivors are treated like sexual objects; this inhumanity causes them to believe that the body does not belong to them, their value is only in their appearance and how they can serve another, their needs are nonexistent, and they cannot trust their bodies. Body image disconnect is a way to survive abuse by denying the self completely.

The expression of cognition, emotions, and the physical body that make up one's body image, are shaped by sexual experiences (Wiederman, 2002). Body image is a concern for sexually abused females as they have a tendency to develop insecure attachment and struggle with weight; survivors have a disrupted view of self and a negative body scheme, and these negative beliefs elicit self-harm and hate towards their violated body (Fallon & Ackard, 2002). Disordered eating may result from sexual violence (Smolak, 2011), as it is common for survivors to either restrict or increase their intake of food to decrease attractiveness and deter potential advances of abuse (Fallon & Ackard, 2002).

Survivors may experience shame and self-blame for what they endured and were forced to do while being trafficked, and this is closely connected to low self-esteem (Polaris, 2014). ST negatively impacts the victim's body image, body perception, body concept, and personal identity. Beyond body reintegration, ST severely disrupts a person's sense of self and self-worth, quality of life, self-development, the morals and beliefs that guide them, and it alters their outlook on the world.

TREATMENT FOR SEX TRAFFICKED SURVIVORS

When treating survivors of ST, there are some recommended approaches:

- Survivor-informed therapy entails survivor implementation of plans and policies based on their concerns, needs, and opinions.

- Culturally competent treatment allows effective care across cultures (e.g., language, beliefs, customs, and values of various races, ethnicities, and religions).

- Trauma-informed care works to not re-traumatize by recognizing the impact of trauma and its symptoms and signs, while prioritizing safety, choice, and empowerment (U.S. Department of State, 2022).

- Strength-based care realizes an individual's talents and possibilities in an empowering community that recognizes that every client has strengths that help facilitate positive change (Saleebey, 2013).

POST-TRAUMATIC GROWTH, EMPOWERMENT, AND POSITIVE BODY IMAGE

Post-traumatic growth (PTG) is perceived as a significant experience of cognitive and emotional growth following a traumatic experience through:

- personal strength/new awareness of power

- new possibilities/new interest

- emotionally relating to others and increased connection with supportive individuals

- appreciation for life's pleasures

- religious/spiritual development that can lead to wisdom from life experience

- increased meaning in life (Calhoun & Tedeschi, 2013).

For survivors of body-based trauma, PTG is demonstrated through newfound trust and reliance in the body, investment in new areas of life, and experiencing support, gratitude, and renewed purpose. While recovery is unique to each survivor, research suggests that support and empowerment may be a crucial part of improving body image (Gattario & Frisén, 2019). Experiencing control, feelings of adequacy and love for their bodies, a more positive body image, and decreased disordered eating are the benefits of empowerment for survivors of sexual abuse (Smolak, 2011).

Survivors may also gain improved body image by experiencing self-compassion, positivity, self-care (Tiggemann, 2015), body acceptance, self-worth, and healthy lifestyle changes (Bacon *et al.*, 2002).

ART THERAPY THEORY AND GOALS

Talk therapy alone does not adequately meet the needs of ST survivors because of the complicated nature of body image that encompasses sensory, mental, and somatic components; these need to be addressed through experiential and expressive treatment for advancement to occur (Danylchuk, 2015; Rabinor & Bilich, 2011). Art therapy (AT) has proven to assist in survivors' recovery (Kometiani & Farmer, 2020; Spring, 1993; Tan, 2012) and also accomplish change through accessing the non-verbal aspects of body image (Rabinor & Bilich, 2011). AT offers the potential to build community, process loss and reintegrate the past, and increase self-worth while restoring the parts of the lost self and providing voice and power back to an individual who experienced no control. Current AT research has demonstrated that:

- structured AT groups provided experiences of emotional processing of trauma and loss, empowerment, and establishing community, leading to an increased sense of self-worth and hope through developing purpose and vision for the future (Kometiani, 2020b, 2021)

- for male youth who were sex trafficked, AT assisted in reducing shame, guilt, trauma, anxiety, and depression while providing coping mechanisms (Drosdick, 2020)

- with Nepalese female youth, an AT and reproductive health program provided a deeper sense of appreciation for the self and reduced shame, isolation, loss, and fear (Tan & Moore, 2020).

AT is a vital part of the recovery process for individuals who have survived ST due to the benefits of empowerment gained from creating, externalizing emotions, and using visual communication of trauma, especially when words cannot be expressed due to the effects of trauma on the verbal centers of the brain. Also, AT can gradually reconnect the client to their body for the release of trauma memories to create healthy connections or introduce perceptions of how to relate to the body differently from what they were taught by the sex traffickers, in order for the survivor to find new purpose in self and life.

ART THERAPY, CULTURAL HUMILITY, AND INCLUSIVITY

Cultural humility is maintaining respect and equality when working with a client who is of a different culture; the therapist is encouraged to be open, curious, and interested in learning about the survivor's belief system, cultural background, personal values, experiences, and worldview; they're cautioned to not assume from previous experience, education, or knowledge (Hook *et al.*, 2013). By practicing cultural humility, art therapists can develop a stronger sense of understanding for those they serve (Jackson, 2020).

Talwar (2010) cautions art therapists to be inclusive towards all aspects of identity the client has, recognize the unequal relationship in the AT setting, honor the individual's image and its cultural significance, and apply an intersectional framework for race, class, sexuality, and gender as something that is fluid in its complexity. To apply this while working with ST survivors, art therapists are encouraged to remember that the art that is made in therapy has worth (like the survivor); to acknowledge and ensure that the power difference between therapist and client is not re-traumatizing; to not judge the survivor regarding what they were forced to do while being exploited or their decisions afterward; and to use non-triggering art supplies and media that represent the client's personal beliefs, gender, and background.

ART THERAPISTS AND SOCIAL ACTION

Kaplan (2007) states that social action addresses societal issues, and while AT facilitates inner personal change, social action intends to make collective change. Just as it is crucial for survivors to experience an inner change in the healing process, art therapists need to become advocates for change in ST, as this global issue violates basic and fundamental human rights and destroys communities. The ripple effect extends from the survivors and their extensive mental, emotional, and physical states of distress, how they react and function in the community, and beyond to how we attune to the needs of these survivors, affecting changes in our neighborhood and the society that we build that further help our clients.

This is a global issue affecting all of us, and art therapists need to work together to bring about social change—to join the anti-trafficking movement—and take action, as every life has value and every human person deserves the right to be free and safe.

CASE EXAMPLES

The following two case examples describe various aspects of survivorship and share how art was used to help the individuals process and heal from the body trauma of being sex trafficked as children. In these cases, trafficking altered the individuals' perception of their self and body, and their unique responses were explored through art materials and interventions. The art treatments were individualized and specific to these two survivors. Even though other cases of ST may be similar, the human mind and personal experience are exclusive to each individual, so flexibility, compassion, and empathy are required from the art therapist.

Warning: Some details in these case examples are disturbing due to the nature of the crimes committed. Be sure to follow self-care measures and access resources available to you.

VERONICA

Veronica Wanchena is a middle-aged, cisgender, white female from the United States (full consent given). As a result of being sex trafficked, Veronica suffered from STIs, emotional trauma, depersonalization, and derealization. She did not experience a meaningful existence and had no awareness of self as an individual or her body as being her own. "I had been driven insane, and I did not know who I was, male or female, child or adult" (Wanchena, 2015, p.36). The extreme dissociation Veronica needed in order to survive this repetitive torture caused a natural response of dissociative identity disorder (DID) as a means of protection against aspects and events of the various traumas.

At 18, even though she was able to escape from her father's cruelties, she blamed herself for the abuse she suffered throughout her life. After decades of therapy, she realized she had separated from her body and was completely unaware of how it changed over time in shape and size due to the significant tortures. She wrote in the first trilogy book *This White House: Recovery from Incest through Painting My Story*, which was published under the pseudonym of one of the dissociative parts, "As an obese woman most of my life, I can tell you that inside I constantly felt the insatiable, desperate hunger of a starving person" (Marie, 2015, p.104). The weight gain appeared to be a defense mechanism to expand her personal space that had been stolen, a way to disguise the sexuality of her body and/or dissociate from what she was forced to do and the effects of depersonalization. With at-home, self-guided art creation and in-therapy art sharing, she could finally see herself, and an awareness of her body developed with a need to care for, respect, be grateful for, and love it as part of the whole self. "In my body, I no longer feel like a stranger living in a strange house" (Marie, 2015, p.108).

Approaches

Survivor-informed psychotherapy supported the use of at-home, self-guided art production. In between therapy sessions, Veronica and the other dissociated parts created what they were incapable of expressing aloud; they created what each dissociated part needed to convey and brought the art into therapy to discuss. Due to the many parts needing different support, the focus here will be on the overall body and self-image disconnect. Figures 6.1 and 6.2 were created as process art related to their trauma by the dissociated parts named Lume and G.O.M. It was through the artwork that a new *voice* was discovered, along with an awareness of no longer being isolated. The recreated traumas in the art allowed Veronica and the other dissociated parts and their tormenting memories to be held externally through therapy. Veronica learned to self-advocate by discovering language through visual, verbal, and written expression. Similar to how a child naturally develops communication skills in a healthy environment (Chapman, 2014), Veronica was able to develop a sense of self and process the traumas in a way that brought her back into the body and connected with the dissociated parts.

Figure 6.1, Holes, personified Lume and showed the holes that penetrate deep into their psyche and physical form with every abuse. Holes is a visual description of the emptiness and lack of existence felt due to the history of perpetual abuse, lack of being seen, and being unprotected. The monochromatic nature of the painting gives an outstanding representation of the disparaging emotional disconnect that was created out of necessity to endure all of the torturous encounters and "holes" of her enslavement. This image displays a dissociation and separation from the entire body that was required for survival.

FIGURE 6.1: HOLES

Figure 6.2, Boy knocked over, was completed by the dissociative parts G.O.M. and Lume, showing body dysmorphia with depersonalization, derealization, and possibly dissociative fugue. These terms are defined by the American Psychiatric Association (2022) and explained here in regard to Veronica:

- Body dysmorphia is when Veronica saw the body differently from what it was physiologically, even unable to see it as her own.
- Depersonalization is a form of dissociation that occurred when Veronica disconnected from self and did not feel as though she was within the body or even aware of the body.
- Derealization is a form of dissociation, where Veronica disconnected from the environment and people around her.
- Dissociative fugue occurred when Veronica lost track of time and events throughout the day(s) because another dissociated part took

charge of the body as she was going places or doing things that were triggering.

The description for this painting in Veronica's book (2015) explains how the torture by her father forced her into creating many personas of the opposite gender to survive and combat insanity. "It knocked me over inside and I often lost any sense of reality regarding my own gender, age, and orientation to time and place" (Wanchena, 2015, p.32).

FIGURE 6.2: BOY KNOCKED OVER

Art mediums

Primarily, Veronica and the dissociated parts liked to use paint for expression. Each painting unconsciously represented the emotional state of the dissociated part and provided a platform to see the self as they imagined, as they felt, and perhaps even as they were. The visual imagery created by any of the parts allowed them to be their own witness, as if looking into a mirror of their soul for healing from the inside out. Once the inside was seen, the body on the outside could be seen for what it was, and the depersonalization and altered views of the body faded away.

Post-traumatic growth and future goals

Veronica was terrorized with continued extreme abuse while trafficked by her father; she was forced to sell her body and remain idle within her mind as she was consumed by the offenders. No doubt, these traumas caused the need for body disconnection, as well as the dysmorphia needed to be either male or female for the perpetrators' demands. In addition to receiving therapy as an adult, Veronica found that at-home self-guided art creation gave her a voice and opened the opportunity for a witness to the traumas to come forward. She gradually returned to the body that had been over-looked, enslaved, and insecure. Veronica rediscovered her physical being, its functions, and her control, and became a healthy weight, with reduced ailments. She learned to not only see herself but to love herself and her body. "More and more, I am coming to know that I AM, and that my body, mind and soul are one whole me" (Marie, 2015, p.101).

Veronica still experiences healing as she goes back to look at the art-work done during therapy and as new life paths emerge. The post-traumatic growth Veronica experienced helps her advocate for others who have been abused as she shares her story in her published books and professional pre-sentations at conferences. Outside this work, she helps others by providing care and empathy through her nursing license. Veronica's current career path as an artist, author, speaker, and registered nurse remains greatly ful-filling. The art process was the necessary tool that gave her the voice and reflection she needed to get to where she is today.

Amy Anna

Amy Anna Soto is a middle-aged, cisgender, white female from the United States (full consent given). Amy Anna was in primary school, between 5–12 years old, when she was first sexually assaulted by her biological father; she was later sexually abused by her stepfather, her family's friends, and by a stalker—posing as her boyfriend—who kidnapped and assaulted her on her way to school. Many liberties were taken in abusing her throughout her childhood and teenage years. Through visual art, poetry, and journaling, she processed her trauma and communicated about the long-term abuse she suffered. Although she does not identify as a survivor of ST, her abuse meets the definition as she was forced to engage in sexual acts, and manipulated into relationships as a sex slave, all while she was a juvenile. During social gatherings, Amy Anna was sexually assaulted and witnessed sexual abuse to others. This led her brain to defend the traumas by separating the events, emotions, and various aspects of the torture with dissociation, and instinctively she developed DID.

As an adult, Amy Anna intentionally made a conscious choice to grow her body larger as a defense mechanism against abusive threats and actions. She strategically thought that if she had been heavier when she was raped and molested as a child, perhaps the abusers would not have been able to knock her down, or she could have overpowered the men who assaulted her. Amy Anna also thought that if she was larger in size, she would be more likely to be noticed walking around in public places; for example, if ever she were to be abducted, perhaps people in the area would remember seeing her and be able to identify where she was last seen and even with whom, so she could be more easily rescued from her abuser.

Approaches

Trauma-informed, survivor-informed, cognitive behavioral art therapy (CBAT), trauma-focused cognitive behavioral therapy (TF-CBT), and sensorimotor psychotherapy were intertwined to address body image distortions, among other healing needs.

While the AT shifted over a decade in treatment, a core element was the subtle/gentle body feeling and sensory check-ins (listed below) to help gauge Amy Anna's physical presence, increase self-awareness, and discover subconscious messages from different dissociated parts. During therapy, the different dissociated parts were in various healing stages and responded differently to particular approaches. Being aware of the dissociative parts is similar to being attuned to the emotional and developmental shifts that occur during or between sessions. This is vital in ensuring that the needs of the dissociated parts are met. However, the dissociative parts and their messages for treatment were usually acknowledged and conveyed through Amy Anna. They were either agreed on between the dissociated parts to further work with or disregarded because it was not something for Amy Anna to be aware of yet, so further work in that direction would pause or stop.

To achieve greater awareness of self/existence, Amy Anna used mindfulness and body outline check-ins of how she felt in the moment/environment after a dream/nightmare/memory or after the sessions. Bilateral scribbles for grounding into the environment and body, narrative visual processing (Chapman, 2014) to integrate and heal the body trauma, and spontaneous visual and written journaling, Emotional Freedom Technique (EFT/Tapping) and sensory-motor psychotherapy to gently connect to the physical body were routinely used. These opportunities, with an array of flexibility, allowed for discovery, grounding, and processing in the AT, where a wide assortment of interventions was required to meet the distinct needs of the dissociative parts that were present during treatment.

Art mediums

Writing was the first expression when words of childhood horrors could not find the pathways to their lips. Amy Anna remained dedicated to writing about her dreams and creating imagery to coincide with this. The images and words presented clues from her subconscious as to what she needed to see, acknowledge, and process further. As seen in Figures 6.3 and 6.4, the poems and images were powerful for processing, as she found a voice that had been gagged by the abusers' exploits and threats.

Other mediums used during therapy included explorative work with more fluid mediums, such as stained glass or acrylic paint pours and abstract painting. These were times when Amy Anna mentally needed a break from the insufferable details of the trauma or when she was further from directly connecting to the trauma processing but still had very layered and deeply hidden subconscious messages to slowly uncover. For the sensory-motor or expressive processing, materials like glass, ice, or paint that could be safely thrown, splattered, hammered, or shattered were provided, so that Amy Anna could release the body memories or express an emotion she had been forbidden to feel. She reconnected to herself in a way that allowed her to find a place in the world and, therefore, no longer left alone in the secret darkness of the abuse.

Amy Anna most commonly chose drawing materials such as crayons, colored pencils, and markers when depicting details of trauma memories or body sensations. The controlled nature of these materials supported her in remaining grounded in the present moment while entering the trauma of the past. Figure 6.3, Untitled, was drawn to depict the lack of connection to the body and the remnants of body images that were left after the abusers had their way. A couple of dissociated parts were needed to get this picture drawn as they came together to help process and connect to the abuse that had been hidden away for safekeeping through dissociation.

FIGURE 6.3: UNTITLED

Figure 6.4, And the Rain Wouldn't Come—published under the pseudonym Nicolette Lucid, a dissociated part who writes poetry—describes her experience of suicidal disconnection from self, life, and the body that was needed during the life of physical, sexual, and emotional torment. Her body endured deceit from the adults who were supposed to care for her, and her mind was locked in a jail where she had to hide from the abusers. The body became a place of fear and pain that moved with her forever. Poetry offered a way to express how she had to discover a path to survive this dual reality of being within a body that felt unsafe, with an imprisoned mind, while also opening the doors for other dissociated parts to read it, discover more details of the traumas, and be supportive to the emotional anguish.

TREATMENT APPROACHES FOR BODY IMAGE IN ART THERAPY

She reached up to the stars,
walking out of the dust
Leaving the world behind, there was
no one there she could trust
Love as sweet as an unripe lemon
Alone against her own storm
And she would battle, even if alone she swore
She walked through the desert
The sky was black and grey
Lightning flashed thunder roared
She wasn't scared but rather bored
She seen all this before
Tornados fell from the sky
But still no a drop of rain
Everything remained bone dry
The wind and the tornados swept away the path
And took out any landmarks to find her way
You could hear her say to the wind
So this is the aftermath
From all that I;ve been through
And the rain wouldn't come
There was no drenching water
to fall on the thirsty land
She began to run
It didn't matter where
Just as long as it was far away from there
And them and their confusing lies and
conflicting beliefs and theories
You must first admit you were a victim to heal
But to fully heal you must admit
you are not a victim
TO HELL WITH ALL THEM!!!!
She ran on and on racing the wind
That nipped at her heels
Her family's voice still yelling strong in her head
You stupid lying bitch!
You are brainwashed, you are
brainwashing others
You fucking little bitch! You
liar! You klutz! You pig!
She stopped running and her legs began to itch
She looked back and noticed she had
run through a cactus patch
The needles in her legs, the blood running down
At last the physical pain she so wanted!
You could hear her say to the wind
So this is the aftermath
For From all that I've been
Through
And the rain wouldn't come
There was no drenching water
to fall on the thirsty land
And she began to run again
TO HELL WITH ALL THEM!!!!

And their stinging remarks and hard blows
She left the cactus needles in,
somehow they filled a need
To heal you must tell them all what
they've done to hurt you
And how it made you feel.
And she had thrown her head up
and yelled LIKE HELL I WILL!
She remembered all too well the look of
satisfaction and happiness in their eyes
When they found her hurt or crying
She learned how to cover the
bruises and began lying
It was her satisfaction to never
let them see her hurt
The only thing in her turbulent
life she could control
They would get no satisfaction of knowing
How bad they hurt her so
They hit hard, harder still,
And she learned to laugh instead of cry
Which brought on more blows, it was still death
But they wouldn't see her dying!
Words couldn't be trusted and
pain could no longer be felt
She was more than anticipating
anyone else to attack
Until she was almost killed
You could hear her say to the wind
So this is the aftermath
From all that I've been
Through
And the rain wouldn't come
There was no drenching water
to fall on the thirsty land
The ever-present nightmares
waiting for her to sleep
What's wrong what's right? Do this
and survive that's all she knew.
Survive, take the pain, it would be over soon
She wonders if it ever really ended
As she ran on into the storm
Until she could no longer go on
She fell into the sand
With desire to move again
You could hear her say to the wind
So this is the aftermath
From all that I've been
Through
And the rain came in torrents, in floods
And washed her away
After surviving so much pain
They found she had simply drowned that day.

FIGURE 6.4: AND THE RAIN WOULDN'T COME (PAGES 23–27)

Post-traumatic growth and future goals

AT provided Amy Anna a platform to communicate when her mind could not verbalize the trauma and the other dissociated parts were disconnected; the art process was an avenue towards healing in addition to finding deeper connections to the dissociated parts, allowing them to gently share information about the abuse with Amy Anna. Primarily, she now has the ability to see self and body, say "No," safely explore emotions, and speak her truth.

Amy Anna has published poetry to process the traumas of abuse and advocate for her and others' recovery. She self-published a poetry book, *Before the Rain, After the Storm,* in addition to her contribution to a book of poems about domestic violence, assault, trafficking, and sexual violence called *Hush No More! Healing through Words* (Guyton, 2022). She gives talks about DID to college psychology classes in the areas where she lives, as well as on podcasts or anywhere she is invited to speak about abuse. Amy Anna exemplifies DID as a natural self-protective defense from horrendous childhood trauma. The less judgmental she is about her own appearance and the more she becomes grounded in her body with acceptance and love, the more she is able to speak out, having others see her and her body in whatever shape it may be. Amy Anna's story is an example of post-traumatic growth through AT by building connections and re-establishing a supportive community, feeling safe, and experiencing empowerment (Kometiani, 2020b).

CONCLUSION

Although awareness of ST has advanced publicly and politically in recent years, and while many communities are more aware of trafficking crimes, some professions lack research and tools to assist victims and survivors of this physical and mental abuse. AT should be a leader in dealing with mental health and body-related issues of trafficked survivors because of its intrinsic potential to empower, facilitate change, and assist in recovery even when words are not available. ST negatively impacts the survivor's body image, body perception, body concept, personal identity, and perspective on life; survivors' quality of life diminishes due to negative self-worth, shame, and self-blame. For survivors like Veronica and Amy Anna, addressing body image was a crucial way to access parts of the self that were covered/hidden/isolated, and visual art expression provided them with the necessary opportunity to express, gain control, experience empowerment, and reconnect with the self through the body. AT can aid survivors of body-based trauma to not only confront the past and face their pain but break through to post-traumatic growth, acceptance, belonging, and a newfound love for self.

RECOMMENDATIONS FOR ART THERAPISTS

- Check your local government organizations for assistance or hotlines, and in the United States, contact the National Human Trafficking Resource Center at 1 (888) 373-7888 to report information regarding a trafficking situation or search the referral directory.

- Preserving hope is a key component of working with the complexities of survivors of ST; therapists are encouraged to seek support through supervision/consultation and self-care strategies.

- Attend trainings on ST, be aware of legislative issues for survivors, and consult with local anti-trafficking organizations to learn more about ST. See Kometiani's (2020a) *Art Therapy Treatment for Sex Trafficked Survivors: Facilitating Empowerment, Recovery and Hope* for more information.

REFERENCES

Abas, M., Ostrovschi, N. V., Prince, M., Gorceag, V. I., Trigub, C., & Oram, S. (2013). Risk factors for mental disorder in women survivors of human trafficking: A historical cohort study. *BMC Psychiatry, 13*(204), 1–11. https://doi.org/10.1186/1471244X-13-204

American Psychiatric Association (2022). *Diagnostic and Statistical Manual of Mental Disorders* (5th ed., rev. ed.). https://doi.org/10.1176/appi.books.9780890425596

Bacon, L., Keim, N., Loan, M., Derricote, M., *et al.* (2002). Evaluating a "non-diet" wellness intervention for improvement of metabolic fitness, psychological well-being and eating and activity behaviors. *International Journal of Obesity, 26*, 854–865. https://doi:10.1038/sj.ijo.0802012

Bloom, S. (2018). The Sanctuary Model and Sex Trafficking: Creating Moral Systems to Counteract Exploitation and Dehumanization. In A. Nichols, T. Edmond, & E. C. Heil (eds), *Social Work Practice with Survivors of Sex Trafficking and Commercial Exploitation* (pp.241–273). Columbia University Press.

Calhoun, L. G. & Tedeschi, R. G. (2013). *Posttraumatic Growth in Clinical Practice.* Routledge.

Chapman, L. (2014). *Neurobiologically Informed Trauma Therapy with Children and Adolescents: Understanding Mechanisms of Change.* W. W. Norton.

Courtois, C. A. & Ford, J. D. (2013). *Treatment of Complex Trauma: A Sequenced, Relationship-Based Approach.* Guilford Press.

Danylchuk, L. (2015). *Embodied Healing: Using Yoga to Recover from Extreme Stress.* Difference Press.

Davidtz, J., Haskamp, C. M., Millen, D. H., Plombon, B., Basilio, G., & Kennedy, T. D. (2022). *Sex Trafficking: Best Practices for Assessment and Intervention*. SpringerBriefs in Psychology.

Drosdick, C. (2020). Art Therapy Treatment for Survivors of Sex Trafficking, Boys. In M. K. Kometiani (ed.), *Art Therapy Treatment for Sex Trafficked Survivors: Facilitating Empowerment, Recovery and Hope* (pp.113–138). Routledge.

Fallon, P. & Ackard, D. M. (2002). Sexual Abuse and Body Image. In T. F. Cash & T. Pruzinsky (eds), *Body Image: A Handbook of Theory, Research, and Clinical Practice* (pp.117–124). Guilford Press.

Fredrickson, B. L. & Roberts, T. A. (1997). Objectification theory: Toward understanding women's lived experiences and mental health risks. *Psychology of Women Quarterly, 21*(2), 173–206. https://doi.org/10.1111/j.1471-6402.1997.tb00108.x

Gattario, K. H. & Frisén, A. (2019). From negative to positive body image: Men's and women's journeys from early adolescence to emerging adulthood. *Body Image, 28*, 53–65. https://doi.org/10.1016/j.bodyim.2018.12.002

Gerassi, L. B. & Nichols, A. J. (2018). *Sex Trafficking and Commercial Sexual Exploitation: Prevention, Advocacy, and Trauma-Informed Practice*. Springer Publishing Company.

Guyton, V. D. (2022). *Hush No More! Healing through Words*. R. D. Whitehead Rudolph (ed.). Consulting Experts and Associates.

Herman, J. (1992). *Trauma Recovery: The Aftermath of Violence—From Domestic Abuse to Political Terror*. Basic Books.

Hook, J. N., Davis, D. E., Owen, J., Worthington, E. L., & Utsey, S. O. (2013). Cultural humility: Measuring openness to culturally diverse clients. *Journal of Counseling Psychology, 60*(3), 355–363. https://doi.org/10.1037/a0032595

International Labour Organization, Walk Free, & International Organization for Migration (2022). *Global Estimates of Modern Slavery: Forced Labour and Forced Marriage*. www.ilo.org/wcmsp5/groups/public/---ed_norm/---ipec/documents/publication/wcms_854733.pdf

Jackson, L. (2020). *Cultural Humility in Art Therapy: Applications for Practice, Research, Social Justice, Self-Care and Pedagogy*. Jessica Kingsley Publishers.

Kaplan. F. F. (2007). Introduction. In F. F. Kaplan (ed.), *Art Therapy and Social Action* (pp.11–20). Jessica Kingsley Publishers.

Kometiani, M. K. (ed.). (2020a). *Art Therapy Treatment for Sex Trafficked Survivors: Facilitating Empowerment, Recovery and Hope*. Routledge.

Kometiani, M. K. (2020b). Beauty in the Disorder: Art Therapy with Sex Trafficking Survivors in Ohio, United States. In M. K. Kometiani (ed.), *Art Therapy Treatment for Sex Trafficked Survivors: Facilitating Empowerment, Recovery and Hope* (pp.97–112). Routledge.

Kometiani, M. K. (2021). Addressing Motherhood Issues of Sex Trafficking Survivors through Art Therapy. In N. Swan-Foster (ed.), *Art Therapy and Childbearing Issues* (pp.261–277). Routledge.

Kometiani, M. & Farmer, K. (2020). Exploring resilience through case studies of art therapy with sex trafficked survivors and their advocates. *The Arts in Psychotherapy, 67*, 101582. https://doi.org/10.1016/j.aip.2019.101582

Lucid, N. (2009). *After the Rain, Before the Sun*. Lulu Press.

Marie, G. O. (2015). *This White House: Recovery from Incest through Painting My Story*. Gabriel Orion Marie.

National Human Trafficking Hotline (2021). National Human Trafficking Hotline Data Report. https://humantraffickinghotline.org/sites/default/files/2023-01/National%20Report%20For%202021.docx%20%283%29.pdf

Oram, S., Stockl, H., Busza, J., Howard. L. M., & Zimmerman, C. (2012). Prevalence and risk of violence and physical, mental, and sexual health problems associated with human trafficking: Systematic review. *PLoS Medicine, 9*(5), 1–13. https://doi.org/10.1371/journal.pmed.1001224

Polaris (2014). *In their shoes: Understanding victims' mindsets and common barriers to victim identification*. www.nova.edu/create/projectheat/forms/section3.pdf

Rabinor, J. R. & Bilich, M. (2011). Experiential Approaches to Body Image Change. In T. F. Cash & L. Smolak (eds), *Body Image: A Handbook of Science, Practice, and Prevention* (2nd ed., pp.424–433). Guilford Press.

Saleebey, D. (2013). *The Strengths Perspective in Social Work Practice*. Pearson.

Scarce, J. & Wilson, C. (2022). Art Therapy for Trauma Recovery and Response. In M. Rastogi, R. P. Feldwisch, M. Pate, & J. Scarce (eds), *Foundations of Art Therapy Theory and Applications* (pp.413–447). Elsevier.

Smolak, L. (2011). Sexual Abuse and Body Image. In T. F. Cash & L. Smolak (eds), *Body Image: A Handbook of Science, Practice, and Prevention* (2nd ed., pp.119–128). Guilford Press.

Spring, D. (1993). *Shattered Images: Phenomenological Language of Sexual Trauma*. Magnolia Street Publishers.

Sukach, T., Gonzalez, N., & Cravens Pickens, J. (2018). Experiences of female sex trafficking survivors: A phenomenological analysis. *The Qualitative Report, 23*(6), 1422–1440. https://doi.org/10.46743/2160-3715/2018.3242

Talwar, S. (2010). An intersectionality framework for race, class, gender, and sexuality in art therapy. *Art Therapy: Journal of the American Art Therapy Association, 27*(1), 11–17. https://doi.org/10.1080/07421656.2010.10129567

Tan, L. A. (2012). Art therapy with trafficked women. *Therapy Today, 23*(5), 26–31.

Tan, L. A. & Moore, T. M. (2020). The Women's Transformational Program: An Art Therapy, Life Skills, and Reproductive Health Program in Nepal. In M. K. Kometiani (ed.), *Art Therapy Treatment for Sex Trafficked Survivors: Facilitating Empowerment, Recovery and Hope* (pp.163–186). Routledge.

Tiggemann, M. (2015). Considerations of positive body image across various social identities and special populations. *Body Image, 14*, 168–176. https://doi:10.1016/j.bodyim.2015.03.002

Tsutsumi, A., Izutsu, T., Poudyal, A., Kato, S., & Marui, E. (2008). Mental health of female survivors of human trafficking in Nepal. *Social Science & Medicine, 66*, 1841–1847. https://doi.org/10.1016/j.socscimed.2007.12.025

U.S. Department of Health and Human Services (2017). *Fact sheet: Human trafficking*. www.acf.hhs.gov/otip/fact-sheet/resource/fshumantrafficking

U.S. Department of State (2017). *Trafficking in persons report*. www.state.gov/wp-content/uploads/2019/02/271339.pdf

U.S. Department of State (2022). *Trafficking in persons report*. www.state.gov/wp-content/uploads/2022/10/20221020-2022-TIP-Report.pdf

Victims of Trafficking and Violence Protection Act of 2000, Pub. L. No. 106–939, 114 Stat. 1464 (2000). www.congress.gov/106/crpt/hrpt939/CRPT-106hrpt939.pdf

Wanchena, V. C. (2015). *Art as Alchemy; An Inside View of the Transformational Process*. Gabriel Orion Marie.

Wiederman, M. W. (2002). Body Image and Sexual Functioning. In T. F. Cash & T. Pruzinsky (eds), *Body Image: A Handbook of Theory, Research, and Clinical Practice* (2nd ed., pp.287–294). Guilford Press.

Williamson, C., Karandikar-Chheda, S., Barrows, J., Smouse, T., *et al.* (2012). *Ohio trafficking in persons study commission research and analysis subcommittee report on the prevalence of human trafficking in Ohio to Attorney General Richard Cordray*. www.researchgate.net/publication/260335516_Ohio_Trafficking_in_Persons_Study_Commission_Research_and_Analysis_Sub-Committee_Report_on_the_Prevalence_of_Human_Trafficking_in_Ohio_To_Attorney_General_Richard_Cordray_Research_Committee_Members_At

Wilson, C. & Coleman, S. R. (2020). Recommendations for Working with Individuals Affected by Sex Trafficking. In M. K. Kometiani (ed.), *Art Therapy Treatment with Sex Trafficking Survivors: Facilitating Empowerment Recovery and Hope* (pp.55–94). Routledge.

World Health Organization (2019). *International Classification of Diseases* (11th ed.) https://icd.who.int

Zimmerman, C., Hossain, M., Yun, K., Gajdadziev, V., *et al.* (2008). The health of trafficked women: A survey of women entering post trafficking services in Europe. *American Journal of Public Health, 98*(1), 55–59. https://doi.org/10.2105/AJPH.2006.108357

CHAPTER VII

Body Image

From the Victim's Lens

—— LINDA ADENIYI ——

INTIMATE PARTNER VIOLENCE

Domestic violence (DV) and intimate partner violence (IPV) continue to be prevalent issues in our society, affecting millions of individuals globally (National Coalition Against Domestic Violence, 2018). The term domestic violence resulted from new laws that accompanied the Women's Movement in 1973. The common perception is that partner violence is uniquely limited to male dominance in heterosexual relationships, and violence perpetrated by women is assumed to be an act of self-defense. This type of gender paradigm dismisses the 1–2% of men who report being abused (Rakovec-Felser, 2014) and many others who fear reporting. Partner violence is not trivial or insignificant but an immense and wide-ranging problem with grave consequences for victims. It is important to remember that partner violence does not discriminate; it happens to individuals in all age groups, genders, cultures, religions, and across educational and socio-economic statuses (National Coalition Against Domestic Violence, 2018).

IPV gained attention in 2000 as researchers and advocates recognized the need for a more inclusive definition of DV. It was recognized that abusive relationships occur between romantic partners (same sex or opposite sexes), who may or may not be living together in the same household, and have been married, divorced, separated, are dating, or have previously dated, and that violence can occur between parents, children, siblings, and/or roommates. This required expanding the existing definition of DV and broadening the term to IPV (Saltzman *et al.*, 2000). Currently, the terms DV and IPV are often used interchangeably, although IPV will be used for the remainder of this chapter.

Abusive relationships have devastating and long-lasting effects on physical, mental, spiritual, and emotional well-being (Saltzman *et al.*, 2000), with death as the most severe consequence of IPV.

> The journey through and out of IPV is often marked by an initial erosion of sense of self (identity deconstruction) followed by identity reconstruction through an extended process of change aimed at rebuilding self-esteem, mental wellness, self-efficacy, and ultimately self-identity. (Matheson *et al.*, 2015, p.561)

This chapter includes an understanding of violence perpetrated within the context of significant interpersonal relationships and the impact it has on the victim's body image, including the social and cultural influences that reciprocally affect the ongoing relationship with the body. Additionally, the use of art therapy in individual and group sessions is presented as an effective psychological intervention for victims of IPV to address body image distress, trauma symptoms, and cognitive distortions, and foster positive thinking, self-esteem, and self-worth.

Victim or survivor

The labels of *victim* and *survivor* and the connotations that come with them remain debatable. Labels have the potential to impact an individual's self-concept, self-esteem, and help-seeking behaviors. For some, the label of *victim* may imply helplessness and perpetuate a stigmatizing view of IPV (e.g., someone is weak or deserving of abuse), while the label of *survivor* may be empowering; emphasizing strength and resilience. But the term *survivor* for an individual leaving an IPV situation may not adequately identify how they are feeling (Dunn, 2005). They may struggle with not feeling strong or healed enough to be empowered by the label *survivor*. In addition to *victim* and *survivor*, *overcomer* and *thriver* have been added to further expand the terminology. But, for some, none of these words accurately reflect their experiences and they prefer not to use labels to help describe what they have been through (Papendick & Bohner, 2017).

Working within this field for over 18 years, I witnessed the terminology debate. For example, I worked for an agency whose subtitles were victim advocacy, and this was consistently questioned. The founder/CEO would answer, "We want to provide immediate aid to an individual who has experienced violence. If we said survivor advocacy, they might wait until they felt qualified to seek our services." The decision to identify as a victim or survivor is a personal one, and it may impact the way services are sought and provided. It is important for society, service providers, and families to recognize that individuals who have experienced IPV may use specific labels to describe their experiences, but they do not define them, and they do not diminish their strength or resilience. Specifically, providers should use the labels and terms adopted by the individual. And, as the client evolves in their therapeutic journey, so may the label they identify most with. For this chapter, I will use the term *victim* for those who have experienced IPV.

Both terms, *victim* and *survivor,* are laden with certain images, stigmas, or associations that can be effectively addressed in art therapy (Dunn, 2005). Images and image creation have a significant impact on our bodies. Images created in art therapy invite victims to reframe their feelings, respond to their traumatic experiences of IPV, and work towards emotional and behavioral changes. Artmaking in a therapeutic setting provides a safe space for an individual to rehearse, and experiment with, a desired change using tangible objects that can be physically altered, providing a sense of control that was not experienced during their trauma (Malchiodi, 2011). Dunn (2005) points out that creating a *survivor identity* is an attempt to focus on a person's strengths and to support their capability to cope with their experiences, focusing on the positive aspects and ways to change to carry on with their lives. Furthermore, centering mental health in IPV victims may lead to increases in self-worth and body image.

Research, research, research

Suffering from IPV affects the way people see themselves. One specific area of impact is body image, which not only refers to a person's subjective perception of their physical appearance but includes perceptual, affective, cognitive, and behavioral impacts on their concept of self. Empirical studies found that IPV affects victims' emotional appraisal regarding their body image beyond the violence-related injuries. Given the interwoven experiences of physical violence, psychological maltreatment, and injury inherent in IPV, it creates a "virulent environment for body image due to the negative, body-focused interpersonal experience" (Weaver *et al.*, 2007, p.1001). When body image and self-acceptance are impacted by societal views, individualism is diminished.

Weaver *et al.* (2007) conducted a study exploring the association between appearance-related residual injury, body image distress, and PTSD in female IPV victims compared to women who had experienced a similar level of violence but had not experienced an appearance-related residual injury. They determined that body image distress was not significantly different within the appearance-related residual injury group than within the comparison group. Additionally, body image distress emerged as a distinct predictor of PTSD. PTSD is characterized by attentional bias towards reminders or cues associated with the trauma-related stressor, and emotional reactivity within encountering reminders (American Psychiatric Association, 2013). It is possible that cues from past IPV injuries can act as tangible reminders for victims. Avoiding these reminders or having flashbacks to when and how they occurred could cause body image distress, leading to PTSD.

Mental and physical injuries created by an abuser can alter an individual's appearance and result in differential responses to identity development. Weaver *et al.* (2007) anticipated that body image distress would be a unique predictor of PTSD and the results indicated that dominance and isolation were significantly associated with PTSD and body image distress. Due to limited research, the connection between body image distress and PTSD remains unclear, and further research is needed to replicate Weaver *et al.*'s findings.

Matheson *et al.* (2015) explored the impact of IPV on mental well-being among low-income women to gain a broader understanding of the effects on self-esteem and self-identity. They interviewed low-income women who experienced violent abuse and housing instability and discovered that for these respondents, physical injuries healed faster, whereas damage to self-esteem and identity lingered. They noted that advocates have primarily focused on depression, substance abuse, and PTSD, excluding the problems of low self-esteem and loss of self-identity resulting from IPV. Furthermore, Matheson *et al.* (2015) concluded that IPV-related training is needed for physicians, allied health professionals, and supportive programs to holistically address the comorbid needs of those leaving or living with IPV.

Sáez and colleagues (2021) researched IPV victims' emotional appraisal regarding their body image beyond the violence-related injuries.

IPV victims often report poor physical self-concept, which is included in the Battered Women's Syndrome as a condition within PTSD. Body image is negatively affected by experiencing sexual and physical abuse. Empirical studies have found that IPV victims with violence-related injuries experienced higher body image concerns, which are predictors of depressive symptoms. IPV also affects women's emotional appraisal regarding their body image because psychological violence involves attacks and insult towards the victims' body image, leading to feelings of shame towards their body. (p.2)

Sáez *et al.*'s goal was to explore the effects of a new multicomponent program to improve self-concept and self-esteem among IPV victims utilizing cognitive-behavioral therapy and outdoor adventure activities on affective and emotional variables (2021). As a groundbreaking project, they anticipated that the combination of psychological intervention, outdoor activities, and nature exposure would lessen the negative effects of IPV victimization, and there would be an improvement in self-concept, self-efficacy, self-esteem, and body image, as well as a reduction of depressive symptoms.

DYNAMICS OF IPV

IPV involves power and control, as the abuser seeks to maintain dominance over their partner, and the partner learns to oblige due to duress. This involves any manner or behavior within an abusive intimate relationship that causes physical or psychological harm, such as intimidation, verbal and emotional abuse, physical violence, financial control, stalking, sexual abuse, confinement, and other forms of coercion (National Coalition Against Domestic Violence, 2018). There are many reasons why a victim does not leave the relationship, including but not limited to, feeling trapped, financial dependence on the abuser, limited resources, guilt, shame, and fear for their safety. This leaves the victim with no ownership of their own body.

Sometimes I feel paralyzed..., like a paralysis of feeling, you, that you can't (pause) I. I can't, you know, I want to do something but I, I just can't feel, I don't feel like I can do it. Even going out of my house... It's very hard for me...I don't really do that unless it's necessary and, uh, I guess, I guess sometimes, the worthless, the feeling of worthless. (Matheson *et al.*, 2015, p.566)

Bargai *et al.*'s (2007) study explained that abusers control their victims, resulting in learned helplessness. Learned helplessness is a psychological trait resulting from repeated exposure to uncontrollable and aversive events. Women who suffer in IPV relationships are at risk for negative psychological outcomes and are likely to engage in a multitude of coping strategies (e.g., alcohol, drugs, self-harm) to survive in their relationship. These coping strategies ultimately affect factors related to depression, PTSD, and self-esteem. Loss of self-esteem becomes embedded with abuse, leading to emotional exhaustion and a sense of erosion of the self (Matheson *et al.*, 2015).

> Not so much like being sick or flu like in that, but I always felt nauseous. No self-esteem. No self-respect. No dignity. No pride. Like I didn't care what I looked like. I didn't take care of myself; hygienically as well. Just the small things count, you know, just brushing your teeth when you get up in the morning. I didn't care. I didn't even care to get out of bed. (Matheson *et al.*, 2015, p.566)

A victim who has a substantial decrease in associating an action with positive outcomes eventually has a marked reduction in the range of responses to external demands (Matheson *et al.*, 2015). Constant worry and fear manifest as nausea and can erode a victim's capacity to care for their physical self and their belief in their own ability to succeed in any given situation. Loss of self-esteem becomes embedded with abuse and can affect somatic health. Body image distress is multidimensional and not exclusively about appearance but encompasses behavioral, perceptual, cognitive, and affective phenomena (Weaver *et al.*, 2007).

> I didn't even recognize what he was doing as abuse, because I thought I wasn't black and blue or broken bones or anything. It was more psychological. He had weapons and threatened to shoot me all the time, too... It was more stuff that happened that didn't leave marks. (Matheson *et al.*, 2015, p.565)

Learned helplessness and loss of self-efficacy contribute to submissiveness and reluctance to leave an abusive relationship. Bargai *et al.* (2007) suggested that learned helplessness modifies the relationship between violence and mental health by changing the victims' perceptions and beliefs in the relationship, leading them to believe the abuser's spoken or unspoken messages and inducing changes in behavior via negative reinforcement. As a result, the victim stays or returns to the abuser.

> My self-esteem isn't very good. And I don't want to be alone for the rest of my life... And they always say it gonna be different, and it never is, and I know that, I know that I've seen it, I've done it, but it's just a really hard decision. (Matheson *et al.*, 2015, p.567)

Specifically for female victims, Bargai *et al.* (2007) focused on the affective dimension and concluded that victims have lower self-esteem compared to non-abused people, and the victim's self-esteem was completely crushed to the point where they lacked the confidence to maintain autonomy.

THE ABUSER, THE ABUSED AND SOCIETY

The type of abuse is rarely constant in IPV relationships; some abusers exhibit passive characteristics such as withdrawing emotionally, stonewalling, and giving silent treatment. This creates a sense of insecurity and self-doubt for the victim. Cultural, social, and individual standards of behavior significantly affect how certain issues are perceived and addressed (Cabrera, 2014). Through media, culture, and religion, messages conveyed can reinforce or challenge existing norms around IPV, machismo, and gender roles. In some cases, the media can perpetuate harmful stereotypes and promote unhealthy behaviors (Cabrera, 2014). For example, popular music lyrics, music videos, advertisements, and movies may depict violence against partners as acceptable or even desirable, while other forms of media advertisements may objectify women and reinforce gender roles that limit their opportunities and potential. Commonly used catchphrases—love hurts, sex is better after a fight, you made your bed now lie in it, man up—convey negative messages that continue to perpetuate violent and unhealthy behaviors.

Similarly, cultural and religious beliefs may support the idea that men are superior to women and that women should be subservient to men, contributing to the acceptance of abusive relationships. Machismo, a cultural concept that values traditional masculine traits such as dominance and toughness, can also play a role in perpetuating IPV (Cabrera, 2014). Individuals who adhere to this ideal may feel entitled to use violence as a control tactic. This can be especially problematic when combined with gender roles that emphasize female submission and male authority, creating a power dynamic that can make it difficult for victims to escape abuse. The victim may succumb to the belief that if they remain in their body, they will be controlled, abused, and dismissed by their abuser, society, and culture (Cabrera, 2014).

According to Matheson *et al.* (2015), "cultural expectations can magnify how a victim reacts to the disempowerment of IPV relationship" (p.567). Abuse damages an individual's sense of self and cultural expectations to persevere, creating a sense of failure. Sáez *et al.* (2021) recounted previous studies where self-efficacy is negatively affected by IPV, and lower levels of self-efficacy are associated with higher levels and more severe symptoms of depression. IPV not only negatively affects body image but also the belief in the ability to successfully execute behaviors that will lead to desired outcomes or self-efficacy.

Sáez *et al.* (2021) suggest that given the psychological outcomes, it is imperative to distinguish between the benefits of individual and group therapy offered in shelters, clinics, and community counseling centers. They state that individual therapy restores self-esteem and reduces depression; however, group interventions are most beneficial for IPV. In addition to these services, they suggest that psychoeducational and supportive groups improve self-esteem and depression, reduce social isolation, and address body image concerns and self-imposed limitations (Sáez *et al.*, 2021).

COUNSELING SERVICE PROVIDERS

Despite the prevalence of IPV in the general population, it is underrepresented in mental health services, in part because victims rarely voluntarily self-identify or seek treatment due to feelings of shame, guilt, and denial. These factors are compounded by a sense of pointlessness, resulting from learned helplessness, a profound unraveling of self-esteem, and body image distress endured from violent relationships (Bargai *et al.*, 2007). Victims seeking help in the form of shelter, medical, or counseling services may be hesitant if their previous attempts were unsuccessful; for example, seeking housing but the shelters are full, seeking crisis therapy but the wait time is more than ten days, or services being unaffordable. Most victims of IPV have experienced terrible and humiliating situations and in therapy, it might be hard to describe their experiences in words (van der Kolk, 2015). Physical and psychological abuse can cause cognitive distortions and can negatively affect a victim's sense of self, including self-esteem and self-image (Kubany et al., 2004). Even if a victim is successful in finding timely counseling services to address their abuse, IPV may hinder rapport, feelings of support, and therapeutic progress.

Physical and psychological consequences of abuse do not cease when the abuse ends. The individual is now a container for all the messages from their abuser. Therefore, those who survive abusive relationships are much more likely to suffer from body image distress and negatively distorted perceptions of the self, even after the abusive relationship has ended (Sáez et al., 2021). The experience of IPV involving physical abuse, and particularly sexual violence, could result in an increased negative body image and contribute to low self-esteem. The abuser controls the victim's body physically and mentally, and the individual is left with the names they have been called, the doubt, the blame, the hits, the looks, the assumptions, and the humiliation. Their body is the vessel of their experiences.

ART THERAPY

The philosophy of art therapy is founded on the premise that human experience cannot be entirely reduced to words and that some emotional states are beyond words. Therefore, verbal processing for a survivor of IPV is challenging and often unsuccessful due to the need to recall and organize traumatic events that occurred during their violent relationship. Van der Kolk (2015) explains that somatic memories are stored in the right hemisphere of the brain, which regulates emotions, intuition, imagination, and sensory experience. Traumatic memories are not ordinary memories; they are stored in the body. The issue with processing trauma in traditional talk therapy is that language is stored in the left hemisphere of the brain (van der Kolk, 2015). Art therapy offers something that cannot be provided by many other disciplines outside expressive therapies. It enables individuals to effect personal change and growth using art materials and images to understand and communicate events, associations, and feelings. For that reason, art therapy has been influential in trauma work, and an integral part of the interdisciplinary team of providers for individuals working through trauma.

Clay art therapy/IPV individual and group

When I worked as an art therapist in a co-ed IPV shelter facilitating groups, clay was introduced in individual and group settings as a tangible transformation to address body image distress, self-esteem, self-acceptance, positive thinking, cognitive distortions, and PTSD symptoms. As a material, clay has the flexibility and organic factors that provide a unique opportunity for IPV victims to address body image and self-efficacy.

Clay art therapy is beneficial because it requires touching, modeling, developing a sense of creativity, and non-verbal communication. Suputtitada (2021) identified that individuals who participated in clay art therapy experienced rehabilitating neurological effects of self-confidence, aesthetic sensibility, patience, a gained sense of cooperation and solidarity with others, disciplined working, and reduced impulses of anger and revenge. Due to the nature of IPV, gaining autonomy through clay art therapy seemed quite appropriate since the reality of a fired finish piece cannot be denied. Therapists need a thorough understanding of art materials because they are the main tools by which meaning is communicated and the dynamics of art therapy unfold alongside symbolization and metaphor (Moon, 2010). Just the same, the client benefits from an understanding of how to effectively use the material to process emotions, experience success, build confidence, and gain hope from the art therapy session.

The group members had the opportunity to transform something while reclaiming a part of themselves. In reclaiming oneself, a sense of efficacy and possibility is gained. Additionally, clay engages one's mind, muscles, and energy. This group of five women from both the shelter and the community experienced five 90-minute group therapy sessions. Most participants were active in individual therapy or participated in other group therapy services through the shelter. All participants voluntarily received individual therapy services with an art therapist in addition to participating in the group. Individual art therapy sessions and art therapy groups were free to all participants and facilitated by two Master's level registered art therapists employed by the not-for-profit shelter and counseling center.

Creative journaling

Creative journaling was encouraged at the start of each group session. Creative journaling is a mixed media form of self-expression using words and creating art in a journal. Participants could use the journal to express their thoughts and feelings about the group or their day, form ideas and sketches about the clay pieces they planned to create, take notes, and respond to prompts.

Prompts were written on a whiteboard available at the start of the group. Participants could use their journal to calm down and connect to the space before the group began. The supplies for creative journaling included pre-cut magazine collage, markers, pens, pencils, rulers, tissue paper, acrylic paint markers, and pastels. Participants were given the option to leave their journals secured in the art room or take them home. All participants chose to leave their journals.

Session 1: Introduction to clay and creative journaling
Prompt
What is the one joy you have? Or what are you looking forward to having the freedom to do that your abuser (rules) or relationship prevented you from doing?

Goal
Introduction to the properties of clay.

Process
Participants had limited to no knowledge of working with clay/ceramics. This session began with an introduction of the facilitators, participants, and group rules. Participants were introduced to creative journaling and given their first prompt.

The facilitator introduced the clay to the participants and shared the importance of starting off correctly to ensure that the clay did not explode or crack in the kiln. The group discussed what happens in life when the proper steps are not taken. Participants reflected on how they felt when they met their abuser, grew up and left home too soon, or were not fully present in their body in the past. Working with clay allowed participants to become fully present. The facilitators phased in examples of kneading, pounding, rolling, removing bubbles from the clay, and keeping the clay moist. Participants pounded their clay aggressively to force out air bubbles, letting their frustrations and stress from the abuse out on the clay. As participants became comfortable releasing their tension onto the clay, some verbally expressed the release of energy.

After artmaking was concluded, the stations were cleaned and cleared of clay, and participants journaled and shared. They discussed their journal prompt about what they were free to do without their abuser, like singing in the shower, spending time with their parents/family, going skating, cooking, knitting, taking a bath, and many other common joys that individuals should experience without fear. Hope plays an important role in allowing patients to add meaning to their lives, strengthen their motivation, and avoid anxiety, depression, and even suicidal tendencies (Suputtitada, 2021).

Rationale

The connection to clay and the understanding of the properties was imperative to cover in the first session, to create success for the next session. "Clay products are well known in human history since prehistoric times in such forms as vases, pots, and symbolic figures, including human figures" (Sholt & Gavron, 2006, p.66). This reiterates the benefits of using clay with victims of IPV to address body image distress by caring for the substance from which their natural body was derived and creating a vessel. Since reality cannot be denied, coping with illnesses by gaining autonomy through clay art therapy seems quite appropriate.

Session 2: Creating with clay

Prompt

What is the one joy you have? Or what are you looking forward to having the freedom to do that your abuser (rules) or relationship prevented you from doing?

Goal

Hand-building techniques.

Process

This session began with creative journaling. Participants used the kneaded clay from the last session and worked alongside the art therapists as they demonstrated fundamental hand-building techniques: rolling a ball, coils, slabs, and using slip. As participants experienced the flexibility and forgiveness of clay, they could also heal from the succumbed beliefs created by their abuse that they did not own their body and that their body would be controlled, abused, and dismissed by their abuser, society, and culture

(Cabrera, 2014). The clay was a symbol of their body and life that they now owned and controlled. Participants determined how they wanted to represent this new freedom, simultaneously allowing unprocessed feelings to shape the clay as they made detailed decisions about how to create their piece. For most participants, feeling supported by their group members and the therapist was new; they were not alone, and could work on gaining control of their lives and mitigating the feelings of isolation.

Rationale

It was important to continue a dialogue paralleling the change process of clay to the participants' journey after abuse. This process required patience and care for both. If clay is not properly prepared for firing, it can crack or explode in the kiln or while drying. Emotional distance to their trauma, such as the avoidance of reminders of the event, emotional numbing, denial, and dissociation, can be damaging. Keeping the creative journaling prompt the same for the second session helped participants stay connected and fully present in their bodies and minds. Creating something of value for themselves was crucial to their healing because IPV victims often feel like damaged goods, not valued by their abuser (Matheson *et al.*, 2015).

Session 3: Building clay and strength

Prompt

On a piece of paper, write down any shame or guilt that holds you back from owning and reclaiming your body and personal joy.

Goal

Create greenware and burn their burden.

Process

Individuals were not asked to share their prompt responses. They were written, folded, and, once the vessels were completed, placed inside these. During this session, participants learned that their leather-hard clay piece was now greenware ready to be bone dry for the first firing. Participants made their final steps to create clean and smooth lines with a damp cloth on their drying clay.

Rationale

Their prompt response was added to the inside of their clay piece and burnt during the bisque firing. This permanently changes the chemical and physical nature of the clay. The symbolism of burning their prompt response was emotional. Participants supported one another and journaled about the experience.

Session 4: Glazing and no more shaming

Prompt

Reflect on the process of writing and containing your shame or guilt in the fired piece.

Goal

Trusting the process and the self.

Process

Participants reflected on the previous week's response to seeing their fired pieces for the first time and acknowledging the guilt and shame papers that were destroyed. The session was spent choosing glaze colors and glazing their pieces. Trust was the goal. Unlike acrylic paint, the color of glazes is not obvious. The individual has to trust that the color will be what is indicated on the bottle, whether it looks white or muted; the firing process brings out the color. This process is similar to attending therapy and discussing difficult and uncomfortable issues while trusting that the end result will be better, improving one's mental health and self-esteem. Trust is lost in abusive relationships due to fear, so rebuilding trust in the self and in their supporters is imperative in the healing process.

Rationale

The four clay art therapy group sessions allowed abuse survivors to have a bridge between their body and mind that was an effective psychological intervention to address body image distress, PTSD symptoms, positive thinking, self-esteem, self-worth, and cognitive distortions. The process of admission to self, writing it down, and then burning their shame and guilt was therapeutic to their healing. Their created clay piece was a reminder of letting go of that burden.

Session 5: Celebration
Prompt
Reflect on the introduction of clay to build a piece that represents your new life, new body, and mind, free of abuse.

Goal
Identify successes.

Process
The participants' pieces were displayed in a separate space on a table in a gallery style, along with light refreshments, and revealed to the participants after journaling. The art therapist supported the participants as they were united with their new clay bodies. The members had successfully demonstrated the control they wanted in their bodies without fear. Abusive relationships are embedded with extreme stress and intense fear, including experiences of harm or threat of harm to themselves, their loved ones, or pets. The participants were excited and responded as if they did not recognize their own creativity. The process of using clay with survivors to address body image was powerful and spiritual.

Rationale
The trust they had to give in order for their ceramics to be displayed was immense. This was most represented in comments about all the glaze colors finishing as they desired. All participants were amazed at their accomplishment.

PARTICIPANT CASE EXAMPLE: Tina

Tina was a young adult female who identified as Black but was not born in the United States. She was a victim of IPV who later identified as a survivor. Tina described her abuser as controlling mentally and physically, and sexually abusive. Her final creation in the clay art therapy group was a video game controller (Figures 7.1, 7.2a, and 7.2b). During her abusive relationship, she was not permitted to play video games or do anything she considered enjoyable. Tina created her video game controller to be as realistic as possible. She took a photograph of her actual controller to use while building it during the group session. She wrote her shame and guilt list and placed it inside the controller so that the burned ashes remained locked inside. Tina chose a box to be the container for her video game controller. She decorated her box with puzzle pieces to represent putting her life back together.

Simultaneously, in individual and group art therapy sessions, Tina's goal was to own her body, mind, and spirit. Her body image had been controlled by her parents, her culture, her religion, her abuser, and society. After a year of court hearings, therapy, and self-determination, she gained her own identity and self-image and considered herself a survivor of IPV.

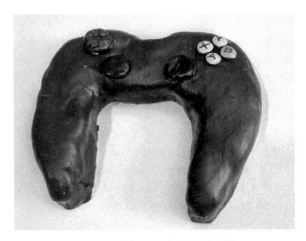

FIGURE 7.1: THE CONTROLLER

FIGURE 7.2A: VIEW OF THE CONTROLLER IN THE BOX

FIGURE 7.2B: FRONT VIEW OF THE BOX

CONCLUSION

Art therapy is beneficial to victims and survivors of IPV because of its ability to address non-verbal issues of body image, and build self-trust and awareness. This allows the individual to experience control of their body, mind, and spirit. More research is needed to gain a better understanding of the phenomenon surrounding the development of the capacity for three-dimensional representation in clay in art therapy (Sholt & Gavron, 2006). Victims of IPV with low self-esteem may also have a heightened fear of being alone or being rejected by their abuser, making it harder for them to leave the relationship. Also, they struggle with feelings of shame and guilt, believing that the abuse is somehow their fault. Low self-esteem is not a personal failure but a result of past experiences or circumstances.

In sum, there is a shortage of mental health providers, shelters, affordable outpatient counseling, and/or a support group for individuals who have experienced IPV.

> One of the big things is... Emotional abuse is so downplayed...having suffered from all the above, it's the worst...it's the one that gets the least amount of attention, and the least amount of help. Or you really have to jump through some hoops to get help with it. (Matheson *et al.*, 2015, p.564)

Consistently attending individual therapy and/or a support group can be helpful in building self-esteem, processing body image distress, and developing the confidence to leave an abusive relationship safely. It is also important for society to work towards ending the culture of victim-blaming and instead create a culture of support and empowerment for victims of IPV.

REFERENCES

American Psychiatric Association (2013). *Diagnostic and Statistical Manual of Mental Disorders* (5th ed.). https://doi.org/10.1176/appi.books.9780890425596

Bargai, N., Ben-Shakhar, G., & Shalev, A. Y. (2007). Posttraumatic stress disorder and depression in battered women: The mediating role of learned helplessness. *Journal of Family Violence, 22*(5), 267–275. https://doi.org.10.1007/s10896-007-9078-y

Cabrera, R. (2014). *Violence against women and machismo: A research study of how machismo justifies cases of violence against women and the psychological process that influence women to remain in abusive relationships in the city of Fortaleza.* Independent Study Project, SIT Study Abroad. SIT Digital Collection. https://digitalcollections.sit.edu/isp_collection/2007

Dunn, J. L. (2005). "Victims" and "survivors": Emerging vocabularies of motive for "battered women who stay." *Sociological Inquiry, 75*(1), 1–30. https://doi.org/10.1111/j.1475-682X.2005.00110.x

Kubany, E. S., Hill, E. E., Owens, J. A., Iannce-Spencer, C., *et al.* (2004). Cognitive trauma therapy for battered women with PTSD (CTT-BW). *Journal of Consulting and Clinical Psychology, 72*(1), 3–18. doi:10.1037/0022-006X.72.1.3

Malchiodi, C. A. (2011). *Handbook of Art Therapy* (2nd ed.). Guilford Press.

Matheson, F. I., Daoud, N., Hamilton-Wright, S., Borenstein, H., Pedersen, C., & O'Campo, P. (2015). Where did she go? The transformation of self-esteem, self-identity, and mental well-being among women who have experienced intimate partner violence. *Women's Health Issues, 25*(5), 561–569. https://doi.org/10.1016/j.whi.2015.04.006

Moon, C. H. (2010). *Materials & Media in Art Therapy: Critical Understandings of Diverse Artistic Vocabularies.* Taylor & Francis.

National Coalition Against Domestic Violence (2018). *Domestic violence and the LGBTQ community.* https://ncadv.org/blog/posts/domestic-violence-and-the-lgbtq-community

Papendick, M. & Bohner, G. (2017). "Passive victim – strong survivor"? Perceived meaning of labels applied to women who were raped. *PLoS ONE, 12*(5), e0177550. https://doi.org/10.1371/journal.pone.0177550

Rakovec-Felser, Z. (2014). Domestic violence and abuse in intimate relationship from public health perspective. *Health Psychology Research, 2*(3), 1821. https://doi.org.10.4081/hpr.2014.1821

Sáez, G., López-Núñez, C., Carlos-Vivas, J., Barrios-Fernandez, S., *et al.* (2021). A multi-component program to improve self-concept and self-esteem among intimate partner violence victims: A study protocol for a randomized controlled pilot trial. *International Journal of Environmental Research and Public Health, 18*(9), 4930. https://doi.org/10.3390/ijerph18094930

Saltzman, L. E., Green, Y. T., Marks, J. S., & Thacker, S. B. (2000). Violence against women as a public health issue: Comments from the CDC1. *American Journal of Preventive Medicine, 19*(4), 325–329. doi:10.1016/s0749-3797(00)00241-5

Sholt, M. & Gavron, T. (2006). Therapeutic qualities of clay-work in art therapy and psychotherapy: A review. *Art Therapy, 23*(2), 66–72. https://doi.org/10.1080/07421656.10129647

Suputtitada, P. (2021). *Clay Art Therapy for Physical, Psychological, and Cognitive Improvement.* Research Gate. www.researchgate.net/publication/353445946_Clay_Art_Therapy_for_Physical_Psychological_and_Cognitive_Improvement van der Kolk, B. A. (2015). *The Body Keeps the Score: Brain, Mind, and Body in the Healing of Trauma*. Penguin Books.

Weaver, T. L., Resnick, H. S., Kokoska, M. S., & Etzel, J. C. (2007). Appearance-related residual injury, posttraumatic stress, and body image: Associations within a sample of female victims of intimate partner violence. *Journal of Traumatic Stress, 20*(6), 999–1008. doi:10.1002/jts.20274

CHAPTER VIII

Using Art Therapy to Address Body Image with Queer Clients

—— CHELSEA LEEDS ——

A NOTE ON LANGUAGE

This chapter focuses on addressing body image for individuals who are members of the queer community. This includes folks who identify as gay, lesbian, bisexual, intersex, asexual, pansexual, demisexual, transgender, gender fluid, gender-nonconforming, queer, nonbinary, questioning, and any other identity related to sexuality and gender characterized by being not heterosexual and/or cisgender. I chose the term queer for two reasons. It is a more inclusive and comprehensive term, and it is the term chosen by both clients featured in this chapter. It is important to start this chapter with an acknowledgment that writing about the intersection of body image and queerness as a monolith is impossible. This nuance is unfortunately not always considered or reflected in research.

BODY IMAGE IN THE QUEER COMMUNITY

Body image for all people is impacted by personal history, microsystems such as family and friends, larger systems such as healthcare and education, and cultural influences such as media and advertising. People who identify as queer experience additional adverse and traumatic influences described in more detail in the following section. An important difference for clinicians to keep in mind when working with this population is that for individuals who identify as gender diverse, body dissatisfaction—connected to body dysphoria— is not an unhealthy phenomenon (Dalzell & Protos, 2020). Body dysphoria can present similarly to an eating disorder and should be considered carefully, with the whole person in mind.

TRAUMA AND THE BODY IN THE QUEER COMMUNITY

The nature of queerness is tied to the body: how it exists, presents, appears, and changes. Traumatic experiences for queer folks may include discrimination, systemic oppression (e.g., sexism, misogyny, transmisogyny, homophobia and transphobia), internalized versions of these issues, physical violence and bullying, isolation and rejection, attachment trauma, medical trauma, puberty, dysphoria itself, objectification and dehumanization, and self-injurious behaviors. These traumatic situations may lead to eating disorders, self-hatred, self-harming, anxiety, depression, dissociation, suicidal ideation, loneliness, and post-traumatic stress disorder (PTSD) or similar trauma-related diagnoses. These findings align with the work of trauma expert Bessel van der Kolk (2014), who proposes that the presentation of trauma in people who have experienced continuous, relational trauma—especially in early childhood—does not generally fit the diagnostic criteria for PTSD and yet those individuals are still impacted by trauma and exhibit symptoms mentioned above.

Stigma

Stigma is the origin of much distress for queer clients. In 2013, Sevelius created the gender affirmation framework for conceptualizing risk behaviors among transgender women of color. This model effectively demonstrates the link between stigma, social oppression, and psychological distress that is experienced by other members of the queer community. Sevelius asserts that stigma leads to social and systemic oppression such as transphobia, sexual objectification, victimization and healthcare barriers, and psychological struggles such as internalized transphobia, depression, anxiety, body shame (Geilhufe *et al.*, 2021), low self-esteem, and self-objectification. For gender nonconforming individuals, Sevelius links these experiences of psychological distress to an increased need for gender-affirming care and increased difficulty accessing such care due to the factors of social oppression. Stigma also exists within the queer community, including expectations of promiscuity, polyamory, prejudice based on body size, and judgment of feminine presentation (Hammack *et al.*, 2022). These areas of stigma and associated challenges are related to the body—accessing healthcare for one's body, dressing one's body, how one's body loves and experiences desire. Unsurprisingly, these stigmas often end up negatively impacting one's body image.

Systemic oppression and discrimination

Minority stress theory, created by Meyer (2003), proposes that chronic exposure to minority stressors (stigma, prejudice, and discrimination) increases an individual's risk for mental health difficulties. This theory may explain why sexual minority populations are more at risk for mental health issues than their heterosexual or cisgendered peers (Camp *et al.*, 2020). Minority stress theory asserts that individuals who hold more than one type of minority stress, such as queerness and disability, or queerness and being a person of color, are more likely to experience mental and emotional distress (Nagata *et al.*, 2020). Minority stress theory links the high rates of eating disorder behavior and body dissatisfaction among queer individuals with their experiences of discrimination and sexual objectification (Nagata *et al.*, 2020).

When queer-identifying individuals internalize their experiences of oppression, meaning they believe that experiencing oppression indicates something negative about themselves as opposed to the systems at play, multiple forms of distress may emerge and create a barrier to self-acceptance (Meyer, 2003). Camp *et al.* (2020) found that decreased self-acceptance due to internalized minority stress is associated with psychological distress. Symptoms may include shame, maladaptive coping or self-destruction, self-loathing, self-neglect, depression, and anxiety (Carmel & Erickson-Schroth, 2016; Darke & Scott-Miller, 2021), all of which can intersect with body image and the relationship to one's body. The impact of internalized oppression on one's body is explored further in the case studies in this chapter.

Violence and bullying

Sexual and gender minority individuals are more likely to experience interpersonal violence than heterosexual and cisgendered individuals (Flores *et al.*, 2020). Queer individuals may experience physical violence as endangering the body as well as being prompted by how one's body exists in the world. A lack of physical safety at home and homelessness are also increased risks for queer individuals, particularly minors (Darke & Scott-Miller, 2021). Transgender and gender-expansive teens and adults are more likely to experience harm due to harassment, violence, or institutionalized discrimination such as homelessness or unemployment (Carmel & Erickson-Schroth, 2016). In a 2013 study by Sevelius, 23% of transgender participants reported fear for their own emotional and physical safety if they were to be "outed." Camp *et al.* (2020) found that suicidality among queer individuals may be correlated with victimization.

Rejection and attachment trauma

Acceptance, specifically from one's family, is a potential indicator of positive physical and mental health and a protective factor for queer individuals (Tankersley *et al.*, 2021). Children who identify as transgender and who socially transition, such as dressing in a way that aligns with their gender identity, fare better emotionally (Darke & Scott-Miller, 2021), and this involves the support of parents/family. Parental or societal rejection of one's identity when tied to the body, as with gender and sexuality, can lead to internalization of this rejection. If someone you love dismisses you because of your body, disliking and blaming your body subconsciously may be a way to keep yourself safe.

Gender dysphoria

The traumatic experience of existing in a body that is not aligned with one's identity is unique to some members of the queer community. Decreased congruence between one's gender and how one's gender is perceived is associated with increased likelihood of body dissatisfaction and restrictive eating (Mitchell *et al.*, 2021). Denying one's own gender identity "due to societal pressure can lead to anxiety, eating disorders, depression and/or suicidality" (Darke & Scott-Miller, 2021, p.85). Puberty can be particularly traumatic, with the arrival of secondary sex characteristics. At times, gender diverse individuals may resort to disordered eating behavior to prevent secondary sex characteristics (Geilhufe *et al.*, 2021; Jones *et al.*, 2018). Treating eating disorder symptoms for transgender individuals may look different from cisgendered individuals because the body dissatisfaction has a different foundation (Geilhufe *et al.*, 2021). It is important that disordered eating behavior is treated concurrently with other issues such as gender dysphoria, instead of as a separate issue (Protos, 2021).

Medical trauma

Trauma related to medical care can occur due to discrimination, stigma, a lack of support for gender-affirming care, or medical treatment that worsens an individual's already existing gender or body dysphoria (Carmel & Erickson-Schroth, 2016). Since medical care is all about the body, it is not hard to understand how these issues in a healthcare setting could lead to disdain or complicated feelings about one's body. Fifty percent of transgender and gender-nonconforming respondents report having to educate their medical providers (James, 2021), and uninformed medical providers may replicate discrimination and stigma that patients experience in the world at large. Individuals seeking gender-affirming care often have challenges around accessibility. For example, I live in a large city in the United States where there is only one hospital system that has a department dedicated to providing gender-affirming care and procedures for adults. This state currently has legislation banning minors from gender-affirming care.

Providers and medical centers without gender-affirming protocols and procedures can negatively impact medical care. For example, eating disorder and body-image-related treatment presents potential challenges for queer folks because treatment is generally based on cisgendered individuals, for example gendered weight charts (Nagata *et al.*, 2020). In inpatient psychiatric care, transgender individuals taking hormones are at risk of being denied them. Carmel and Erickson-Schroth (2016) state that "discontinuing a person's hormones risks worsening the person's mood symptoms, damaging the therapeutic alliance, and sets up the person for bullying and violence on the inpatient unit" (p.45) by other patients, mirroring the discrimination and stigma of the outside world. The medical system in the United States is already difficult to navigate, and these additional challenges can perpetuate queer individuals feeling othered, rejected, and unsafe.

Objectification and dehumanization

Objectification theory is also one of the prevalent theories used as a lens for examining the intersection of body image concerns and objectification with queer experiences and the resulting psychological impact (Brewster *et al.*, 2019; Zullig *et al.*, 2019). Transgender and nonbinary individuals often report experiences of cisgendered people objectifying and dehumanizing their bodies (Anzani *et al.*, 2021; Sevelius, 2013). Additionally, objectification and fetishization, a subset of objectification, happen often within the queer community (Anzani *et al.*, 2021). Fetishization of queer individuals is associated with experiences of disgust, distress, fear, avoidance, sexual objectification, and microaggressions (Anzani *et al.*, 2021).

Maladaptive coping resulting in bodily harm

Maladaptive coping related to bodily harm can include self-injury, substance abuse, self-neglect, risky sexual behavior, and eating disorders. As previously mentioned, controlling one's body can become a coping skill beyond the goal of appearance (Geilhufe *et al.*, 2021). In adolescence, self-loathing, self-neglect, and self-destruction become more common among gender-expansive individuals (Darke & Scott-Miller, 2021) and can present as violence, harm, or neglect of one's body because of complicated feelings around body image. Sevelius (2013) found that 59% of transgender participants reported heavy substance abuse and many of those expressed that it was a way to cope with rejection, transphobia, or avoid dealing with stress related to transitioning. In their review of the literature, Carmel and Erickson-Schroth (2016) found that transgender and gender-nonconforming people are at higher risk for engaging in self-injurious behavior as well as attempting suicide.

Protective factors for body image

There is some research to indicate that being a sexual minority may be a protective factor for body image at times. For example, "Bears" are a subset of the male sexual minority community who value and celebrate larger bodies (Mijas *et al.*, 2020). A study focusing on gay men in Poland found that "higher BMI was associated with increased self-esteem only among men who identified as Bears, which suggests that unique processes associated with claiming Bear identity may be responsible for this effect" (Mijas *et al.*, 2020, p.8). Alvy (2013) asserts that identity as a lesbian woman protects one against risk factors related to body image such as disordered eating behavior, while Smith *et al.* (2019) found that sexual minority women do not exhibit different levels of body dissatisfaction.

CASE STUDIES

The following two case studies provide examples of the ways body image and trauma may intersect for queer individuals; however, it will not be an exhaustive list. Both participants were given the choice of two prompts: "How has coming out to yourself impacted you physically, mentally, and emotionally?" and "How is your relationship with your body impacted by your identity as a queer person?" (Millen, 2019). The first question was chosen based on Darke and Scott-Miller's (2021) statement that "to optimize treatment, art therapists should focus on gender identity as a whole, not just body image, including aspects of their client's identity, such as social, intellectual, vocational and interpersonal development" (p.101). Participants were encouraged to use whatever art materials they preferred to allow for a sense of control. Both sessions used a secure teletherapy platform and lasted 90–130 minutes. Therapists should keep in mind that clients may struggle with viewing an image of themselves throughout the session (Shaw, 2020) and should be allowed to use modifications such as turning off their camera or minimizing the window.

EMMA

Emma (she/they) is a middle-aged femme/woman who describes her sexuality as queer. Emma resides in a large metropolitan area in the United States. Emma chose to answer prompt number two and created three pieces of artwork using computer paper and a box of 24 crayons. The first piece (Figure 8.1) Emma described as representative of her time in high school, during which they considered their body to be a problem and worked to cover it. Emma shared that both her queerness and experiences of childhood abuse contributed to this view of her body. Emma shared that it felt good to cover their body because it was their own choice and gave her a sense of autonomy.

Emma said the second piece (Figure 8.2) focused on freedom and actively not fitting in. Emma stated that in college she was allowed to step outside norms, represented by the cage. They stated it was liberating to be with others who shared their values. Emma talked about finding a small group of queer and multiracial folks at her college. Emma explained that the small brown and orange boxes within the cage represent the binary of masculine and feminine while the hand reaching to the right is trying to pull her back into the cage.

USING ART THERAPY TO ADDRESS BODY IMAGE WITH QUEER CLIENTS

FIGURE 8.1: EMMA 1

FIGURE 8.2: EMMA 2

The third piece (Figure 8.3) contains a large white, vertical oval on the left side of the page with a black line in the middle. There is nothing to the right of the black line. Emma stated that the white oval being difficult to see is symbolic of being unseen within queerness because of their femme identity. Emma identifies as having a 'hard femme' aesthetic which can lead to people making incorrect assumptions about their sexuality. Emma shared that, at times, she feels as if others believe she has an insufficiency of queerness. Emma expressed frustration with the queer community creating their own cages, mimicking cisgendered heterosexual communities. Emma stated she worries about having to 'signal' her queerness through how she presents. Emma expressed a resistance to perform their gender or sexuality when part of the strength of queerness is to escape the need to perform. Emma described her experience of body acceptance. The one exception to this self-acceptance is the fear of physical harm that comes with existing in a female-presenting body in a misogynistic society.

FIGURE 8.3: EMMA 3

Emma said that attractiveness for them is not tied to their worth, which allows for more space to be themselves. She is part of the powerlifting community and noticed that she is potentially insulated by her queer identity in that space. Female powerlifters often lose their breasts because of losing weight and having a leaner body. Emma stated that women who powerlift often get breast implants because of societal expectations placed on women's bodies. Emma feels protected from this pressure because of different expectations placed on bodies within the queer community. Emma stated that, as she is aging, she believes queerness also protects her from some of the issues around body image that other aging women experience.

JANE

Jane (she/he/they) is a middle-aged individual living in a major metropolitan area in the United States. Jane identifies as genderfluid and states that her sexuality is fluid, most closely defined as pansexual. Jane used pencils, erasers, colored pencils, and paper. Jane's artwork (Figure 8.4) responded to a combination of both questions. The final product has an illustration-like appearance, with multiple drawings on one page.

FIGURE 8.4: JANE 1

Jane has experience using internal family systems in therapy and on her own, which she said impacted how she approached this directive. Jane talked about connecting with her internal system before creating art. Jane identified the image on the top left side of the page as her inner critic. Jane associated their inner critics with a vulture, and so this figure has a human head with the body of a vulture. Jane chose birds because she considers herself to have always been a "strange bird." Jane explained that the figure looking in the mirror is examining themselves and trying to determine if they "look like a queer person." Jane then moved on to the image in the bottom left of the page, a bird who is on fire, and focused on its human-like genitals.

Jane shared that she grew up in a house where genitals were associated with shame, and she received the message that women are seductresses, and arousal is to be regarded as bad. This messaging around genitals and arousal led to fantasies of self-mutilation of their genitals at an early age. I asked Jane if this messaging was related to religion and she responded that it was more "Freudian" in nature, and it seemed based on her mother's own struggles and jealousy of the attention that Jane's father paid to them. His mother never said this directly, but Jane can remember feeling bad as a child for being cute and that he received messages early on about being seductive. She also remembers receiving positive feedback from her mother as a teenager for not overtly expressing her sexuality.

Jane explained that the figure whose ribs are visible represents Jane's eating disorder. Jane said she developed an eating disorder in childhood due to shame about her body, genitals, and arousal. It was a way to "take herself out of her pelvis into her head," where she could focus on restricting and controlling her body. Jane stated that the eating disorder became the "front man" so that arousal could fly under the radar from parents, giving Jane control and boundaries around sexuality. At one point in time, Jane believed her interest in women's bodies to be about thinness and related to her eating disorder. However, the bottom center image represents her realization that it was not about thinness, but attraction to women's bodies. The two figures within the bottom center image represent the part of her grieving this realization and an old woman who will never be able to express or experience this part of herself.

Jane officially came out to herself in her early thirties. Jane stated that, at this time, she experienced moving from dysphoria to euphoria. This period is represented by the peacock in the upper right-hand part of the page. Jane described the peacock as being symbolic of the need to proclaim their sexuality. It also represented the sense of competition within the queer community and the objectification that occurs. Jane described having a "gay mom" (mentor) "coaching" her as she came out. Magnified by this relation-ship, Jane had anxiety around signaling queerness to others. Jane struggled with the labels, anxiety about not being "gay enough," and the sense that nothing had changed aside from the audience for whom he was performing. Jane experimented with online dating and felt it was too objectifying for her. Jane stated it was important to her that queerness is about who you love, not who you lust after.

Jane stated that she has struggled with expectations within the queer community to be promiscuous. Separately from promiscuity, Jane briefly shared about experiencing pressure within the queer community to be polyamorous or non-monogamous, which she stated she does not identify with. Jane said their desire for connection is represented by the heart in the hands on the right side of the page. Jane expressed frustration with the queer community's desire to put everyone in "buckets" while acknowledging that compartmentalization and labeling are part of how human brains work.

In the top center of the page is a young child who Jane said represents her wounded masculine energy. This part is aware that Jane has been harmed and betrayed by the masculine energy of others in the past. Jane stated that this wounded part has taken on the shame of these men. Jane stated that she has pride in her masculine energy, that this is where her confidence and power lie, not to be confused with hubris or infallibility.

These case study examples included themes of stereotyping within the queer community, stigma, internalized oppression, signaling queerness through presentation, objectification within the queer community, and feeling protected against some heteronormative expectations because of queerness.

PSYCHOTHERAPY APPROACHES

It is important that therapists collaborating with queer individuals are informed by a systems approach. Intersectionality and minority stress theory are important for the therapist to understand. As individuals in a position of power, therapists must be mindful of and address this power differential directly (Darke & Scott-Miller, 2021). Systems approaches uniquely equip therapists to address the goal of helping clients increase their critical consciousness of systemic oppression and how it has impacted their experiences with their body as a queer person (Chmielewski, 2017).

Following the client's lead when they are not interested in a suggested directive is important in creating a supportive environment (Darke & Scott-Miller, 2021). This stance aligns well with person-centered approaches. It can help to address power differentials in the therapeutic relationship, centering the client's experience over the knowledge of the therapist. Affirming and strength-based therapies are clinically indicated because they "acknowledge(s) and encourage(s) the resiliency in clients who break gender norms" (Darke & Scott-Miller, 2021, p.54). While traditional interventions for body image are not always appropriate for queer individuals, loving self-care continues to be important (Dalzell & Protos, 2020). Compassion-based approaches such as compassion-focused therapy, positive rational acceptance, and internal family systems can potentially address goals of increasing body flexibility and increasing self-compassion, as well as promoting self-acceptance. However, no research was found on using these approaches to address body image in the queer community.

Multiple sources promote the use of acceptance and commitment therapy (ACT) and cognitive behavioral therapy (CBT). ACT is specifically "well aligned with body image flexibility" (Walloch & Hill, 2016) and can assist with promoting acceptance and mindfulness. CBT can increase an individual's awareness of the impact of minority stress on their mental health as well as challenge negative beliefs and behaviors (Pachankis, 2014).

ART THERAPY GOALS

This section must begin by acknowledging that research that includes queerness, art therapy, and addressing body image is severely lacking. The art therapy goals included here are based on therapy goals for addressing body image within the queer community or art therapy goals for addressing body image broadly.

There are a few art therapy goals for addressing body image unique to the queer community. One of these is receiving external acceptance from the therapist and creating internal acceptance of queerness (Camp et al., 2020; Darke & Scott-Miller, 2021; Mustanski *et al.*, 2015). Art therapy has the unique advantage of symbolic acceptance of the art image by the therapist, leading to acceptance of the individual (Darke & Scott-Miller, 2021). Expressing self through art can be experienced as safer for queer individuals because of previous life experiences of rejection (Darke & Scott-Miller, 2021).

A second goal for a portion of the queer community is decreasing gender dysphoria (Dalzell & Protos, 2020; Darke & Scott-Miller, 2021), which may increase body satisfaction (Jones *et al.*, 2018). The fact that art is non-linear can be helpful for better understanding the experience of gender dysphoria (Darke & Scott-Miller, 2021). The process of exploring gender dysphoria can feel safer when done non-verbally through artmaking.

Understanding one's identity is another key art therapy goal for addressing body image for members of the queer community. This includes exploring one's values, core beliefs, and worldview (Darke & Scott-Miller, 2021; Metzl, 2017; Mustanski *et al.*, 2015; Walloch & Hill, 2016). Artmaking specifically can provide "a neutral holding space for the client to imagine what is...engaging with the art as part of a schema and correction process, moving from the response of others (projected and internalized) and the client's ongoing and unique molding of self" (Metzl, 2017, p.70). Art allows for exploration of identity, even playing with new versions of self in a safe environment (Darke & Scott-Miller, 2021). The subjective nature of artwork, including that it may be unclear or vague to the viewer, can allow for a sense of agency and safety for the creator (Millen, 2019). As with trauma-focused treatments, integration of queer identity into the overall concept of self was mentioned as a subset of this goal (Darke & Scott-Miller, 2021; Metzl, 2017; Mustanski *et al.*, 2015).

A fourth goal unique to working with queer individuals on body image is acknowledging experiences of trauma related to queerness and the body. Therapists are charged with helping individuals increase critical consciousness of how their experiences are rooted in homophobia, transphobia, misogyny, transmisogyny, and more (Chmielewski, 2017; Mustanski *et al.*, 2015). Darke and Scott-Miller (2021) stated that in order "to cultivate emotional resilience, the art therapist must openly address the emotional toll from consistent negative experiences" (p.22).

Other common goals, while not unique to this community, include increasing sense of control/choice and fostering a sense of empowerment (Darke & Scott-Miller, 2021; Hetherington *et al.*, 2021; Millen, 2019; Zullig *et al.*, 2019), decreasing self-harm and suicidal behaviors (Camp et al., 2020; Geilhufe *et al.*, 2021), understanding and changing one's relationship to one's body (Camp *et al.*, 2020; Soulliard & Vander Wal,

2020), increasing self-compassion (Dalzell & Protos, 2020; Nagata *et al.*, 2020), and decreasing a sense of isolation through increasing support (Chmielewski, 2017; Dalzell & Protos, 2020; Mustanski *et al.*, 2015).

Clinicians should keep in mind that focusing on body image flexibility and positive body image may have unique challenges for transgender and gender-expansive folks. Focusing on body pride may be more beneficial because of the focus on what their body is able to do for them (functional awareness) and how it allows them to connect with other human beings (Webb *et al.*, 2015). It may also be especially protective for groups who have traditionally been marginalized and therefore have a lack of positive representation that is affirmed by society at large (McHugh *et al.*, 2014).

ART THERAPY DIRECTIVES

Specific directives found within the literature include body tracing (Hetherington *et al.*, 2021), creating art about experiences that affect sexual or gender identity/affiliation, or relationship to body (Millen, 2019), creating an image that represents one's strengths, and creating a drawing of self as a character (Darke & Scott-Miller, 2021).

Body tracing can identify and integrate subjective and objective ideas of self and body, providing opportunity for the transformation of relationship with one's body (Hetherington *et al.*, 2021). The process of "delegat[ing] agency to another in the process of representing one's body on paper seems to parallel social cisgendered norms concerning meaning attributed to the body" which creates the opportunity for the client to take that experience and transform it (Hetherington *et al.*, 2021, p.56).

Millen (2019) created and wrote about her directive asking participants to create art about their experiences that affected their sexual or gender identity/affiliation and/or their relationship to their body. The goal of Millen's protocol is to "help the participant develop a more cohesive sense of their own identity and increase one's awareness of the intersections between developmental, social, sexual, environmental, aesthetic, behavioral and internal dimensions" (p.206). Millen specifically suggests that clients be allowed to use any desired media. Art therapists should keep in mind that asking a client to create a self-portrait may be difficult or triggering (Darke & Scott-Miller, 2021; Shaw, 2020).

Alternative directives can include creating an image that represents one's strengths and creating a drawing of self as a character (Darke &

Scott-Miller, 2021). While not yet documented as art therapy directives, Dalzell and Protos (2020) include a list of reflective questions that could be beneficial as directives. These include: "What has it been like coming out to yourself? Others?" and "Do you have concerns about body image? Do body image pressures in the LGBTQ+ community affect you?" (p.84).

MEDIA AND MATERIALS

Research suggests that art therapists provide clients with a wide array of materials (Millen, 2019) including approachable materials such as collage, controlled materials such as markers and pencils, and more fluid and flexible materials such as paint, clay, or tissue paper (Metzl, 2017). Choices can give clients a sense of control. It is also important to provide high-quality, appealing art materials that encourage play and experimentation. Media such as collage and the colors of drawing materials should also be representative (Metzl, 2017). Textiles and jewelry-making have also been suggested as they align well with goals of self-expression and can be a healthy way to exert control over appearance rather than trying to control the physical body (Darke & Scott-Miller, 2021).

SPECIAL CONSIDERATIONS

It is of the utmost importance that therapists be aware of their "own perceptions and expectations of gender and sexuality, paying attention to check with the client about her/his identity needs, places of ease, and areas where more struggle or 'stuck-ness' might be experienced" (Metzl, 2017, p.69). To prevent further harm, therapists must challenge and deconstruct their beliefs around sexuality and gender (Darke & Scott-Miller, 2021). Therapists are also responsible for learning about developmental milestones in gender and sexuality, which can begin as early as 18–24 months old (Darke & Scott-Miller, 2021).

FUTURE PLANNING

More research on using art therapy with queer individuals to address body image is needed, separate from eating disorder research. There is also a lack of research on those who are questioning, intersex, asexual, demisexual, or pansexual. Potential areas for further or future research include protective factors. Research has largely focused on risk factors and challenges within the queer community. Another topic that would benefit from further focus would be the experience of positive body image within the queer community. Other potential subjects include studying attunement, body responsiveness, and mindful self-care within the queer community, especially for those impacted by body dysphoria.

REFERENCES

Anzani, A., Lindley, L., Tognasso, G., Paz Galupo, M., & Prunas, A. (2021). "Being talked to like I was a sex toy, like being transgender was simply for the enjoyment of someone else": Fetishization and sexualization of transgender and nonbinary individuals. *Archives of Sexual Behavior, 50*, 897–911. https://doi.org/10.1007/s10508-021-01935-8

Alvy, L. M. (2013). Do lesbian women have a better body image? Comparisons with heterosexual women and model of lesbian-specific factors. *Body Image, 10*(4), 524–534. https://doi.org/10.1016/j.bodyim.2013.06.002

Brewster, M. E., Velez, B. L., Breslow, A. S., & Geiger, E. F. (2019). Unpacking body image concerns and disordered eating for transgender women: The roles of sexual objectification and minority stress. *Journal of Counseling Psychology, 66*(2), 131–142. https://doi.org/10.1037/cou0000333

Camp, J., Vitoratou, S., & Rimes, K. A. (2020). LGBQ+ self-acceptance and its relationship with minority stressors and mental health: A systematic literature review. *Archives of Sexual Behavior, 49*(7), 2353–2373. https://doi.org/10.1007/s10508-020-01755-2

Carmel, T. C. & Erickson-Schroth, L. (2016). Mental health and the transgender population. *Journal of Psychosocial Nursing and Mental Health Services, 54*(12), 44–48. https://doi.org/10.3928/02793695-20161208-09

Chmielewski, J. F. (2017). A listening guide analysis of lesbian and bisexual young women of color's experiences of sexual objectification. *Sex Roles: A Journal of Research, 77*(7–8), 533–549. https://doi.org/10.1007/s11199-017-0740-4

Dalzell, H. & Protos, K. (2020). *A Clinician's Guide to Gender Identity and Body Image: Practical Support for Working with Transgender and Gender-Expansive Clients.* Jessica Kingsley Publishers.

Darke, K. & Scott-Miller, S. (2021). *Art Therapy with Transgender and Gender-Expansive Children and Teenagers.* Jessica Kingsley Publishers.

Flores, A. R., Langton, L., Meyer, I. H., & Romero, A. P. (2020). Victimization rates and traits of sexual and gender minorities in the United States: Results from the National Crime Victimization Survey, 2017. *Science Advances, 6*(40). https://doi.org/10.1126/sciadv.aba6910

Geilhufe, B., Tripp, O., Silverstein, S., Birchfield, L., & Raimondo, M. (2021). Gender-affirmative eating disorder care: Clinical considerations for transgender and gender expansive children and youth. *Pediatric Annals, 50*(9), e371–e378. https://doi.org/10.3928/19382359-20210820-01

Hammack, P. L., Grecco, B., Wilson, B. D. M., & Meyer, L. H. (2022). "White, tall, top, masculine, muscular": Narratives of intracommunity stigma in young sexual minority men's experience on mobile apps. *Archives of Sexual Behavior, 51*, 2413–2428. https://doi.org/10.1007/s10508-021-02144-z

Hetherington, R., Della Cagnoletta, M., & Minghini, F. (2021). Not female-to-male but shadow-to-human: An exploration of body tracing in terms of embodiment and identity definition during gender transitioning. *International Journal of Art Therapy, 26*(1–2), 55–64. https://doi.org/10.1080/17454832.2021.1889626

James, S., Herman, J., Rankin, S., Keisling, M., Mottet, L., & Anafi, M. (2021). *The Report of the 2015 U.S. Transgender Survey.* https://transequality.org/sites/default/files/docs/usts/USTS-Full-Report-Dec17.pdf

Jones, B. A., Haycraft, E., Bouman, W. P., Brewin, N., Claes, L., & Arcelus, J. (2018). Risk factors for eating disorder psychopathology within the treatment seeking transgender population: The role of cross-sex hormone treatment. *European Eating Disorders Review: The Journal of the Eating Disorders Association, 26*(2), 120–128. https://doi.org/10.1002/erv.2576

McHugh, T. L., Coppola, A. M., & Sabiston, C. M. (2014). "I'm thankful for being Native and my body is part of that": The body pride experiences of young Aboriginal women in Canada. *Body Image, 11*(3), 318–327. https://dx.doi.org/10.1016/j.bodyim.2014.05.004

Metzl, E. (2017). *When Art Therapy Meets Sex Therapy.* Routledge.

Meyer, I. H. (2003). Prejudice, social stress, and mental health in lesbian, gay, and bisexual populations: Conceptual issues and research evidence. *Psychological Bulletin, 129*(5), 674–697. https://doi.org/10.1037/0033-2909.129.5.674

Mijas, M., Koziara, K., Galbarczyk, A., & Jasienska, G. (2020). Chubby, hairy, and fearless: Subcultural identities and predictors of self-esteem in a sample of Polish members of Bear community. *International Journal of Environmental Research and Public Health, 17*(12), 4439. https://doi.org/10.3390/ijerph17124439

Millen, M. (2019). Exploring Gender Identity and Sexuality through Portraiture and Mixed Media. In B. Macwilliam, B. T. Harris, D. George Trottier, & K. Long (eds), *Creative Arts Therapies and the LGBTQ Community Theory and Practice* (pp.201–216). Jessica Kingsley Publishers.

Mitchell, L., MacArthur, H. J., & Blomquist, K. K. (2021). The effect of misgendering on body dissatisfaction and dietary restraint in transgender individuals: Testing a misgendering-congruence process. *International Journal of Eating Disorders, 54*(7), 1295–1301. https://doi.org/10.1002/eat.23537

Mustanski, B., Greene, G. J., Ryan, D., & Whitton, S.W. (2015). Feasibility, acceptability, and initial efficacy of an online sexual health promotion program for LGBT youth: The queer sex ed intervention. *Journal of Sex Research, 52*(2), 220–230. https://doi.org/10.1080/00224499.2013.867924

Nagata, J. M., Ganson, K. T., & Austin, S. B. (2020). Emerging trends in eating disorders among sexual and gender minorities. *Current Opinion in Psychiatry, 33*(6), 562–567. https://doi.org/10.1097/YCO.0000000000000645

Pachankis, J. E. (2014). Uncovering clinical principles and techniques to address minority stress, mental health, and related health risks among gay and bisexual men. *Clinical Psychology, 21*(4), 313–330. https://doi.org/10.1111/cpsp.12078

Protos, K. (2021). Restricting the gendered body: Understanding the trans-masculine adolescent with anorexia. *Clinical Social Work Journal, 49*, 380–390. https://doi.org/10.1007/s10615-020-00758-9

Sevelius, J. M. (2013). Gender affirmation: A framework for conceptualizing risk behavior among transgender women of color. *Sex Roles, 68*(11–12), 675–689. https://doi.org/10.1007/s11199-012-0216-5

Shaw, L. (2020). 'Don't look!' An online art therapy group for adolescents with anorexia nervosa. *International Journal of Art Therapy, 25*(4), 211–217. https://doi.org/10.1080/17454832.2020.1845757

Smith, M. L., Telford, E., & Tree, J. J. (2019). Body image and sexual orientation: The experiences of lesbian and bisexual women. *Journal of Health Psychology, 24*(9), 1178–1190. https://doi.org/10.1177/1359105317694486

Soulliard, Z. A. & Vander Wal, J. S. (2019). Validation of the Body Appreciation Scale-2 and relationships to eating behaviors and health among sexual minorities. *Body Image, 31*, 120–130. https://doi.org/10.1016/j.bodyim.2019.09.003

Tankersley, A. P., Grafsky, E. L., Dike, J., & Jones, R. T. (2021). Risk and resilience factors for mental health among transgender and gender nonconforming (TGNC) youth: A systematic review. *Clinical Child & Family Psychology Review, 24*(2),183–206. https://doi.org/10.1007/s10567-021-00344-6

van der Kolk, B. (2014). *The Body Keeps the Score: Brain, Mind, and Body in the Healing of Trauma.* Penguin Books.

Walloch, J. C. & Hill, M. L. (2016). Treating Disordered Eating in Gay Men and Other GSM Clients Using DBT and ACT. In M. Skinta & A. Curtin (eds), *Mindfulness & Acceptance for*

Gender & Sexual Minorities: A Clinician's Guide to Fostering Compassion, Connection & Equality Using Contextual Strategies (pp.109–130). New Harbinger Publications.

Webb, J. B., Wood-Barcalow, N. L., & Tylka, T. L. (2015). Assessing positive body image: Contemporary approaches and future directions. *Body Image, 14*, 130–145. https://doi.org/10.1016/j.bodyim.2015.03.010

Zullig, K. J., Matthews-Ewald, M. R., & Valois, R. F. (2019). Relationship between disordered eating and self-identified sexual minority youth in a sample of public high school adolescents. *Eating and Weight Disorders, 24*(3), 565–573. https://doi.org/10.1007/s40519-017-0389-6

CHAPTER IX

Art Therapy with Veterans Who Have Experienced a Combat-Related Amputation

— DEBORAH ELKIS-ABUHOFF AND MORGAN GAYDOS —

Before discussing the target population and body image for this chapter—that of veterans—it is first important to understand the active-duty soldier and what brings a person to join the military. There are many reasons why a person chooses to enlist in the military as the next step in their career. Some of the most common reasons include a desire to serve their country; a sense of duty; a craving for adventure, excitement, or travel; a need for financial stability or educational opportunities; a yearning for personal growth, structure, or self-improvement; and a sense of camaraderie and belonging. For some individuals, joining the military may also be a way to continue a family generational tradition or to honor the memory of a loved one who served. Additionally, some people may join the military to escape a difficult life circumstance, such as poverty, family turmoil, or a lack of opportunities available to them. Ultimately, each person's decision to join the military is influenced by a unique combination of personal, cultural, and societal factors. However, the military creates an even playing field where all become comrades and *battle buddies*.

There are six different and unique branches related to the United States military (U.S. Department of Defense, 2023). They include The United States Army, which is responsible for ground-based combat operations. It includes those trained to engage in warfare on land and is usually the first branch called on to engage in combat. The United States Navy is responsible for naval warfare and maritime operations. It includes both ships and submarines and becomes involved in global operations. The United States Air Force is responsible for air-based combat operations. It comprises pilots and other personnel who are trained to operate and maintain military aircraft. The United States Marine Corps is responsible for providing rapid response and strategic mobility and is tasked with support of naval operations. Marines are highly trained for both land-based and amphibious operations. The United States Coast Guard is responsible for maritime law enforcement and search and rescue missions. It is also responsible for maintaining ports and waterways, and conducting environmental protection operations. Lastly, the United States Space Force is the newest branch of the military, established in 2019. It is responsible for space-based operations, including missile warning, satellite operations, and space surveillance. Although each branch has its own very specific missions, they all work together to support the national security of the United States, and those enlisted all have a common philosophy (U.S. Department of Defense, 2023).

The ethos of active-duty individuals is to present with strengths such as courage, honor, and integrity. There is a perception that the United States military is infallible. When a unit is called to a combat zone, the expectation is to protect the country and return unharmed and unscathed. Unfortunately, this is not always the case, and soldiers return with both physical and emotional wounds. Those in combat are often faced with traumas that stem from self-sacrifice, and the belief that their responsibility is to the men and women who serve beside them, at all costs. When put in harm's way, soldiers approach danger rather than retreating.

In today's combat zones, soldiers are faced with roadside bombings, encountering an improvised explosive device (IED), or having their compound ambushed, among many other dangers. As a result, soldiers risk the loss of life, witnessing friends, comrades, and innocent civilians dying, and experiencing their own traumas as a result of military actions. This trauma includes traumatic brain injuries, burns, and loss of appendages (legs, arms, etc.), and often ends their military career and changes how they perceive themselves and how they look in the mirror. When they return from a combat zone, having been wounded, they face the medical board and, if found *unfit to serve*, are forced to discharge. This leaves the now veteran to reacclimate to civilian life and learn to live with a physical disability, and in most cases, a comorbidity with post-traumatic stress disorder (PTSD) and other diagnoses that can affect their overall identity, specifically that of body image.

For veterans who have experienced changes to their physical appearance during their service, such as the loss of limb, a number of factors can contribute to poor body image. These factors include, but are not limited to, decreased sense of masculinity/strength, depleted self-worth, difficulty with relationships, and an inability to see themselves as the same individual who once served their country (Keeling *et al.*, 2021; Keeling *et al.*, 2023). As many veterans struggle to adapt back into civilian society, the importance of establishing a healthy body image can be crucial to one's overall mental health.

BODY IMAGE WITHIN THE VETERAN POPULATION

Body image can be defined as an individual's mental representation of themselves that may or may not coincide with outward appearance (Psychology Today, 2023). It is also a component of an individual's level of self-esteem and well-being, as it relates to beliefs and attitudes about one's body. One of the main factors within body image is body perception, which is directly linked to one's own physical characteristics and subjective knowledge towards one's body (Choudhary *et al.*, 2022). Global factors that can promote, or damage, an individual's body perception can include, but are not limited to, culture, societal standards, media, and personal experiences. With these considerations, body image can therefore be viewed as multidimensional, where an individual's behaviors, thoughts, and emotions can be affected by their body perception in a positive or negative manner (Rodgers *et al.*, 2023). Certain populations, such as service members, face additional pressures that can lead to the deterioration of body image as they face a greater risk of physical exhaustion and harm.

For active duty and veterans, body image dissatisfaction is generally associated with an injury sustained in combat, which can range from scars and burns to loss of limbs. In addition, the notion of having a strong, resilient body is viewed as a requirement within the soldier community (Keeling *et al.*, 2023). Keeling and colleagues (2021, 2022, 2023), whose research efforts have focused on body image and service members, report that individuals who sustain appearance-altering injuries can be prone to psychological symptoms/diagnoses such as depression, generalized anxiety and social anxiety, and decreased emotional well-being in response to body image distress. Societal and military expectations for service members further contribute to discontent towards one's body image (Choudhary *et al.*, 2022), as perceived strength and resilience become directly affected when there is a negative physical change to the body.

In addition to the loss of a limb, military sexual trauma (MST) has also been linked to decreased body image and a veteran's perception of their physical appearance. Freysteinson *et al.* (2018) explored MST among women veterans and found the impact of *invisible scars* to be a prevalent theme among participants, in addition to transitioning from feelings of pride to feelings of shame and mistrust of others after service. *Invisible scars* pertain to the psychological and emotional wounds experienced within combat or service, which might not be apparent to others, and can leave a lasting impact on one's body image. These internal battles can negatively change the way a veteran perceives their body, and their sense of control, and can lead to additional mental health concerns similar to physical injuries.

If not properly addressed, veterans experiencing negative body image are at greater risk when transitioning back into the community and are in need of supportive mental health resources. Engagement in complementary therapies, such as art therapy, can help a veteran develop a more positive relationship with their body and learn to reframe negative thoughts about their body's appearance and ability to function.

THE ROLE OF ART THERAPY

Therapy for veterans is an essential service that can help address the unique challenges faced by these individuals and can make a significant difference in their mental health and overall quality of life. Specialized therapies, such as cognitive behavioral therapy, exposure therapy, and art therapy, can help the veteran focus on specific issues related to their military service. Art therapy is a recognized mental health profession that has been known to help treat complex mental health issues with diverse and vulnerable populations; through the alternative mode of visual communication and expressive materials, art therapy can empower an individual to work towards wellness and establish emotional resiliency (American Art Therapy Association, 2017). When working with veterans who have experienced trauma resulting in PTSD, which could be related to being wounded, witnessing death and destruction, or an accumulation of their combat experiences in general, Lobban and Murphy (2018) found that veterans were able to utilize the art therapy process to explore new ways of perceiving and responding to these traumas and their new life situation.

Furthermore, it has also been found that a group art therapy process can provide a container for painful emotions, thoughts, and pre-conceived, often rigid, perceptions from their time serving in the military (Lobban & Murphy, 2018; Smith, 2016). Utilizing essential dynamics within the group process, such as relatedness and humor, can therapeutically challenge ideologies regarding a warrior or defender, and the strength within this population, leading to more effective conversations regarding trauma and how one's physical body has been affected (Kopytin & Lebedev, 2013).

It is important to note, however, that the journey to building a positive body image is unique to each veteran; it is a process that will require time and patience as the individual works through physical and emotional challenges within their self-perception. The act of creating art can help compensate for any resistance, hesitation, or loss of words when attempting to express the traumatic experience (Lobban, 2018). Various materials, sensory engagement, and colors can all play a role in symbolic representation for a veteran to work towards self-acceptance and self-compassion as they can begin to perceive a different definition of *strength*. Additionally, expressive and adaptive techniques within art therapy can also help veterans work towards a new found acceptance by providing a safe, judgment-free space to express and work through their trauma.

Adaptive art therapy

Adaptive, mechanical art supplies are those that have been designed specifically to accommodate the needs of artists with physical disabilities or limitations. These supplies are intended to make the process of creating art more accessible and enjoyable for individuals who may have difficulty using traditional art tools due to a physical limitation. One example of an adaptive mechanical art supply is a specialized easel that can be adjusted to different heights and angles, making it easier for artists with limited mobility to work comfortably. Another option is a specially designed brush or pen holder that can be attached to a wheelchair or other assistive device, allowing individuals with limited hand function to create intricate designs and patterns. In addition, adaptive art materials can include large-grip paintbrushes and pencils for limited dexterity; lightweight, ergonomic scissors that require less force to cut through materials; textured grips or modifications to traditional art tools that improve grip and stability; assistive devices that can hold canvases or paper in place while an artist works; and magnifying lenses or other visual aids to help artists with low vision work more effectively. Adaptive techniques and tools have been found to be essential in enhancing the communication of complex populations and avoiding power dynamics that can affect an individual's level of engagement (Lazar *et al.*, 2018).

Additionally, the use of computer-based technology, including tele-health, has been found to support the adaptive needs of veterans when incorporated into the art therapy process. Traditionally, art therapy has been associated with drawing and painting, which can be limiting to an individual with specific needs (Elkis-Abuhoff, 2018). Art therapists often embrace the use of technology and digital applications, specifically within a medical setting, to facilitate accessible creativity and break down barriers within treatment (Elkis-Abuhoff, 2018; Levy *et al.*, 2018). For veterans experiencing physical trauma, such as a loss of limb, the use of digital technology can help accommodate for range in mobility, use of hands, and other considerations that can be associated with traditional and direct artmaking. Adaptive digital art tools come in many forms, including drawing and painting software, three-dimensional modeling software, graphic design software, and video-editing software that can be downloaded onto a tablet for use (Elkis-Abuhoff, 2018). These digital tools can allow an individual to create intricate designs and artworks that were previously impossible or very difficult to achieve with a physical limitation. When exploring the role of technology within medical art therapy, Elkis-Abuhoff (2018) and colleagues (2017) found that individuals were able to explore changes within their bodies and visually represent their sense of self through creative apps within the art therapy session. This finding can be directly applied to an art therapist's work with veterans, as it is yet another creative avenue to explore in the journey to adapt to a new way of living.

Overall, adaptive materials and techniques within art therapy considerations can greatly enhance the creative process for individuals with physical disabilities and/or bodily trauma, enabling them to pursue their artistic passions and express themselves in new and exciting ways. Encouraging an individual to overcome creative challenges is one of the many benefits of adaptive art therapy, as it can easily transition outside the therapeutic session and empower an individual to work through additional obstacles. Adaptive tools and techniques are also highly customizable, allowing an individual to personalize their creative experience and develop a sense of autonomy through the therapeutic process.

The following case study is a composite in order to protect the identity of real clients.

STEVE'S STORY

Steven Jones is a 37-year-old male veteran who served in the Army (2010–2013) during Operation Enduring Freedom (OEF). Steven grew up in a military family; both his parents served during the Cold War, and were stationed in Germany. In fact, that's where they met, and Steven was born. His grandfather served in Korea, and his great grandfather in World War II. They were proud of their service and viewed themselves as strong and "ready for action."

Steven grew up, just like his two older brothers, counting the days he could enlist and follow his family line of military service. He made sure to stay fit and played many school sports, such as baseball, football, basketball, and track. Steven was also very creative, and his mother gave him an appreciation of art history through museum visits and discussing artwork. In fact, Steven enjoyed fully engaging in the creative process, and learning about different artists was a favorite pastime he had with his mother during the time his father was deployed. Steven loved to paint and would paint in detail his life experiences, such as when his team won a game, things that he saw hiking, and the fun he had with his dog. In fact, many of these created artworks were sent, instead of written letters, to his father while he was away at training or on a deployment.

Steven finally became a senior in high school and, on his 18th birthday, celebrated by going to the recruitment office and enlisting in the Army. He went to boot camp in the July of that year and was trained in communications. He was proud to be serving his country and following his family's legacy.

After training, Steven received his orders to deploy to Afghanistan to serve in OEF. He remembers arriving at night, and it was an overwhelming experience. It was the darkest night he can remember, and he heard booms and saw flashes in the sky. Within a week, Steven was joining transport convoys as their communications person. It was his responsibility to maintain the unit's communication to base when "out of the wire and in transport." These were very stressful times because there was always the sound of firefighting, and he always needed to be on alert for ambushes and roadside bombs. However, Steven found comfort in returning to base and escaping the war with his sketchbook.

On September 12, one day after the 9/11 anniversary, his unit was set to transport equipment to another base. His convoy was on the road when his Humvee hit a roadside IED and was thrown down an embankment and overturned. Steven was knocked out. When he came to, he looked over and saw three of his men above him and as he assessed the damage, he noticed that his "brother"—someone he had known since basic training and who had been deployed with him—was not moving. He was full of blood and Steven realized that the explosion had killed him. Steven attempted to get up but was unable to move. He noticed that he was covered in blood and realized it was his own. The rescue team finally arrived and stopped his bleeding, which stabilized him. He was medevaced to a field hospital, where they further stabilized and prepared him for transport to Germany for medical attention in the hope of saving his leg and repairing his arm.

After all attempts, it was decided that Steven's leg was not repairable and needed to be amputated below the knee. His arm was able to be saved, but there was permanent nerve damage limiting his strength and fine motor skills. As a result of the impact from the accident, and Steven hitting his head during the rollover, he also received a diagnosis of a traumatic brain injury (TBI). This caused him to have difficulty with his short-term memory and word retrieval. During this time, he became increasingly depressed and frustrated and felt a heavy weight of guilt, as he was alive and his buddy who died would not be returning to his family. As a soldier, you are taught to make sure you protect those fighting beside you, and Steven was not able to prevent his buddy from being killed. In addition, he was going through the emotional and physical pain of healing from the loss of his leg, was having difficulty lifting and maintaining his grip on items, and was increasingly frustrated as he struggled with keeping his thoughts clear. Steven also struggled with flashbacks, night terrors, and hypervigilance, eventually leading to a diagnosis of PTSD. Steven stayed in Germany for another month after his surgery before being transported to a United States military hospital for three additional surgeries and to begin his recovery and rehabilitation.

Steven's time in the hospital was filled with appointments. He was in occupational and speech therapy, was fitted for a prosthetic, and started physical therapy. However, there was one therapy he really looked forward to: art therapy. Steven had difficulty finding words and verbalizing. He found it impossible to discuss his trauma, the loss of his leg, and his struggles with memory, flashbacks, and hypervigilance. However, engaging with art materials helped him feel safe. Creating visually was Steven's comfort zone, a familiar space for him, as it had been many times in the past. His visual communication was important to him, as he was able to express himself and share his art, just as he did with his parents as a child, and during his deployment to escape the war. Although some of his fine motor skills and memory were affected, Steven found visually expressing himself with a different approach, and with the support of the art therapist, to be healing. Together, Steven and the art therapist were able to target his changed body image, thought processes, and PTSD.

Art therapy with Steven

As it was difficult for Steven to verbally discuss his experience, he was offered expressive materials to promote non-verbal communication and foster emotional engagement. One of the materials that Steven gravitated towards was painting. However, he was no longer able to utilize smaller brushes to produce the type of detailed artwork he had previously created. This did not stop Steven from engaging with paint, and he explored different approaches and large brushes that were easy to grasp. When Steven painted, he appeared to immerse himself in the creative process and remained in the moment with each focused brushstroke. Steven was able to naturally adapt his painting from his fine details to a new approach with broad strokes and large canvases. Over several weeks, it was observed that he had found "favorite" brushes in a variety of sizes, widths, and grips, allowing him to find a brush that fitted comfortably in his hand to support his current motor abilities. He also enjoyed the soft, silky bristles on the largest brush and often stated that he was surprised that using a tool so large felt so "delicate."

Steven would paint with kinesthetic movements, utilizing the range of his arm to create large brushstrokes with vibrant and often contrasting colors. Repetitive arm movements within the act of painting can be described as a satisfying and grounding experience that can lead an individual to feel fulfilled in the artmaking process (Gaydos, 2018). Painting provided a safe space for Steven to express his emotions and experience a sense of control within the art therapy sessions; it also became a supportive outlet for self-discovery and acceptance over the loss of his leg. As seen in Figure 9.1, Steven chose to gravitate towards rich dark tones in his color choice, with sporadic bursts of red and orange. Additionally, the large, adaptable brushes also contributed to his thick line quality. Both features created visual contrast and became a discussion point within his verbal processing. Steven became better able to discuss his trauma within the safe setting of the art therapy studio and relied on the art process when words were not enough. He often spoke about the physical pain, and remembered being in "that moment" where he was unsure whether or not he would survive. Those thoughts and feelings stayed with Steven, as his physical abilities and body image dramatically shifted after his injury. However, he was able to process his trauma through the creation of art. It became evident that Steven was able to work towards establishing a sense of empowerment and resilience as he continued to attend art therapy, and started to explore additional materials for expression.

FIGURE 9.1: EXPRESSIVE PAINTING[1]

Steven regularly had art therapy sessions after physical therapy and also participated in occupational therapy. Prior to this scheduled art therapy session, his physical therapist spent time discussing his current prognosis and the

---

1   The artwork has been recreated by the authors to protect the identities used in this composite case.

different adaptive supports available. When Steven entered the art studio in his wheelchair, he seemed quiet and frustrated. He went over to the table and started exploring the paints that he had been fully engaged with in the past. However, after a few minutes of contemplating, he expressed to the art therapist that he had a lot on his mind and he felt painting required too much energy. It was apparent that Steven needed a safe and controlled medium. The usual painting that he seemed to really enjoy was too threatening and regressive. Steven was in a different place and was observed to be deep in thought. The art therapist sat quietly next to Steven's wheelchair, allowing him to contemplate and hopefully find words to discuss his current state. After a short time, Steven did start to open up and began to explain that after his three surgeries to amputate his leg below the knee and the skin grafts, he was starting to realize that the IED he encountered had forever changed his life. His life had not simply changed, but all the physical activities he used to engage in prior to his injury would need to be adapted or possibly never engaged in again in the future.

Steven had a lot to communicate, but he was not able to find the words. He just sat as his energy was low, and he was introspective. The art therapist decided that a different approach was needed and offered Steven a series of collage materials, including words, images of people and animals, textured paper, and recycled materials. Steven asked if he could use the computer to find specific visuals that spoke directly to him and his current situation. He spent time on the computer pulling up images and printing them out. He seemed to know what he wanted to communicate, but he could not find a way to express himself in words. However, he was able to find images that helped with this. Steven moved his wheelchair to the table and appeared to use the collage materials to communicate his emotional state. He included specific and impactful images and words that he collected in the pile offered to him by the art therapist, as well as what he had pulled off the computer.

As Steven was working on his collage, he started to become visibly more engaged and focused. As he pulled together the images, he sat and planned how to position them (Figure 9.2). When Steven finished his collage, he sat and viewed the outcome with deep thought. The art therapist positioned herself across the table from Steven and asked if he would like to share what he created. Steven looked up and started crying, and then, with a slight smile, said, "A lot has changed since the injury, and my life will never be the same. I've been going day to day to physical therapy and occupational therapy, and keeping up hope. I used to run and play basketball and cycle. However, now

I see that between my leg being gone, having trouble thinking and focusing, and just simply coordinating and holding things with my arm, I will never be the same."

FIGURE 9.2: COLLAGE-MAKING

Together, he and the art therapist looked at his collage. It was apparent that he was concerned about his mobility and the photos he found online were related to amputation and different prosthetics. Steven explained that his goal was to be as independent as possible moving forward. However, he was concerned that he would no longer be able to go and do things as before. He was also concerned about the optics of having "half a leg," and his ability to be intimate with a partner. Steven opened up, and together, through the art, he was able to find words that helped explain his thoughts, fears, and obstacles. Steven had been working hard in physical therapy and occupational therapy to get his fine and gross motor skills moving forward. In the past, Steven had been able to engage in the art therapy studio with his kinesthetic large brush paintings. He enjoyed the visual expression again, and this was the perfect place to process his current thoughts. The art therapist observed the different types of prosthetics, the outdoors, a comforting dog, and trail markings that Steven included in his collage. However, there were statements included in the work that the art therapist felt were important to discuss. These included "The journey might have gotten longer, but the destination is still the same," "Disaster Planning," and "A guide to amputee running for beginners: Part I." Steven discussed that he has been working with his new prosthetic, and learning how to walk again. He focused on increasing his fine motor skills in occupational therapy related to damage from the physical injury and his TBI. He shared that the words he included spoke to him because he did have goals to move forward and increase his functioning. He was not yet sure what his path would look like in the future, but he knew that "the destination" was "still the same."

Through the collage, Steven was able to express his goals and fears. He was able to find the words for how he was feeling and realized that he had a direction. Even if things took longer, "the destination" could be reached. In the end, Steven realized that he was on the path he needed to follow, and that as he moved forward, although not a smooth trail ahead, things would fall into place. In fact, Steven decided that he would design the graphics for his next prosthesis to be personal and he would be able to wear his own artwork in an important and meaningful way. With the intention of increased visual expression, and incorporation of words, Steven was able to explore his bodily trauma in a non-judgmental and safe manner and start to accept his new body image.

Overall, the art therapy sessions allowed Steven to use his body to create despite his loss of a limb, contributing to feelings of resilience and empower-ment. Steven was able to work through his limitations and begin to develop a new self-perception.

Through the art therapy process, veterans have the ability to view their artwork with empathy as the visual imagery becomes an antidote to the emotional suffering and loss of self that can be present within trauma (DeLu-cia, 2016). This phenomenon adds to the value of art therapy as a treatment intervention and allows veterans to be an active part of the healing process through a creative, individualized manner, which can be adapted as needed.

CONCLUSION

When we look at Steven, we see someone who was very proud to serve their country and be part of a family history of military service. After his injury, Steven had difficulty with his day-to-day life, due to his injuries, receiving a TBI and loss of a limb, as well as his experienced symptoms of PTSD. Steven naturally gravitated to the art therapy sessions, because as a young child he utilized visual creation to process things. The big change that the art therapist had to be aware of, and sensitive to, was that Steven's previous artwork was detailed and realistic, utilizing his fine motor skills. The art therapist had to focus on the creating aspect and offer materials that were appropriate and easy to handle, and allowed Steven to manage and feel successful. Steven was open to these new materials and re-established himself as an artist. He was able to express his feelings and utilize words in his artwork, as verbalizing was difficult, and words did not come easily. In the end, Steven found the art therapy studio was a place where he could relax and process his thoughts and feelings through media.

When working with veterans who have experienced combat trauma and physical disability, it is important to get to know and understand the person who is sitting across the table. Each veteran has their own specific story. In the case of Steven, he was following his family legacy; for others, it might be that they didn't know what their next step was going to be and they decided to enlist in the military. What is their story? How do they see themself since the injury? Are they experiencing loss of fellow soldiers, survival guilt, flashbacks, nightmares, hypervigilance, learning to walk again, or how to use a prosthetic, dealing with nerve damage, and so on? When an art therapist learns about their veteran clients, it's important to consider the materials presented. Even though Steven utilized art as a means of processing his feelings, offering him the materials that he used prior to his disability that required fine motor skills would have only frustrated him and brought to the surface his limitations. However, the art therapist offered him large brushes as an adaptive tool, paint, large canvases, and collage materials to allow for Steven's abilities to shine, and this increased his self-esteem and self-worth. Since the art therapist was thoughtful in the media presented, Steven became curious and creative, which in turn allowed him to express his feelings openly through his artwork.

REFERENCES

American Art Therapy Association (2017). *About art therapy.* https://arttherapy.org/about-art-therapy

Choudhary, P., Upadhyay, S., & Kar, S. K. (2022). Concept of body image and its mental health implications. *Odisha Journal of Psychiatry, 18*(1), 11–20. http://doi.org/10.4103/OJP.OJP_3_22

DeLucia, J. M. (2016). Art therapy services to support veterans' transition to civilian life: The studio and the gallery. *Art Therapy: Journal of the American Art Therapy Association, 33*(1), 4–12. https://doi.org/10.1080/07421656.2016.1127113

Elkis-Abuhoff, D. (2018). The Application of Technology within the Medical Environment: Tablet, Apps, and Stylus. In D. Elkis-Abuhoff & M. Gaydos (eds), *Art and Expressive Therapies within the Medical Model* (pp.13–23). Routledge.

Elkis-Abuhoff, D., Gaydos, M., & Goldblatt, R. (2017). Using Tablet Technology as a Medium for Art Therapy. In S. L. Brooke (ed.), *Combining the Creative Therapies with Technology: Using Social Media and Online Counseling to Treat Clients* (pp.53–73). Charles C. Thomas Publisher.

Freysteinson, W. M., Mellott, S., Celia, T., Du, J., *et al.* (2018). Body image perceptions of women veterans with military sexual trauma. *Issues in Mental Health Nursing, 39*(8), 623–632. https://doi.org/10.1080/01612840.2018.1445327

Gaydos, M. (2018). Material Considerations to Providing Art Therapy within a Medical Model. In D. Elkis-Abuhoff & M. Gaydos (eds), *Art and Expressive Therapies within the Medical Model* (pp.188–196). Routledge.

Keeling, M. & Sharratt, N. D. (2022). (Loss of) the super soldier: Combat-injuries, body image and veterans' romantic relationships. *Disability and Rehabilitation, 45*(2), 209–219. https://doi.org/10.1080/09638288.2022.2026499

Keeling, M., Williamson, H., Williams, V., Kiff, J., & Harcourt, D. (2021). Body image concerns and psychological wellbeing among injured combat veterans with scars and limb loss: A review of the literature. *Military Behavioral Health, 9*(1), 1–10. https://doi.org/10.1080.21635781.2020.1792013

Keeling, M., Williamson, H., Williams, V. S., Kiff, J., *et al.* (2023). Body image and psychosocial well-being among UK military personnel and veterans who sustained appearance-altering conflict injuries. *Military Psychology, 35*(1), 12–26. http://doi.org/10.1080/08995605.2022.2058302

Kopytin, A. & Lebedev, A. (2013). Humor, self-attitude, emotions, and cognitions in group art therapy with war veterans. *Art Therapy: Journal of the American Art Therapy Association, 30*(1), 20–29. https://doi.org/10.1080/07421656.2013.757758

Lazar, A., Feuston, J. L., Edasis, C., & Piper, A. M. (2018). Making as expression: Informing design with people with complex communication needs through art therapy. In *CHI 2018*. CHI Conference on Human Factors in Computing Systems, Montreal, QC, Canada. https://doi.org/10.1145/3173574.3173925

Levy, C. E., Spooner, H., Lee, J. B., Sonke, J., Myers, K., & Snow, E. (2018). Telehealth-based creative arts therapy: Transforming mental health and rehabilitation care for rural veterans. *The Arts in Psychotherapy, 57*, 20–26. https://doi.org/10.1016/j.aip.2017.08.010

Lobban, J. (2018). The Development and Practice of Art Therapy with Military Veterans. In J. Lobban (ed.), *Art Therapy with Military Veterans: Trauma and the Image* (pp.9–25). Taylor & Francis.

Lobban, J. & Murphy, D. (2018). Using art therapy to overcome avoidance in veterans with chronic post-traumatic stress disorder. *International Journal of Art Therapy, 23*(3), 99–114. https://doi.org/10.1080/17454832.2017.1397036

Rodgers, R. F., Laveway, K., Campos, P., & de Carvalho, P. H. B. (2023). Body image as global mental health concern. *Cambridge Prisms: Global Mental Health, 10*, e9. https://doi.org/10.1017/gmh.2023.2

Psychology Today (2023). *Body image.* www.psychologytoday.com/us/basics/body-image?page=2

Smith, A. (2016). A literature review of the therapeutic mechanisms of art therapy for veterans with post-traumatic stress disorder. *International Journal of Art Therapy, 21*(2), 66–74. https://doi.org/10.1080/17454832.2016.1170055

U.S. Department of Defense (2023). *Our forces.* www.defense.gov/About/Our-Forces

CHAPTER X

Body Image during Peri/ Postpartum Period

Reconciling Grief and Betrayal—Mother and Body: Utilizing Creative Arts Therapy

— ALISON SILVER —

Prior to her appointment as Associate Justice of the Supreme Court of the United States, Ruth Bader Ginsburg offered a critique of the ruling of Roe versus Wade (Roe v. Wade, United States Supreme Court, 1973) before the House Judiciary Committee. Ginsburg stated, "It is essential to woman's equality with man that she be the decisionmaker, that her choice be controlling. If you impose restraints that impede her choice, you are disadvantaging her because of her sex" (Nomination of Ruth Bader Ginsburg, 1994).

Can Winnicott's (1958) good-enough mother theory hold weight within a culture that does not acknowledge the importance of "good enough" and pushes the community towards perfection? This question influences a review of body autonomy and strong identity due to inflections of societal judgment. Societally, if you do not experience the birthing process or identify as a mother, the concern of *good enough* cannot be achieved or is threatened. Good enough and perfection are subjective and abstract concepts that impact the initial mother/child bond and can exacerbate the relationship due to the societal pressures of being better than good enough. Are females held to an ideal that is unattainable? These are repeating themes within my practice working with mothers experiencing peripartum mood and anxiety disorders (PMADs) while simultaneously processing the grief they harbor due to the inability to have a vaginal birth, the inability to breastfeed, or the loss of a child due to infertility challenges, miscarriage, stillbirth, or birth trauma.

Culturally, within the United States, we are raised to believe in a sequential order of life. First, we attend school or enter the workforce, find our forever partner, then get married. After a year of marriage, or sooner depending on the age of the bride, the expectation is to produce off-spring—1.9 to be exact according to the 2020 United States Census Bureau. Expectations are to be followed in that order and in a timely fashion to be accepted by community standards. This expectation was set in place by a white, heteronormative, upper-middle-class community and was set up for me during my formative years in the seventies. Although we have grown exponentially as a society and norms are not followed explicitly today, the undertones of systemic and institutional expectations of the white male persist. In practice, I hear the disappointment of the older generation in their children's inability to follow societal rules appropriately: a persistent cultural reflection that judges the quality of life and identity of a woman.

While being approached to participate in this book, I was working within a peri/postpartum outpatient program. The program provides services for women and families with the symptoms of peri/postpartum depression, anxiety, and mood disorders. The center provides roughly a year-long program, beginning at the birth of the child; though sometimes the program begins at conception if persistent symptoms are impeding or debilitating the daily activities of the mother-to-be. If a mother comes to the program during pregnancy, the timeline for services remains in place and the program will continue for that family for one year, postpartum, or until the child's first birthday. The program includes a multidisciplinary methodology to assist the whole family system rather than just the identi-fied patient. The center offers numerous services, including peer-to-peer support groups, infant massage, infant CPR, introduction to first foods, trauma support groups, sleep training, and individual sessions. Other services include creative arts therapy (individual, couples, and group), medication evaluation and management, psychiatric evaluations, and referrals to supportive services outside the scope of the practice if a cli-ent requires more support than the program can allocate.

The large pool of skilled clinicians ranges from advance practice nurses, registered nurses, and social workers. I provided creative arts therapy and specialized (pregnancy/birth) trauma work with individu-als, groups, and their families (couple's therapy) within the program's holistic paradigm. I remained vigilant in my approach, which is rooted in a Freudian framework. Understanding their past, or the schemas built during the developmental phases of childhood allows the individual to cope with and adapt to their environment or inadvertently paralyzes them due to utilizing strategies that no longer satisfy an effective outcome. These concepts assist in identifying patterns of behavior that no longer work advantageously for the individual, thus establishing a structure for change where the individual can ground themselves. Mischel and Shoda (1995) categorized the theory as, "identifying the meaningful patterns that categorize the person's behavior across seemly diverse situations, and to discover the dynamics—the interactions among mediating process variables—that underlie the patterning and that can explain it" (p.247).

I maintained a strength-based approach as it has proven effective and necessary for this population. These mothers have unequivocally been tested by society; exploring and challenging capabilities to cultivate healthy, adapted, well-adjusted *perfect* babies—with no margin for error. Support from a therapist who institutes these theories can be beneficial for a healthy transition into motherhood/parenthood. Pattoni (2012) defines strength-based approaches as, "a collaborative process between the person supported by services and those supporting them, allowing them to work together to determine an outcome that draws on the person's strengths and assets" (p.10). Combined, these approaches support the exploration of identity that are inclusive of body and self-image.

The program's structure works toward the overall health and well-being of the mothers, partners, and the whole family construct. The agency focuses on the psychological needs of the families but also the physical health of the family, for example eating frequency as well as quality (e.g., protein versus sugar), exercise routines, and sleep hygiene. The program is integral to the mission of women and family health and is housed within the Anne Vogel Family Care and Wellness Center. The center focuses on the complete care and well-being of clients throughout their entire developmental stages, from conception to death.

Pregnancy has been categorized as an experience that affects the mind and body, with drastic changes in the physical body, such as weight gain, as well as transitions that force psychological distress among pregnant women due to an overall sense of loss of control and dissatisfaction with body image and perception of self in physical embodiment (Watson *et al.*, 2017). The American Psychiatric Association's (2013) *Diagnostic and*

Statistical Manual of Mental Disorders (5th ed.; *DSM-5*) has structured the diagnosis of postpartum as an addendum to depressive disorder and is coded as follows:

- Postpartum Mood and Anxiety Disorder (PMAD) is defined within the DSM-V as DSM-5; Other Specified Depressive Disorder (311 [F32.9]) Major Depressive Disorder with postpartum onset. (p.94)

- Presentations in which symptoms characteristic of a depressive disorder cause clinically significant distress or impairment in social, occupational, or other important areas of functioning. Due to the predominate criteria being met, the unspecified category affords the clinician to not specify and includes presentations that may have insufficient information for a more specified diagnosis. (p.184)

- With peripartum onset: This specifier can be applied to the current or, if full criteria are not currently met for a major depressive episode, most recent episode of major depression if the onset of mood symptoms occurs during pregnancy or in the 4 weeks following delivery. (p.186)

The diagnosis presently does not include the other intricate facets and possible expressions of symptomology (e.g., generalized anxiety disorder, obsessive-compulsive disorder, psychosis). This leaves the families of those suffering the effects of PMADs without a clear idea that the symptoms they are experiencing are not *baby blues* and they are not going *crazy* during the peripartum period. Antiquated notions of hysteria are still categorized by the medical field. It is not until the client comes into a mental health facility that the term hysteria is deleted from the case file. Numerous clients break down in tears when they finally enter our program after experiencing invalidation from their doctors and healthcare providers, thanking us for witnessing their disturbances and validating the experience, and simultaneously labeling the dysfunction in a way that can be organized and corroborated by the external world of insurance providers and family members, and within themselves.

The complex social inferences on the psyche and ego of an expecting or new mother are detrimental to the well-being of the individual and the bond between mother and child. As the mother's body changes and adapts to allow for the embryo/fetus to grow, the woman's body becomes further from the standard in American culture that has been deemed acceptable. Hodgkinson and colleagues (2014) specified, "Pregnancy-related changes have a significant impact on women's body image by transgressing the socially constructed ideal image" (p.10). Antonie *et al.* (2020) reported, "The image that women have regarding their body can also be influenced by the way mass media presents information about beauty ideals" (p.194).

Cognitive dissonance has become prevalent due to the marketing of American beauty standards. Festinger (1962) conveyed, "This theory [cognitive dissonance] centers around the idea that if a person knows various things that are not psychologically consistent to one another, he will, in a variety of ways, try to make them more consistent" (p.93). During the pandemic, a singer named Jax released a song titled "Victoria's Secret," which directly references body dissatisfaction resulting from media standards and expectations. Attachment can be thwarted during the peri-postpartum period following the reduction of body satisfaction from cognitive dissonance. A common struggle for new mothers during this transitional stage into their new identity is between body image satisfaction and reconciling perceived failure to meet external societal pressures to be thin enough and reconciling perceived failure to meet external societal pressures and being thin enough.

O'Hara and McCabe (2013) reported, "Difficulties with early mother-baby bonding can negatively influence a child's social, emotional, and mental development" (p.400). This becomes a significant conundrum as the mother and child grow into their new identities individually and dyadically and can lead to complications that persist due to maladaptive attachment styles. Body image satisfaction may lower if the body fails to produce the perfect outcome with pregnancy (e.g., miscarriage, inability to breastfeed, cesarean section). Again, my clients have reported that their community, whether it be family, peers, or religious affiliation, maintains that anything outside the parameters of natural conception, a full-term pregnancy, and a vaginal birth can instill shame, grief, failure, and mistrust in the body; lowering body satisfaction.

Normative constructs of pregnancy and body image hold a multitude of conflicting paradigms. Many of my clients view pregnancy as the one time they are allowed to gain weight and eat without judgment as they nourish the growing embryo. Society deems to mirror this concept, though it walks a narrow tightrope of appropriate and inappropriate. To gain too much weight will be viewed and reported by the obstetric community as unhealthy and unsafe for the fetus, and too little weight gain will be viewed as a possible mental health calamity that is restricting the mother from food intake. For example, a client who was reported to the program by her obstetrician-gynecologist, due to concerns regarding her attitude towards food and body, had inherently been set into a lose/lose structure between healthcare and self. Typically, the discussion with expecting mothers focuses on the choice to ingest everything their body is craving and resist the urge to control food intake to reduce outward judgment. This particular client felt that it was acceptable to gain weight and eat items or quantities of food sources that offered limited nutritional value without including nutrient-dense items.

Some clients encountered body dissatisfaction during pregnancy because they gained minimal weight, typically without cause or intention, and were not viewed as pregnant. These clients stated that they wished their pregnancy was more visually apparent and would frequently choose clothes that emphasized the *baby bump*. Could this timeframe exemplify a maladaptation of self-image and symbiosis between mother and fetus during the development of the fetus that would prompt the mother to begin to individuate herself, ultimately challenging to describe the developmental phase of pregnancy that typically lacks the boundary between self and fetus as stated by Bibring *et al.* (1961)?

At the center, clients are assigned to a therapist and attend their first session with or without their newborn—the choice is theirs—for an in-depth initial intake to assess their current emotional status using the Edinburgh Postnatal Depression Scale (EPDS). Simpson *et al.* (2014) reported that the EPDS is the only screening tool available to clinicians; however, it does not report on anxiety or other mood disorders during the peri/postpartum period. The program requires the mothers to repeat the EPDS before each session to establish a measurable scale of coping during this period. A limitation of the EPDS is that it does not measure generalized anxiety disorder (GAD), a common diagnosis given during this period of transition (organized under the coding of other specified depressive disorder—major depressive disorder with postpartum onset).

During the early phases of treatment, the clients may also receive a diagnosis of generalized anxiety disorder, obsessive compulsive disorder, major depressive disorder, adjustment disorder, and post-traumatic stress disorder for insurance purposes or listed informally by providers to clarify symptomology. Diagnosing is an imperative moment in the rapport-building phase of therapy, as the clinician can facilitate the role of witness and normalize the mother's emotions surrounding her post-partum disruption, as well as institute clinical knowledge to ground the client in theory.

HAIKU AS A CONTAINER

We, as art therapists, have a unique opportunity to present information in a digestible manner to assist in organizing emotions and symptoms, normalizing the difficult transition into motherhood. We have the extraordinary opportunity to tackle therapeutic interventions in an unconventional manner and use novel approaches to confront our clients' ways of thinking and reframe disordered thought processing. Moon (2007) explained, "Art therapists go beyond the verbal limitations of these literary understandings of metaphor by interacting with the metaphors found in visual images, sounds, and movements" (p.18). Levy *et al.* (1974) stated, "Art therapy focuses on the use of art materials to serve the patient's own expressive needs and eschews the manufacture of an arty bag of tricks" (p.13). Levy *et al.* (1974) concretized the approach of art therapy beyond magic, which can be a misconception for those beginning this process for the first time. I instituted haiku but allowed for a deviation from the traditional and modern definitions to establish freedom for my clients.

Haiku is a traditional form of poetry that utilizes an alternating syllabic prose of 5-7-5.

> Haiku uses imagery, affective content, sound values, figurative language, and so forth. Poetic forms in Japanese are generally short; in fact, haiku is the shortest poetry form in the world, 17 sound units divided into a 5-7-5 pattern in traditional Japanese haiku. (Ross, 2007, p.51)

The traditional style of haiku institutes an adherence to the incorporation of a season or seasonal topic. Although I respect the structure of the traditional haiku, the seasonal correlation was not a consideration in my directive. I did not encourage or discourage my clients' flow of emotional outpouring to adhere to the guidelines of the poetic style, as it would not improve the outcome of processing their experience.

There are many reasons haiku was an appropriate intervention for my clients within the PMAD center. The primary reason was to establish a controlled and short form of expression during a time of duress and overwhelming feelings. The structure of the art form established a container for clients to explore the directive within or outside the therapeutic space while maintaining emotional safety for themselves. The restrictive flow of the material and art form inhibits destabilization of the client by restricting the fluidity and looseness of the material. Malchiodi (2007) confirms, "Some media are more resistive (for example, pencils, felt tip markers, and cut paper collage). These materials permit you to be more precise and detailed, and they are easier to control" (p.84). Furthermore, the structure and rules of haiku poetry provide control and containment. The most powerful and necessary element of haiku as an art form is that it is bound in thought and time, zeroes in on emotions, and provides a distinct opportunity to emphasize the present emotions so clients and therapist can process them together. In summary, this directive allows for control and containment through material and art form to mirror what the client desires in their lives that they are unable to establish.

Although haiku is the art form referred to within this chapter, it is not the only form of creativity I institute with my clients. I offer directives organically in the session that resonate tremendously with the population, creating tangible evidence for the client to explore, process, and take with them. Within this process, the client explores prevalent themes, most commonly boundaries, identity, and self-esteem. From there, the client is prompted to create art about the theme and investigate what has been created. Specifically with this population, materials that are more restrictive in feel and production are preferred, as loose materials tend to move clients towards decompensation from a loss of perceived control and generally have been detrimental to success. While not an exhaustive list, I have limited materials including Play-Doh, colored pencils, pastels, oil pastels, gel pens, magic markers, tissue paper, decorative paper, and glue sticks.

It is imperative for the art therapist to convey the importance of process over product within adult trauma cases, specifically in relation to still birth or late-term miscarriages, as fear of embarrassment or failure may override the propensity to explore a new medium of expression. Malchiodi (2007) stated, "It is not necessary that they [client] be trained artists; the process is what is important; they should trust their own intuition and way of working; and they should not worry about what they have created" (p.83). This notion challenges the mothers as their trust in themselves, their body, and their abilities faltered when the body faced interruptions in its functioning. Our role is to build rapport and trust, somewhat quickly, so that the client can examine their internal struggles or maladaptation by disarming their astutely attuned defenses established in their development, leaving them vulnerable during the session. Exploring and processing the art form/product challenges the client in a new fashion.

CASE FINDINGS

Jennifer

There are events that can change the mother's view of self and challenge and/or strain the relationship with the body. Jennifer, at the time of services, was an early 30-year-old female, a competitive athlete and all-around sports enthusiast. Jennifer maintained a healthy sleep and eating regimen and sustained an intimate relationship with her body necessitated by her athletic endeavors. Before her first pregnancy, Jennifer maintained a strong body image. She came to the Postpartum Mood and Anxiety Disorder program due to a miscarriage in the first trimester of her first pregnancy. At our first session, Jennifer reported feeling as though her body had betrayed her and she was having difficulty resolving the overwhelming emotions that she was drowning in.

Jennifer reported understanding every part of her body and that she had held a high standard of body awareness throughout her life to sustain her athletic endeavors. She relied on the symbiotic relationship she had with her body and was dysregulated when she miscarried because her body did not present any signals to alert her to the upcoming tragedy she was about to suffer. Fernlund *et al.* (2021) found in their study that "anxiety levels were highest on the day when the miscarriage was diagnosed but had decreased when the miscarriage was judged to be complete and then remained at a low level for more than a year" (p.763). This, unfortunately, was not the case for Jennifer, as her anxiety continually escalated as she moved further away, in time, from the miscarriage. Jennifer felt out of control, and her body had become unfamiliar as we journeyed through the stages of grief and worked towards achieving a healthy conception again. Freud (1917) conveyed, "The fact is...that when the work of mourning is completed the ego becomes free and uninhibited again" (p.245).

While Jennifer recounted her experience, I worked diligently to validate Jennifer's experience, being cognizant of not redirecting her grief with concepts that could invalidate her experience. Jennifer's grief quickly translated into expressions of anxiety as she lost trust in her body and her desire to get pregnant, and feared she would never carry a fetus to full term. During these sessions, we focused on self-esteem and self/body awareness to strengthen a holistic relationship of mind, body, and soul. Jennifer worked to regain the confidence to try to conceive again. During this stage, Jennifer created her first haiku within the therapeutic space. "I pined for you/Here, gone, never said goodbye/Now I must learn trust."

This was Jennifer's first creative expression where she tried to gain the courage to begin the process of conception again. Jennifer eventually became pregnant after working extensively on her self-esteem, which included strengthening her body image, and afforded Jennifer the space to begin to trust in her body. Garrod and Pascal (2019) stated, "we find the lived experience of a subsequent pregnancy, instead reignites anxiety, guilt, grief, and loss; a profound sense of betrayal by one's body; and the liminality of the double jeopardy" (p.6). This stage of Jennifer's conception/birth story began to shape the continuation of mistrust in her body, even after conceiving and birthing a healthy child within the markers of a healthy gestation period.

After giving birth to her child, Jennifer's body betrayed her once again. She was having difficulty breastfeeding due to the fast and abundant flow of milk. When breastfeeding, Jennifer reported feeling as though she was drowning her newborn as they gagged, choked, and spit up. We explored other options— formula, or pumping and bottle feeding—but Jennifer was vehemently against these options as the research she obtained reported that breastfeeding at the onset of life increases healthy attachment and decreases the risk of sudden infant death syndrome (SIDS). Contrarily, other research has limited or inconclusive data to solidify that breastfeeding is a conclusive remedy for healthy attachment. For example, in their research, Linde *et al.* (2020) concluded there is a small correlation between breastfeeding and healthy attachment and other factors may also play a contributing role.

Throughout Jennifer's first few months postpartum, she continued to experience high levels of anxiety that inhibited her sleep routine and ability to share parental tasks with her partner. Jennifer expressed severe symptoms associated with loss of control, magnified by the uncontrollable flow of breastmilk when feeding. I asked Jennifer to create another haiku surrounding her experience. "Liquid gold they said/Promised safety but denied/ You failed me again."

This haiku reflected Jennifer's conflict with the relationship with her body and challenged the societal concept that the female body will provide for the child in the safest way. Jennifer and I began to explore the concepts of safety within her body and rebuild the trust between herself and her body.

Vera

Vera came to me as a client first through group art therapy, and subsequently we began individual sessions. She was raised in a family that exhibited extreme alcohol abuse, acts of enabling, parentification of Vera as she was the eldest child to several younger siblings, and forms of childhood neglect. Vera processed complex concepts of attachment with her mother and thus motherhood. When I met Vera, she was having difficulty breastfeeding her newborn. She was adamant that breastfeeding was the optimal choice for providing nourishment for her child and expressed a need to overcome this challenge. She felt enormous guilt for a birth deformity that the child attained in utero, although it was correctable with extensive physical therapy, and commitment from both parents.

Vera felt that breastfeeding would be the only opportunity to establish dominance over her circumstances. Her self-worth and body image diminished because her body did not perform appropriately or expectantly. She attended lactation services at the center to assist in forming a strong latch from her child as well as learning methods to increase milk production and express milk via pumping. Due to Vera's decision to breastfeed exclusively, she became the sole source of nourishment as she was unable to effectively pump and store milk to allow bottle feeding by her partner. Applied theories continually explored and processed in sessions of self and motherhood were developed during maturation, at doctor visits, readings preparing her for birth and motherhood, and in prenatal classes. Vera produced a haiku to explore the loss of trust she had with her body. "What is wrong with me/ You won't provide or perform/Help this is too hard."

As Vera continued the arduous path of increasing her breastmilk production, the task became easier and easier for her and her newborn. She became reliant on the act of breastfeeding to establish a healthy attachment for herself and the baby. Simultaneously, she began to feel judgment from the other mothers at the center as they would say, "Breastfeeding is so easy for you; you cannot understand what I am going through." Vera began to exhibit feelings of frustration and anger because she felt her peers minimized her process. Vera wrote, "Judged unfairly/No one knows the toil, I do/Motherhood is harsh."

We processed and explored feelings surrounding the unforgiving reality of our society and the innate need to critique and ridicule the body to afford a semblance of ego repair. This was required due to their own maladaptation during the transition into parenthood in a negative manner towards others. Tangney *et al.* (1998) reported, "Feelings of shame are often accompanied by a sense of shrinking or being small and by a sense of exposure in front of a real or imagined audience" (p.256). In these moments of adjudication, it was critical to remain a vigilant source of safety within the group dynamic for Vera and the other members.

Johanna

Johanna, a first-time mother, faced an unacceptable birth experience that she viewed as an institutionalized, western medical approach via an emergency cesarean section (C-section). Johanna came to the center months after the birth, unable to regulate her emotions. She was unable to perform daily tasks effectively and successfully move past the events that traumatized her and were deemed an unsuccessful birthing process from her perspective. Johanna was a woman of a strict religious sect and reported prejudice within the hospital system post-birth. These events exacerbated her feelings of invalidation and loss of (body) autonomy, and perpetuated the events. The prejudice simultaneously intensified and diminished her perception of body satisfaction due to her religious ideals and principles. This sect's expectations were to have many children throughout the childbearing years, and her C-section altered her vision of her future, thwarting her satisfaction with her body and its ability to perform. During Johanna's birth experience, she felt that she and her baby should have never had to experience a state of duress or medical state that would precipitate an emergency medical intervention.

As clinicians, we see the story through the lens of the individual, and it is important to validate but also challenge the viewpoint to encourage processing and cognitive flexibility while inspiring healing. Johanna was admitted to the hospital for a safe birthing experience at the time of labor. She was prepared and excited to welcome her first child into the world with the support of her partner and doula. Johanna had created an extensive birth plan to anchor herself in space and mitigate symptoms of anxiety heightened by increasing bodily responses to active labor. Johanna remained in active labor for over 48 hours.

The on-call doctor deemed that they had given Johanna ample time to labor naturally and decided to institute a C-section as the standard recourse to her body not dilating within the medically suggested timeframe. The doctor informed Johanna, her partner, and the doula that they would be off duty/shift soon and did not want to hand the case over to the next attending obstetrician for an unknown reason. No further explanation was provided at that time. The choice was taken out of her hands, and she was raced into the operating room for an immediate and, what felt like, an emergency C-section.

We processed her story and experience, providing a safe space to be validated and witness her experience as she remembered it. After many weeks of therapeutic work, I requested that Johanna create a haiku to explore her emotions surrounding her birth experience. "Please listen to me/I need you to hear me—my voice/Lost and silenced." Due to her medical experience, she lost confidence in the medical community. We worked to build trust in self and with medical staff. Another layer of conflict surfaced when Johanna admitted that her partner was presently employed as a medical professional because, from Johanna's perspective, they mirrored behaviors of the medical team during her birthing experience. She reported that they were unable to process emotions verbally surrounding the event, and, at times, she felt, sided with the institution rather than her.

Johanna needed to explore emotions surrounding trust within the medical community, her partner, and her body. The emotions precipitated a feeling of loss and isolation for Johanna, because of the C-section and the lack of empathy from her partner during her postpartum period. During our time together, Johanna processed her grief, around the birthing experience and incongruent emotions surrounding the reality of the birth (C-section) versus her wishful birth (vaginal birth). As we moved through her grief and space for reconciliation, she still pined for the vaginal birth and realized it would not preclude her from having that birth in the future. As a result, we worked towards establishing control over the circumstances in an adaptive and healthy manner. This included finding a new obstetrician who would listen to her concerns and work with her to create a healthy birth plan that did not exclude a vaginal birth and changing hospital systems. Through empowerment, Johanna became emboldened to change her experience for the future of childbearing and to regain a healthy and strong relationship between herself and her body. Happily, Johanna went on to have her second child via vaginal birth with an obstetrician-gynecologist who made her voice the resonant sound of clarity and grounding within the birthing suite.

CONCLUSION

I found limited research on disturbances throughout the stages of conception and pregnancy related to body image. The lack of studies and research leads clinicians to rely on tangential research. This leaves clinicians in a mirrored role with their clients as we cannot fall back on work established thus far but need to forge ahead into unknown territories. We need to recognize a continual theme replaying itself time and time again: loss of voice and trust in the body. Due to the repetitive themes in the postpartum period, educating the birthing partner with information regarding realistic expectations, boundary setting, and effective communication are essential in establishing a tolerable and adaptive means of control and satisfaction of self, including body image satisfaction.

My work has continuously been reparative. With clients that have worked with me after their first birth/loss experience, I can shift from reparative to proactive processing and planning for the subsequent pregnancies during the early stages of pregnancy, sometimes before the time of conception if anxiety becomes intolerable in repeating experiences. However, I am still left with questions, such as: would postpartum symptomology reduce if mothers had a more realistic expectation of the hormonal transitions of pregnancy and birth? Would reparation shift towards empowerment and realistic goal setting if the birthing partner felt inspired rather than victimized? Would women have a safer relationship with their bodies if they were supported with the information available regarding birth, loss, and body image satisfaction? As a clinician who believes wholeheartedly that power comes from transparency and knowledge, I believe that the answer can only be yes. We need to expect more from our healthcare systems, including medical and mental healthcare providers within the role of this extraordinary moment of transition and development in the pre/peri/postpartum period.

REFERENCES

American Psychiatric Association (2013). *Diagnostic and Statistical Manual of Mental Disorders* (5th ed.). http://dx.doi.org/10.1176/appi.books.9780890425596

Antonie, L., Vintila, M., Tudorel, O. I., Tetu, C. C., & Bularca, M. C. (2020). Body satisfaction and self-esteem in pregnant women. *Bulletin of the Transilvania University of Brasov, 13*(62), 193–200. https://doi.org/10.31926/but.ssl.2020.13.62.2.7

Bibring, G. L., Dwyer, T. F., Huntington, D. S., & Valenstein, A. F. (1961). A study of the psychological process in pregnancy and of the earliest mother–child relationship. *Psychoanalytic Study of the Child, 16*, 9–24. https://doi.org/10.1080/00797308.1961.11823197

Fernlund, A., Jokubkiene, L., Sladkevicius, P., Valentin, L., & Sjöström, K. (2021). Psychological impact of early miscarriage and client satisfaction with treatment: Comparison between expectant management and misoprostol treatment in a randomized controlled trial. *Ultrasound in Obstetrics & Gynecology, 58*(5), 757–765. https://doi.org/10.1002/uog.23641

Festinger, L. (1962). Cognitive dissonance. *Scientific American, 207*(4), 93–106.

Freud, S. (1917). Mourning and Melancholia. In J. Strachey (ed. & trans.), *The Standard Edition of the Complete Psychological Works of Sigmund Freud* (vol. 14, pp.237–259). Hogarth Press.

Garrod, T. & Pascal, J. (2019). Women's lived experience of embodied disenfranchised grief: Loss, betrayal, and the double jeopardy. *Illness, Crisis & Loss, 27*(1), 6–18. https://doi.org/10.1177/1054137318780582

Hodgkinson, E. L., Smith, D. M., & Wittkowski, A. (2014). Women's experiences of their pregnancy and postpartum body image: A systematic review and meta-synthesis. *BMC Pregnancy and Childbirth, 14*(1), 1–11. https://bmcpregnancychildbirth.biomedcentral.com/articles/10.1186/1471-2393-14-330

Jax (2020). Victoria's Secret. www.youtube.com/watch?v=F9K5IS-inHs

Levy, B., Kramer, E., Kwiatkowska, H., Lachman, M., Rhyne, J., & Ulman, E. (1974). Symposium: Integration of divergent points of view in art therapy. *American Journal of Art Therapy, 14*(1), 13–17.

Linde, K., Lehnig, F., Nagl, M., & Kersting, A. (2020). The association between breastfeeding and attachment: A systematic review. *Midwifery, 81*, 102592. https://doi.org/10.1016/j.midw.2019.102592

Malchiodi, C. (2007). *Art Therapy Sourcebook.* McGraw-Hill Education.

Mischel, W. & Shoda, Y. (1995). A cognitive-affective system theory of personality: Reconceptualizing situations, dispositions, dynamics, and invariance in personality structure. *Psychological Review, 102*(2), 246–268. https://doi.org/10.1037/0033-295X.102.2.246

Moon, B. L. (2007). *The Role of Metaphor in Art Therapy: Theory, Method, and Experience.* Charles C. Thomas Publisher.

Nomination of Ruth Bader Ginsburg, to be Associate Justice of the Supreme Court of the United States: Hearings Before the S. Comm. on the Judiciary, 103d Cong. 207–208 (1994). (statement of the Honorable Ruth Bader Ginsburg).

O'Hara, M. W. & McCabe, J. E. (2013). Postpartum depression: Current status and future directions. *Annual Review of Clinical Psychology, 9*, 379–407. https://doi.org/10.1146/annurev-clinpsy-050212-185612

Pattoni, L. (2012). *Strengths-based approaches for working with individuals.* www.iriss.org.uk/resources/insights/strengths-based-approaches-working-individuals

Roe v. Wade, 410 U.S. 113, 93 S.CT 705 (1973).

Ross, B. (2007). The essence of haiku. *Modern Haiku, 38*(3), 51–62. www.modernhaiku.org/essays/RossEssenceHaiku.html

Simpson, W., Glazer, M., Michalski, N., Steiner, M., & Frey, B. N. (2014). Comparative efficacy of the generalized anxiety disorder 7-item scale and the Edinburgh Postnatal Depression Scale as screening tools for generalized anxiety disorder in pregnancy and the postpartum period. *The Canadian Journal of Psychiatry, 59*(8), 434–440. https://doi.org/10.1177/070674371405900806

Tangney, J. P., Niedenthal, P. M., Covert, M. V., & Barlow, D. H. (1998). Are shame and guilt related to distinct self-discrepancies? A test of Higgins's (1987) hypotheses. *Journal of Personality and Social Psychology, 75*, 256–268. https://doi.org/10.1037/0022-3514.75.1.256

United States Census Bureau. (2020). *America's Families and Living Arrangements: 2020.* www.census.gov/data/tables/2020/demo/families/cps-2020.html

Watson, B., Fuller-Tyszkiewicz, M., Broadbent, J., & Skouteris, H. (2017). Development and validation of a tailored measure of body image for pregnant women. *Psychological Assessment, 29*, 1363–1375. https://doi.org/10.1037/pas0000441

Winnicott, D. W. (1958). *Through Paediatrics to Psycho-Analysis.* Basic Books.

PART 3

BODY IMAGE AND MEDICAL DIAGNOSES

CHAPTER XI

Body Image in Children Who Encounter Medical Conditions and Hospitalizations

—— JOAN ALPERS ——

Children are hospitalized for an abundance of reasons, from temporary high fevers to challenging and sometimes life-threatening conditions. During a typical hospitalization, children are removed from familiar surroundings and required to navigate the medical environment and culture. Developmental age, attachment style (Bowlby, 1988), support systems, length of hospital stay, number of hospitalizations, and severity of illness or its treatment all contribute to a child's sense of well-being and body integrity (Alpers, 2019; Councill, 2019; Malchiodi, 1999; McCue, 2009: Turner, 2009).

Separation from home, school, siblings, extended family, friends, teachers, and regular support exacerbates this experience. Over the course of a single day at a hospital, nurses, nurse's aides, attending physicians, residents, and medical students may all examine a child's body. Through the lens of a child, plastic tubes are inserted and clear plastic bags hanging from intravenous poles pump fluid into veins. Vulnerability is heightened as clothes are exchanged for hospital gowns. Radiologists take pictures with large, often loud, machines. Some procedures may be anxiety provoking, especially diagnostic scans and radiation therapy because the forces acting on children's bodies are both invisible and intangible (Councill, 2012). Phlebotomists show up, often early in the morning, disrupting sleep, to take blood samples with a needle. Some children begin to associate white coats with pain.

As a child develops, the brain makes a catalogue of the *safe* and *familiar* humans who are supportive. In contrast, an interaction with a stranger activates the liminal stress response (Ludy-Dobson & Perry, 2010). The human brain does not tell us how something feels but how it ought to feel, and so the caress of a loved one or caregiver may feel wonderful, but the touch of a stranger can feel threatening and creepy (Bryson, 2019).

ATTACHMENT, DEVELOPMENT, AND REGULATION IN BODY IMAGE

Body image is a term used to denote the embodied or lived-in experience of the physical (Markey *et al.*, 2020). How a person mentally represents or perceives their body includes an individual's history, attitudes, and feelings about physical, emotional, and interpersonal views of themselves and implicit and explicit memories related to overall health and well-being. Over the course of the first months of life, infants begin the task of understanding the difference between self and non-self (Stern, 1998). From birth, babies are working on a series of overlapping senses of self-image that begin with touch and gaze. From our first experiences of life, the presence of a healthy primary caregiver provides an attuned or *implicit relational knowing* where we learn first how to be with another, and then how to be with ourselves (Stern, 1998). An infant *feels felt* by the significant other who validates their aliveness (Siegel & Hartzell, 2004). Stern (1998) called these exchanges affect attunement. Attachment theorists have shown how this early attunement promotes healthy wiring in the brain that leads to eventual affect regulation and the capacity for integration (Schore, 1994; Siegel, 2009). The capacity for integration promotes flexibility, creativity, and adaptation in everyday coping, mastery, and resilience (Schore, 1994; Siegel, 2009; Stern, 1998). Attachment and mastery are responsible for body and emotional regulation and fear modulation, among other milestones (Ressler, 2010; Siegel, 2009).

THE DEVELOPMENT OF BODY IMAGE AND SELF-CONCEPT IN YOUNG CHILDREN

Young children lead with their limbic brain and senses, visually and non-verbally. Much of early memory is implicit and related to emotions and images (Stern, 1998). By 18 months, children develop a social self and the beginnings of verbal communication (Stern, 1998). An 18-month-old toddler can recognize their own image in a mirror and reach to remove a post-it dot that someone has secretly stuck to their forehead; this is evidence that the child can recognize themselves in a mirror (Rochat, 2003). A developing body schema or body self-awareness remains implicit until the middle of the second year when self-conscious emotions appear. At this time, a child can be shy and consciously aware of being and feeling small (Pivnik, 1997).

Development of a stable sense of self, despite changes in appearance, such as being able to identify oneself in a photo taken at a younger time, happens closer to three (Rochat, 2003). At three to four years, self-conscious awareness means a child can see themselves and also imagine how others in the world see them. Stern (1998) calls this the narrative self. When there is a realization that experiences and people can be good and bad at the same time, children are said to have fully accomplished the task of object constancy, the belief that a relationship is steady, loving, safe, and secure, despite occasional obstacles.

As external language goes inward and becomes thought, the body collects data implicitly and explicitly and children understand that their body and mind belong to them (Stern, 2010). They begin to draw a first representation of the human body, frequently called the cephalopod, consisting of a circle with sticks for limbs coming out of it and marks for facial features, eye, nose, or mouth. Cephalopod means "head foot" in Greek, a reference to the way the cephalopod's head/body connects directly to arms or legs (Merriam-Webster, n.d.). The cephalopod circle is a geometric form composed of three parts: inside, outside, and the line between. Similarly, children are aware of an inside, an outside, and a boundary between. However, a child's mind and body may still be undifferentiated for years (McCarthy, 2015).

BODY IMAGE EVALUATION OF CHILDREN WITH ILLNESS

There are multiple facets of body image for adults and youth alike. Perception of body function is the capacity to move about in the world as well as the organic workings of the inner self, like a heart beating and lungs breathing (Markey *et al.*, 2020). Children are very aware of a body that works or does not work for them. They know when a body hurts.

Body appreciation is what people like about their body (Markey *et al.*,

2020). Children want to look, dress, and act like their peers and worry about being stared at or excluded by others if they are different. Appearance evaluation is comparing oneself to a standard or norm, regardless of its validity, maintained by a culture or group and the acceptance or rejection of that comparison (Markey *et al.*, 2020). Children as young as four are aware of cultural preferences for body shape and attractiveness. Body satisfaction is the overall satisfaction or dissatisfaction with how a body works, looks, and is perceived, and accepted or rejected by its owner (Markey *et al.*, 2020). Children draw bodies showing awareness of differences caused by physical illness and disability (Alpers, 1989; Bach, 1990; Bertoia & Allan, 1988; Furth, 1988).

Kossak (2009) uses the term *embodiment* to describe how a person experiences the world through body-centered intelligence as opposed to knowing the world through the conscious mind. "Embodiment can include awareness of breath, movement, impulses, sensation and associative emotions" (p.14). There are multiple experiences of embodiment, including comfort, competence, appearance, and predictability. Comfort includes pain, tiredness, dyspnea, sleep quality, paresthesia, nausea, and enjoyment of food (Vamos, 1993, as cited in Goodill & Koch, 2019). Competence includes cognitive ability, perceptual clarity, mobility, respiratory, nutritional, and sexual function (Vamos, 1993, as cited in Goodill & Koch, 2019). In the case of younger children, competence is apparent in eating, peeing, and defecating. Appearance involves self-evaluation, other-evaluation, and visibility of disorder. Children are aware of differences like scarring, bloating, weight gain and loss, balding and other outward appearances of illness. The predictability that the body will do what the mind intends it to do, such as running, jumping, walking, reaching, playing, is related to the child's sense of accomplishment (Vamos, 1993, as cited in Goodill & Koch, 2019).

The human body is always influenced by development. A child's body is constantly growing and changing, acquiring new capacities for exploration and play, expanding and striving for mastery and independence. When normal milestones and physical illness compete, there is a challenge to maintain physical and emotional developmental targets.

For children, an age-appropriate understanding of disability or illness is crucial. A child's view and ability to understand illness is related to their developmental level. Very young children will rely on the structure and comfort the parent provides. Preschool children can be egocentric and may view illness as a punishment (Rae, 1981). A five-year-old once said to me, "My mother told me to never go out in our backyard in my bare feet, but I did, and now I have cancer in my leg." Older children may require a more scientific understanding of their illness and how their body works. They use this information as part of their ability to feel and maintain competence. An adolescent, developing identity, may struggle with why this burden has been given to them, as well as how illness fits into their emotional and social world (Erikson, 1950).

SKIN AS THRESHOLD

Whether short or long hospital stays, serious or temporary illness, a common denominator of nearly every hospital experience is the needlestick. Fear of skin penetration is very common in children. The experience of pain during the stick is present in even the youngest infant during a blood draw and is the opposite of the experience of attunement by a supportive primary caregiver. The skin is a liminal or threshold organ. It is the living boundary between me and not me, what is outside and what is inside. It keeps organs, tissue, and blood inside and defends against germs and other bad things outside (Bryson, 2019). It enables one to feel and to touch others and to be felt and touched. A supportive caregiver may use positive touch as a means of attunement. Skin is sensitive to pleasure and caress, pain and foreign intrusion. Skin is one of the most noticeable changes to the body. Changes to skin, rashes, burns, scarring or exposure (as in balding or surgical punctures) impact how children are seen by others and how safe or how whole they feel inside and, in some cases, leave impressions that last into adulthood.

A graduate art therapy reflected on a doll-making art directive in a class about art therapy and medical illness:

> I made my doll in response to a traumatic head injury when I was around two-and-a-half years old. I do not recall the event... The scar from the injury wraps around the right side of my head. I remember being young and feeling petrified of my scar. I was very insecure about the scar showing if my hair parted a certain way. My sister recalls the time I came home from the hospital post-surgery and was scared to look at me because half of my head was shaved, showing off the ugly scar. She used to show my scar off to friends and family to scare and shock them... My impulse

to staple the doll shut reminded me of hearing at a young age how the surgeons had to use staples to close the opening in my head. I could not picture what a staple to the head looked like as a child... I used to be scared of my scar opening and bleeding out if I bumped it because I did not think staples were strong enough. (Zeankowski, 2023)

VITALITY AND PLAY IN BODY IMAGE AND IN ILLNESS

Vitality remains a part of every sensory modality and can be found in every action we take (Stern, 2010). Vitality is "the positive quality of aliveness..." (Goodill & Koch, 2019, p.87), and a lack of vitality is the result of some illnesses. Humans are duration, speed, timing, and force. They are scent, vision, feel, and touch. They reach, grab, hug, create, pull away, struggle, and hide, with embodied felt aliveness. Vitality is life energy, a quality that mobilizes the entire body (Goodill & Koch, 2019). Movement is a most primitive and fundamental experience (Stern, 2010). The very act of being placed in a hospital bed changes life energy. Medicines that create lethargy and nausea, accidents that require surgeries, altered bodily abilities, and physical therapy all impact vitality.

Margaret

Margaret was a toddler who was hospitalized for cancer treatment. She had just participated in an art therapy session. She marched swiftly down the hospital corridor while her mother, balancing her IV pole, hurried behind. She was wearing a foam crown, covered with foam jewels, handmade during her session with the art therapist. "I am the Queen!" she yelled at me as she walked past my office door. "Yes, you are!" I replied. There was an increase in energy that mobilized both of our bodies, an electric pulse. I felt it. I think Margaret felt it too. Later, on her way back from the playroom she stuck her tongue out at me as she passed by again and made a "graaaaaaaaaahhhh" sound. Her mother clarified, "She is an urchin now." "Oh," I said, "Queen of the Urchins!" "Yes, she is!" said her mother. Was she a sea urchin or a child urchin or both? It felt as if we were underwater, somewhere in the unconscious.

Margaret has cancer. Her body is in trouble, but in this moment, one would not know that. In this moment, she is a powerful queen and ruler of the underworld. Body image is empowered by the antidote of play, and by the soothing of her exhausted but ever-present parents who help to provide her with a resilient defense, conscious and unconscious. The serious effects of a cancer diagnosis and treatment are apparent in the nightmares Margaret has which wake her from sleep.

The element of play, deeply imbedded in the work of children, is essential to both fun and mastery (Alpers, 2019; McCarthy, 2015). "Play allows patients and their families to forget serious illness...and focus instead on what it means to be fully incarnate in a child's body" (Crane & Davis, 2018, p.320). Play helps provide a developmentally appropriate tool to regulate, communicate, practice, and master (Gaskill et al., 2014). Creative arts are a form of play that children enjoy in the hospital. There is substantial literature about the use of art therapy within hospital settings to illustrate how children readily communicate concerns about bodies, expressions of actual illness within bodies and within self-images related to their body, as well as enact the work of healing and resilience about their bodies (Itczak, 2021; Malchiodi, 1999; Rode, 1995).

GRIEF, TRAUMA, AND BODY IMAGE

Coping with any illness is essentially a process of grief. In a serious or chronic illness, a loss of the concept of a healthy body must be mourned (Councill, 2019). Primary needs such as safety in the body are predictably challenged by illness and hospitalization. Procedures or new medications may lead a child to ask, "What will be done to me?" Loss of control, loss of the self as healthy and resilient, and loss of the energetic self are perceptions that children endure.

A trauma is an overwhelming intense emotional blow or series of blows that assault the person from the outside (Terr, 1990). "Life threatening childhood illness or injury meets the definition of an Adverse Childhood Experience when adversity includes discrete events or ongoing circumstances that are outside the child's control and are perceived as negative by the child" (Centers for Disease Control and Prevention as cited in Oral et al., 2016, p.227). Perry (2007) discusses multiple painful medical procedures and life-threatening medical conditions when describing kinds of trauma. "Art may...serve as a way to integrate parts of the identity that are temporarily lost or confused when trauma such as illness, injury or impairment is experienced" (Malchiodi, 1999, p.177).

BODY MEMORY

It is the nature of the human brain to store experiences (Perry, 2007). Young children, without sufficient cognitive understanding, can be unaware of how fear, anxiety, and emotional distress take up residence in implicit body memory. A young child who lacks narrative memory of a stressful event may still carry a body schema related to it, especially in the dearth of a soothing and safe intervention at the time of the stressor (Perry, 2007).

Thomas

Thomas, an African American boy, was born with a malformed non-functioning thumb that was amputated at an early age, thereby giving him the opportunity to compensate early on with his other digits. I met Thomas in my private practice for the first time when he was 12, after a referral by his school for issues of anger that took the form of harmless acting out in the classroom. He had several losses in his life, including the death of his father in elementary school and a school system that did not challenge his level of intelligence. His mother, a medical professional, offered a clear and concise case history but neglected to tell me about the surgical removal of his thumb. Later she explained that she didn't think it was important to recount because he was so young. Indeed, he was so adept with his index finger that I only noticed the missing thumb two or three sessions into our work.

Thomas explained that he had no memory of the lost thumb. One week, many months into his art and Sandplay process, he entered, excited about a documentary he had seen on TV about an African tribe whose boys were required, as part of their passage into manhood, to stick their hand into a nest of stinging ants and leave it there, enduring the pain and injury. Thomas, who was also transitioning from boyhood to manhood, spent weeks fixated on the story, often holding up the hand with the missing thumb in illustration, perhaps making a connection to his early, implicit memory of thumb amputation.

BODY IMAGE IN CHILDREN'S ART

Malchiodi (1999) writes about the importance of seeing children as experts of their own experiences: "Art often serves as a way to express that which is not spoken about illness, particularly fears and concerns about being sick or disabled as well as why one is ill and what will happen if one dies" (p.173). She suggests taking a therapeutic stance, phenomenologically, of not knowing, thereby allowing the voice of the child to express itself fully in image.

Jungian analyst, Susan Bach (1990), felt that spontaneous drawings were the best way to support children in medical crisis because they offer choice in the hospital environment, which limits choice and sense of control. Bach (1990) studied the art of life-threatened children, compared it to their medical case histories, and concluded that "not only the mental and psychological state was reflected but also the condition of the body" (p.8). While looking at the art, Bach projected how a child in a particular body state might feel from within, commenting, "there appears to be an inner knowingness running through their life story as reflected in their pictures" (1990, p.23). Using a combination of her interpretive conclusions on the use of color, content, and symbolism, she showed how the unconscious archetypal motifs in a drawing could indicate the course of body illness, past, present, and future, be it for good or ill. Sometimes they could even indicate the location of illness, as in a tumor that doctors could not find until a child's drawing depicted its location (Bach, 1975, p.87).

Using Bach's symbolism, I applied them to the art of several children, including Veronica and Janie, whom I was honored to work with at the time of my graduate thesis (Alpers, 1989).

Veronica

Bach (1990) recognized the bird as a symbol of the soul at critical moments of life, and the gnome, fool, or dwarf as an archetypal messenger who was allowed to enter any house with a message that the occupants may or may not want to hear. Veronica, an 11-year-old child suffering from a malignant tumor in her throat, repeatedly used the bird in her artwork. In a spontaneous drawing completed in the middle of treatment, she created a colorful bird with one leg supporting its body and the other leg supporting the throat, at the site of her cancer. Near the end of her life, and possibly her last image, she created a bird taking flight, from a broken tree (Figure 11.1). The tree is often considered a life symbol (Cirlot, 2001). In this case, the tree may have been a symbol of a broken life.

FIGURE 11.1: BIRD TAKING FLIGHT FROM A BROKEN TREE

Janie

The gnome was depicted as the helper or guide to the land beyond (Bach, 1990). Janie drew an image of a leprechaun, facing the rainbow bridge, archetypally symbolic of the way to heaven (Bach, 1990). In an earlier picture (Figure 11.2), Janie created a self-portrait with a deep worrisome cloud behind her head. At the time, she had just been told she was in remission, but several days later it was found she had relapsed (Alpers, 1989). From a Jungian perspective, the self knows, even if early perceptions of illness and hospitalization are lost to the unconscious.

FIGURE 11.2: SELF-PORTRAIT

BODY IMAGE PERCEPTIONS AND CHRONIC ILLNESS

Chronic illnesses can result in negative body image perceptions. "Body functionality refers not to just physical capacities and athleticism, but to autonomic body functions (e.g., digestion), sensations (e.g., sight), self-care (e.g., showering) and interactions with others (e.g., via body language and eye contact)" (Markey et al., 2020, p.104). When illness carries a stigma, it can mean living with symptoms and disability over the lifespan, resulting in altered lifestyles or beliefs about what the body can and cannot do, and feelings of fragility, powerlessness, and hypervigilance. An image by a teen with severe Crohn's disease (Figure 11.3) speaks of the difficult work of carrying an illness, like a burden, wherever she goes.

FIGURE 11.3: CARRYING THE PAIN

Children often draw body representations of illnesses or the emotional experience of the illness. Gabriels (1999) highlights art interventions with asthmatic children for expression of feelings and to increase a sense of competency and self-efficacy. My own experience with spontaneous drawings by asthmatic children frequently showed a clouding or rain-like marking of available air around a figure and images with scribbled out nose and mouth, suggesting a frightening lack of available air (Alpers, 2019).

Treatment for cancer can go on for months and even years after remission, including follow-ups to safeguard against any chance of recurrence. From the initial diagnosis, a child's associations with the fear of cancer can range from fear of loss of life to adjusting to an attack on the body by the illness and by the treatment. Chemotherapy and other cancer drugs can create lasting problems, including issues with cognition as well as altered body image. Misperceptions of what an illness looks like can exacerbate existing body image concerns for some children. Tara, a teenager diagnosed with a serious cancer, associated the look of sickness with gauntness and fatigue. She said, "Great! I'm going to lose weight!" This was challenged when the medicine she was given caused puffiness and weight gain instead.

Body changes that occur with illness are coped with in a variety of ways. Some children receiving chemotherapy mourn the loss of hair. A few use wigs or hats. Many children wear their baldness proudly. Tara, mentioned above, deliberately posed for her senior picture with a bald head two years later. Other children are bothered by the looks they recount from strangers who stare at their altered appearances. A fifth-grade boy refused tickets to a very popular sporting event because it meant sitting with the other sick kids and he did not want the attention. The same fifth grader was very angry at a helpful stranger who exclaimed, "You're my hero!" He expressed feeling exhausted and sick at the time, not at all like his idea of a hero. A girl explained, "You get some compliments initially about how brave you are, until you lose your eyebrows and you really look sick. Then people avoid you."

The lived-in experiences of the body include perceptions of pain and disfigurement (Markey *et al.*, 2020). Pain is often not visible. Creative work can help patients describe their pain, gain insights into life events that may exacerbate their pain, provide relaxation, and find techniques for coping with the experience of pain (Councill, 2012). Medical teams use visual scales to assess patients' experience of pain. Barton (1999) uses two visual assessments in her work with juvenile rheumatoid arthritis patients. She combines a body outline with her own meaningful pain drawing to better understand both the size and location and the overall quality of the pain.

Chronic pain, loss of physical function, mobility, and sensory functioning can all change how we experience our bodies (Sundaram *et al.*, 1995). Figure 11.4 is a drawing by a seven-year-old girl showing her experience with two bone marrow tests, side by side, as one test required her to lay flat on her stomach and the other required her to lie on her side in a fetal curve. Note the encapsulation of circles, used to represent doctors and nurses in the treatment room, and the size of the needle to the left of the figures, which is as large as the patient. The large black holes in the patient bodies are the exaggerated punctures of the procedures (Alpers, 1989).

FIGURE 11.4: TWO BONE MARROW TESTS

THE INTERFACE OF CHILD LIFE AND ART THERAPY IN THE HOSPITAL SETTING

Pediatric healthcare providers are cognizant of the potential for trauma and stress related to illness, pain management, and intrusive medical treatment on children and their families. Child life work has been described as "fun in the face of crisis" (Towne, 2016). The American Academy of Pediatrics' policy statement on child life services addresses the ways in which child life specialists work as part of an interdisciplinary team to avert trauma proactively through preparation, play, and education (Romito *et al.*, 2021).

Creative arts therapists often work in conjunction with child life programs to lessen the potential harm associated with serious, life-threatening, or chronic illness (Malchiodi, 1999; Rode, 1995). The role of child life and art therapy is to lessen the impact of difficult physical and emotional life challenges caused by illness and its treatments by providing experiences that promote a sense of mastery and return control to the child. The use of play and creative arts interventions proactively helps children of every developmental age to cope and survive hospitalizations with as much resilience as possible.

ARTMAKING TO REDUCE STRESS AND PROMOTE EXPRESSION AND MASTERY

Kossak (2009) compares creative arts work to affect attunement at every developmental level, in that the arts-based activity, shared between the art therapist and the patient, is a non-verbal rhythmic embodied exchange of energy and information and the experience of the body as the unbroken feeling of connectedness between two people. Kossak explains:

> All of the arts by nature affect the body, where meaning formation is created from the corporeal rather than the cerebral. Painting, sculpture, music making, dramatic enactment, and of course movement all involve the body in one way or another. (p.14)

The art therapist, by listening to and tuning into the creation of form, validates the experience of the body in much the same way as energy is exchanged between two limbic systems in infancy, resulting in enhanced ego strength in the forms of relationship and mastery.

"Understood as a way of discovering strengths, art therapy can be a bridge from the sad and lonely places of illness to the joy of human connection and understanding" (Councill, 2012, p.227). As children grow and change, the experiences of illness and hospitalization can help to develop resilience and effective coping techniques. Art therapists can help by providing experiences with materials that are accessible and successful in an environment that limits control and choice.

INTERVENTIONS FOR CHILDREN WHO ARE CHALLENGED IN BODY AND MIND

Children who are not feeling well and who may be frightened and bodily stressed can benefit from calming and soothing activities such as mandala. Kneading model magic clay is a stress-reducing experience for many children who are agitated or worried, as it can soothe both body and mind. Watching colors flow, such as watercolor drip painting on coffee filters, is another relaxing and non-demanding activity. Hospital postcards of imaginary vacations, like a trip to the moon, encourage visualization and relaxation. Making art can decrease the stressful perception of wait time between medical procedures and test results. Where possible, Sandplay is a liminal medium, engaging the skin, hands, and eyes, with sand and miniatures in therapeutic play (Amatruda, 1998).

Spontaneous art, for those who are up to it, will often reveal images about physical disease, diagnosis, and body image (Alpers, 1989; Bach, 1990; Bertoia & Allan, 1988; Furth, 1988). A blank game board, where school-aged children or adolescents can decide the rules and how one wins, and fill in the game cards with hospital challenges, is a great tool for engaging individuals and groups to talk about their hospital experiences, both physical and emotional. Writing game cards provides opportunities for children to share embarrassing moments related to body experiences anonymously (Alpers, 2019). Creating a personal pain scale, locating places of pain within body outlines, or creating images to symbolize pain can help communicate distress (Councill, 2012).

Much of what happens to the body in a hospital happens with the use of medical equipment. The incorporation of medical supplies used on the body into a collage or as tools for making art, as in syringe painting, can create mastery experiences for children in a hospital environment. As medical supplies are expensive, checking with nursing for expired bandages or items that they can spare is always important. Hospital wash bins and cups, empty milk containers, cardboard, and tape are handy for building sculptures. Syringes, googly eyes, felt, and clay can be combined to make tiny people and animals. Longer stay patients enjoy using casting materials on mask forms to make inside and outside feelings masks.

SPECIAL CONSIDERATIONS FOR ART THERAPY IN THE MEDICAL SETTING

Because hospitals are concerned with infection control it is important to remember that the supplies art therapists bring into a hospital room may need to stay in that room. Many supplies, such as paper and cloth, cannot be sanitized. Limiting the number of supplies to any one patient is always advisable for conservation. Finding creative ways to present choices, such as a laminated booklet of simple idea samples, can help a child visualize possibilities. Hospitalized children and their art therapists are frequently beset by interruptions for examinations, procedures, doctor or nursing visits. Children often tire easily as well, so projects which are short term with few steps and easy to dry are best.

Remembering development, understanding diagnosis, and having some history as to the length, severity, and prognosis of a child's illness are vital details when addressing body image in a medically ill child. Familiarity with the care plan that includes what will happen for a child on any given day and what may happen in the near future is also key in decision-making about what creative activities to offer in the hospital setting. Working closely with child life and the medical team can inform the course of treatment or its change due to unforeseen medical events or scheduling.

"Art therapy brings familiar materials and the universal language of visual expression to the foreign land of medicine. Through artwork with a sensitive therapist, ill children can respond to their situation with meaning and purpose" (Councill, 2012, p.238). When children leave the hospital, the team hopes they will say, "Look what I learned! Look what I made!" and be ego-strengthened by their experiences. Even so, the losses and stresses associated with chronic and life-threatening illness may impact body image for many children throughout their lifetime. It is important for every therapist to have a good health history of their client, regardless of the reason for referral, as body history lives implicitly on in all of us.

REFERENCES

Alpers, J. (1989). Art Therapy and Art Diagnosis with Chronically and Physically Ill Children in the Hospital Setting [Unpublished master's thesis]. Pratt Institute.

Alpers, J. (2019). Working with Children Who Encounter Medical Challenges: A Multimodal Approach. In D. Elkis-Abuhoff & M. Gaydos (eds), *Art and Expressive Therapies within the Medical Model: Clinical Applications* (pp.24–35). Routledge.

Amatruda, K. (1998). The liminal world: Threshold between body and psyche [Unpublished manuscript]. Psyche & Soma Psychotherapy & the Body: Sandplay Therapy & Play Therapy.

Bach, S. (1975). Spontaneous pictures of leukemic children as an expression of the personality, mind and body. *Acta Paedopsychiatrica, 41*(3), 86–104.

Bach, S. R. (1990). *Life Paints Its Own Span: On the Significance of Spontaneous Paintings by Severely Ill Children*. Daimon Verlag.

Barton, J. (1999). Comparisons of Pain Perceptions between Children with Arthritis and Their Caregivers. In C. Malchiodi (ed.), *Medical Art Therapy with Children* (pp.153–172). Jessica Kingsley Publishers.

Bertoia, J. & Allan, J. (1988). Counseling seriously ill children: Use of spontaneous drawings. *Elementary School Guidance and Counseling, 22*(3), 206–221.

Bowlby, J. (1988). *A Secure Base: Parent-Child Attachment and Healthy Human Development*. Basic Books.

Bryson, B. (2019). *The Body: A Guide for Occupants*. Anchor Books.

Cirlot, J. E. (2001). *A Dictionary of Symbols*. Internet archive. https://ia801306.us.archive.org/9/items/DictionaryOfSymbols/Dictionary%20of%20Symbols.pdf

Councill, T. (2012). Medical Art Therapy with Children. In C. A. Malchiodi (ed.), *Handbook of Art Therapy* (pp.222–240). The Guilford Press.

Councill, T. (2019). Art Therapy in Pediatric Oncology. In D. Elkis-Abuhoff & M. Gaydos (eds), *Art and Expressive Therapies within the Medical Model: Clinical Applications* (pp.1–12). Routledge.

Crane, J. L. & Davis, C. S. (2018). Child's play: The role of play in mitigating the fear of death among pediatric palliative care team patients, families, and caregivers. *Journal of Loss and Trauma, 23*(4), 317–334. https://doi.org/10.1080/15325024.2018.1446271

Erikson, E. H. (1950). *Childhood and Society*. W. W. Norton & Co.

Furth, G. M. (1988). *The Secret World of Drawings: A Jungian Approach to Healing through Art*. Sigo Press.

Gabriels, R. L. (1999). Treating Children Who Have Asthma: A Creative Approach. In C. Malchiodi (ed.), *Medical Art Therapy with Children* (pp.95–112). Jessica Kingsley Publishers.

Gaskill, R. L., Crenshaw, D., & Perry, B. D. (2014). The Neurobiological Power of Play. In C. Malchiodi (ed.), *Creative Arts and Play Therapy for Attachment Problems* (pp.178–194). Guilford Press.

Goodill, S. W. & Koch, S. C. (2019). Medical Dance/Movement Therapy for Chronic Conditions. In D. Elkis-Abuhoff & M. Gaydos (eds), *Art and Expressive Therapies within the Medical Model: Clinical Applications* (pp.85–98). Routledge.

Itczak, M. (2021). *Pediatric Medical Art Therapy*. Jessica Kingsley Publishers.

Kossak, M. S. (2009). Therapeutic attunement: A transpersonal view of expressive arts therapy. *The Arts in Psychotherapy, 36*, 13–18. https://doi.org/10.1016/j.aip.2008.09.003

Ludy-Dobson, C. & Perry, B. (2010). The Role of Healthy Relational Interactions in Buffering the Impact of Childhood Trauma. In E. Gil (ed.), *Working with Children to Heal Interpersonal Trauma: The Power of Play* (pp.26–43). Guilford Press.

Malchiodi, C. A. (1999). *Medical Art Therapy with Children*. Jessica Kingsley Publishers.

Markey, C. H., Dunaev, J. L., & August, K. J. (2020). Body image experiences in the context of chronic pain: An examination of associations among perceptions of pain, body dissatisfaction, and positive body image. *Body Image, 32*, 103–110. https://doi.org/10.1016/j.bodyim.2019.11.005

McCarthy, D. (2015). Deep Sand: Body-Centered Imaginative Play. In D. McCarthy (ed.), *Deep Play: Exploring the Use of Depth in Psychotherapy with Children* (pp.121–141). Jessica Kingsley Publishers.

McCue, K. (2009). Therapeutic Relationships in Child Life. In R. C. Thompson (ed.), *Handbook of Child Life: A Guide for Pediatric Psychosocial Care* (pp.104–135). Charles C. Thomas Publisher.

Merriam-Webster. (n.d.). Cephalopod. In Merriam-Webster.com dictionary. www.merriam-webster.com/dictionary/cephalopod

Oral, R., Ramirez, M., Coohey, C., Nakada, S., *et al.* (2016). Adverse childhood experiences and trauma informed care: The future of health care. *Pediatric Research, 79*(1–2), 227–233. https://doi.org/10.1038/pr.2015.197

Perry, B. D. (2007). *Stress, trauma & PTSD disorders in children*. Child Trauma Academy. www.childtrauma.org/trauma-ptsd

Pivnik, B. (1997). Wriggles, Squiggles and Words: From Expression to Meaning in Early Childhood and Psychotherapy. In A. Robbins (ed.), *Therapeutic Presence: Bridging Expression and Form* (pp.39–83). Jessica Kingsley Publishers.

Rae, W. A. (1981). Hospitalized latency-aged children: Implications for psychosocial care. *Child Health Care, 9*(3), 59–63. https://doi.org/10.1080/02739618109450686

Ressler, K. J. (2010). Amygdala activity, fear, and anxiety: Modulation by stress. *Biological Psychiatry, 67*(12), 1117–1119. https://doi.org/10.1016/j.biopsych.2010.04.027

Rochat, P. (2003). Five levels of self-awareness as they unfold early in life. *Consciousness and Cognition, 12*(4), 717–731. https://doi.org/10.1016/S1053-8100(03)00081-3

Rode, D. (1995). Building bridges within the culture of pediatric medicine; the interface of art therapy and pediatric medicine. *Journal of the American Art Therapy Association, 12*(2), 104–109. https://doi.org/10.1080/07421656.1995.10759140

Romito, B., Jewell, J., Jackson, M., Ernst, K., *et al.* (2021). Child life services. *Pediatrics, 147*(1), e2020040261. https://doi.org/10.1542/peds.2020-040261

Schore, A. N. (1994). *Affect Regulation and the Origin of the Self: The Neurobiology of Emotional Development.* Lawrence Erlbaum Associates.

Siegel, D. J. (2009). Mindful awareness, mindsight, and neural integration. *The Humanistic Psychologist, 37*, 137–158. https://doi.org/10.1080/08873260902892220

Siegel, D. J. & Hartzell, M. (2004). *Parenting from the Inside Out: How a Deeper Self-Understanding Can Help You Raise Children Who Thrive.* Penguin.

Stern, D. (1998). *The Interpersonal World of the Infant: A View from Psychoanalysis and Developmental Psychology* (2nd ed.). Karnac Books.

Stern, D. N. (2010). *Forms of Vitality: Exploring Dynamic Experience in Psychology, the Arts, Psychotherapy, and Development.* Oxford University Press.

Sundaram, R. (1995). In focus: Art therapy with a hospitalized child. *American Journal of Art Therapy, 34*(1), 2–8.

Terr, L. (1990). *Too Scared to Cry: Psychic Trauma in Childhood.* Harper & Row.

Towne, M. (2016). *Michael Towne. Fun in the face of crisis.* [Video] YouTube. www.youtube.com/watch?v=T_Kvefokrpw

Turner, J. C. (2009). Theoretical Foundations of Child Life Practice. In R. C. Thompson (ed.), *Handbook of Child Life: A Guide for Pediatric Psychosocial Care* (pp.23–35). Charles C. Thomas Publisher.

Zeankowski, J. (2023). The study of medical illness and the human body [Unpublished manuscript]. Department of Counseling and Mental Health Professions, School of Health Profession and Human Services, Creative Arts Therapy Counseling, Hofstra University.

CHAPTER XII

Adolescents and Body Image in Medical Settings

— MICHELLE ITCZAK —

Navigating the intersection of adolescence and body image is an intense process, and medical diagnoses and trauma can create even more complexities for those maneuvering this developmental phase. The experience of adolescence has drastically changed over the last few decades because of a burgeoning world with countless advances and developments in areas such as technology and social media. Rapid changes in our world have only intensified the challenges adolescents face, particularly in regard to body image. Some have established that body image is "a critical area of well-being among adolescents" (Lacroix *et al.*, 2022, p.285) and body image issues are significant for the preponderance of adolescents (Ricciardelli & Yager, 2016).

Adolescents who experience a life-altering medical trauma, a medical diagnosis, a hospitalization, or even an invasive medical procedure are faced with additional tribulations that can contribute to the development or intensification of body image issues. The majority of research and information about adolescents and body image in art therapy is related to eating disorders. While some chronic medical diagnoses or events that include a heavy focus on dietary needs or weight can be an impetus for eating disorders, there is an entire population of adolescents who experience life-altering medical situations that result in other psychological complications and body image issues unrelated to eating disorders. The lack of guidance and direction, or even a standard protocol for working with body image (Schattie *et al.*, 2018), leaves a significant gap for those who work in medical settings with adolescents and body image concerns. Art therapists in medical settings must be flexible, creative, and adaptable in their work with hospitalized patients because the number of sessions that one can offer before a patient is discharged is often unpredictable. The opportunity to address body image issues with this population, in this type of setting, can be fleeting or limited.

IMPACT OF MEDICAL EXPERIENCES

Adolescence is known as the time that one asserts one's independence and autonomy, while also exploring one's identity (Berk, 2004). These tasks can feel monumental to many, and even more so for the hospitalized adolescent who faces medical hurdles that impact development. Hospitalization and medical conditions interrupt the developmental trajectory of an adolescent in a variety of ways. Experienced pediatric medical art therapist Tracy Councill has declared, "The diagnosis of a serious illness or injury is a catastrophic blow to the young patient" (Councill, 2003, p.207). Receiving a diagnosis such as a chronic illness involves dealing with acute stress when diagnosed, as well as chronic stress over the long term when adapting to the diagnosis (Compas *et al.*, 2012). A chronic illness such as cancer will most likely include treatment in the form of chemotherapy or radiation, which has an impact on the physical body. Adolescents receiving treatment for cancer may experience side effects that can alter typical development, such as weight gain or loss, hair loss, damage to organs or nerves, skin changes, delayed or slowed growth, and fertility changes. Teens, who are naturally developmentally egocentric, may struggle to cope with unavoidable bodily changes during these types of medical treatments. Adolescents naturally compare themselves to one another (Kail & Cavanaugh, 2010), so an aggressive treatment regimen that alters their development can negatively impact how they feel about their body.

Not every adolescent who is diagnosed with a medical condition or who experiences a medical trauma develops poor body image, but a long-term illness that is diagnosed in adolescence could increase body image issues (Corbett & Smith, 2020). Researchers have found that a variety of factors can contribute to body image issues in adolescents who experience a medical trauma, such as a burn, or those who have chronic illnesses such as diabetes, thalassemia, or cystic fibrosis (Corbett & Smith, 2020; Darukhanavala *et al.*, 2021; Dhawan *et al.*, 2021; Huang & Su, 2021; Moore *et al.*, 2021; Troncone *et al.*, 2020). Struggles with body image could lead to psychological complications; therefore, medical and mental health professionals must be aware of the potential impact that a medical diagnosis or trauma may have on a patient. All healthcare providers should be mindful of ways they can support adolescents with medical conditions to encourage a positive body image (Hartman-Munick *et al.*, 2020). Art therapists have the ability to apply their distinctive skill set when helping adolescents reintegrate their body image after a life-altering medical experience. "The ultimate goal is to help individuals adapt to changes brought about by chronic illness or disability, integrating those changes into a restructured body image that can be assimilated and incorporated into daily life" (Falvo, 2005, p.13).

Body image is based on individual differences and often changes because of one's ability to adapt to treatment regimens and bodily changes from medical conditions, diagnoses, and traumas (Falvo, 2005; Moore *et al.*, 2021). Medical conditions may or may not have a visible physical effect on someone and every person reacts in an idiosyncratic way when their body is permanently changed or impacted. "Changes do not have to be visible in order to alter body image" (Falvo, 2005, p.12). However, with some diagnoses, "more visibly apparent factors such as ports, gastrostomy tubes, surgical scars, and supplementary oxygen, may further negatively influence one's body image" (Darukhanavala *et al.*, 2021, p.3). Patients who have permanent, visible physical effects, such as burn patients or those who have lost a limb, must navigate the responses, reactions, and comments of people with whom they interact, in addition to wrestling with their own thoughts and feelings about the changes. Concerns about what others may think or how others respond to a permanent physical change can impact socialization and social development. Experiences requiring visible medical equipment or physical changes may lead to a desire to isolate oneself or minimize public exposure.

For adolescents, socialization is a key component of their world. A large part of their ability to socialize is dependent on their ability to interact with same-age peers. Frequent appointments, long-term treatments, and reduced immunity related to medications take time away from the normal routine and can reduce an adolescent's ability to participate in educational experiences, thus decreasing opportunities for socialization. Maintaining a similar level of academic growth and smoothly transitioning into educational or extracurricular settings after treatment is necessary to minimize the impact on a patient's self-esteem.

Some diagnoses or side effects of treatments may alter one's body temporarily. Other medical changes may not be externally visible. Chronic illnesses such as diabetes, scoliosis, inflammatory bowel disease, sickle cell disease, and cystic fibrosis may not always be readily obvious to others. Invisible diagnoses or treatments can be particularly difficult for adolescents to navigate because they may not feel well, but because they appear well, they are expected to participate in activities, express positive emotions, and engage in other activities that healthy adolescents might. Constantly feeling misunderstood, judged, or alone can exacerbate emotional struggles. Body image issues can arise when an adolescent's bodily functioning does not align with what is considered "normal" in society. Frustration, disappointment, and existential questions abound during this highly emotional and egocentric developmental phase. Finding healthy ways to express and explore all of these emotions is vital to an adolescent's ability to successfully navigate the unique challenges of a medical diagnosis.

TREATMENT CONSIDERATIONS FOR ART THERAPISTS
Body image issues arising from medical diagnosis/trauma

Art therapists working with the adolescent medical population need to be familiar with the possible mental health ramifications that can accompany a chronic illness, medical trauma, or hospital experience. Not all adolescents experiencing medical diagnoses or traumas will develop psychological complications and not all develop the same type of struggles. Art therapy interventions and approaches must be individualized. Table 12.1 identifies a small number of chronic conditions and some of the psychological impacts that an adolescent might experience. Note that issues related to body image are identified as potential concerns with each of these diagnoses.

Table 12.1: The psychological consequences of chronic diseases on adolescents

Chronic diseases	Psychological complications
Cystic fibrosis	• Embarrassment or anxiety over medical consequences such as delayed puberty, malnutrition, decreased muscle mass, or ports and surgical scars • Depressive symptoms • Hyperfixation on weight and body mass index (BMI) • Negative parent-child interactions during meals

Chronic diseases	Psychological complications
Diabetes	• More likely to develop eating disorders • When body is perceived as "broken," teen is more likely to have low self-esteem and high body dissatisfaction • Preoccupation with food monitoring • Negative body image
Sickle cell disease	• More likely to have a distorted sense of weight/dissatisfaction with body • Depressive symptoms • Negative body image
Scoliosis	• Negative self-image and body dissatisfaction • Anxiety, behavioral, and mood disorders • More likely to have a mental health disorder than their non-AIS peers

Note. The data for cystic fibrosis is from Darukhanavala et al. (2021). The data for diabetes is from Corbett and Smith (2020). The data for sickle cell disease is from Bhatt-Poulose et al. (2016). The data for scoliosis is from Çubukçu and Bilir (2022) and Lee et al. (2021).

Understanding and successfully working with adolescents who experience psychological effects of a medical condition is vital to patient outcome and prognosis. Researchers studying the effects of thalassemia on adolescents have noted that "chronic illness and hospital experience exerts influence on adolescent's narrative" (Dhawan *et al.*, 2021, p.603). Because many medical conditions require attention to bodily functions, physical activity, and/or diet to manage an illness, the emphasis on these management aspects has the potential to contribute to body image concerns (Darukhanavala *et al.*, 2021; Troncone *et al.*, 2020).

Fortunately, art therapists can use creative approaches to either help prevent body image issues from developing or assess and treat patients who experience disturbance or psychological struggles related to body image (Cameron *et al.*, 1984). Art therapy helps individuals better understand their body image and work through body image and physical changes related to illness or traumatic events. The following sections address goals, directives, and effective art media for the adolescent medical population who may experience body image issues.

Goals related to the population

Art therapists establish goals to help guide the treatment process and prioritize the needs of their patient. Collaborating with an adolescent patient to identify goals for art therapy sessions is necessary for several reasons. Often, a primary goal when working with a medical population is to help the patient develop mastery or a sense of control or power over the situation (Ciucci, 2021; Councill, 2003; Malchiodi, 1999) because the development of the illness or situation that affects them was beyond their control. Asking an adolescent to help create an art therapy goal for themselves can be the first step to re-establishing a sense of control and can be further supported by future art therapy directives. Additionally, including the adolescent in their treatment planning can empower them to take more control of and increase their willingness to adhere to their treatment regimen. Adolescents who experience an illness or situation in which their diet or weight control is a focus of the treatment regimen may need the opportunity to focus on control of external situations and decrease the intense focus on themselves, which is something art therapy can provide.

When working with this population, creating art can help patients deal with their body image struggles from a safe distance to better identify and experience the changes. Directly confronting or talking about a sudden or unexpected medical situation and the feelings surrounding it can be scary or daunting for an adolescent. Simply acknowledging the change can also be a big hurdle that could be addressed through art therapy. Once acknowledged, an additional goal may include assimilating, accepting, and adjusting to the diagnosis, loss, or change in the body. In some cases, a diagnosis or a traumatic injury can elicit a state of shock or denial, especially when the medical situation has physically impacted the body or bodily functions. For example, a teenager who identifies as an athlete and loses a limb or suffers a significant burn may no longer be able to participate in athletics in the same way they previously did. This type of situation could lead to numerous psychological challenges, especially related to body image since the patient relied on the use of their body to engage in activities that were important to their identity. An art therapist working in this scenario would hope to help the patient assimilate and accept the changes and then work toward adjusting to what the patient's future might entail. An art therapist might help an adolescent in this situation explore their identity as an athlete and how that may change.

Art therapists working with adolescents who experience body image issues in relation to medical adversities need to help patients to identify misconceptions about how their body may change or be affected in the short and long term. Misconceptions can be addressed through art directives and open communication, as well as in a safe environment, without necessarily having to verbalize concerns or worries. Art therapists should encourage communication between the adolescent and the medical team for the patient to better understand the disease or injury.

Self-esteem and body image are closely associated because of the emphasis society places on appearance. Although self-esteem is applicable to many ages and psychological concerns, working towards improving self-esteem with this population needs to be prioritized. Helping adolescents identify and focus on the positive aspects of their body may be advantageous in building self-esteem.

Helping an adolescent develop a sense of curiosity, resilience, and a willingness to explore is beneficial for patients who need to adapt to new ways of conducting activities of daily living. When a body is permanently changed, one must approach the challenge with an open mind and be willing to try new ways to accomplish tasks such as brushing teeth, getting dressed, or simply moving about. Art therapists are able to provide directives that help build resilience and encourage exploration of new situations.

The above-mentioned body image goals are not exhaustive for this population, and individualized care supports establishing developmentally appropriate goals aligned with a patient's individual culture and circumstances. Every experience is unique, eliciting a myriad of responses in the hospital setting requiring ongoing assessment of needs and readiness to address body image. Art therapists' knowledgeable selection of specific art directives allows patients to process body image and encourages acceptance of the changes (Cameron *et al.*, 1984). Because body image is an ongoing issue that may be affected at various points in one's development, art therapists in hospitals can encourage caregivers to seek ongoing support for adolescents outside the hospital or post-diagnosis and treatment.

Directives appropriate for the population

"Art therapy is one of few therapies where the individual becomes actively involved in treatment through the process of art making and through the creation of a tangible product" (Malchiodi, 1999, p.16). A tangible art product can help an ill or injured patient move from a passive victim to an active participant in the work of healing (Councill, 2003). Healing from a medical trauma includes accepting and adjusting to the bodily changes or impacts one experiences. The following section will provide art directives that could be used to address body image issues that adolescents with medical diagnoses or traumas may face. Helping adolescents acknowledge and accept the state of their body is a safe starting point. Once acceptance is achieved, helping the adolescent move into appreciation, exploration, and expression of feelings is a key step to healthy coping. Self-compassion and problem-solving directives require more insight and are appropriate for later stages of body image work with adolescents.

Body sculpture

"The visual nature of clay body image sculpture engages with our human need to present ourselves visually to others" (Crocker & Carr, 2021, p.22). Asking a teenager struggling with body image to create a body sculpture from clay can prove beneficial for a variety of reasons. Creating a sculpture of their body immediately establishes a situation where a new perspective must be taken. When they are asked to look at themselves from a different perspective, their self-view can begin to shift, which may help them move towards acceptance. Meaningful processing and insight can result from a sculpture of the former or current body. Processing the grief and loss of what the body once was is an important step in acceptance of the changes. Conversely, a sculpture of their present physical condition can lead to discussions about feelings regarding the changes and an opportunity to explore moving forward or adjusting to the changes. If an adolescent elects to sculpt their former body, the art therapist could then ask them to restructure or manipulate the sculpture into what the body looks like now. This additional directive could help the adolescent process and accept the physical changes they have experienced.

Art therapists in hospitals must be aware of the hazards that natural clay can pose in regard to infection control and take this into consideration when selecting sculpting materials. Proper precautions must be taken when working with natural clay as it grows bacteria and can create dust (Davis, 2021). In some cases, a modeling clay may be a safer choice or may be mandated by hospital policy. Patient safety should prevail when selecting materials.

Body appreciation collage/image

After the adolescent acknowledges and explores their body through a body sculpture, the therapist can help the patient focus on the functions of their body and how their body allows them to interact with the world, which can help establish a positive frame of mind. Initial directives such as, "Create a collage that illustrates what you appreciate about your body" and "Create a collage about what your body helps you do" can serve as an introduction to body image work. In addition to collage materials, drawing or painting materials encourage patients who may want to use those materials to create their own image. Expanding on this directive, the prompts, "Create a collage or image about an experience that reminds you of what your body can do or what helps you appreciate your body" and "Create an image of yourself interacting with the world or environment with your new body" support deeper reflection and problem-solving.

Visual body feelings journal

Adolescence is naturally a time full of emotional ups and downs. Adding a complicated medical diagnosis only increases the amount and frequency of emotions that could include frustration, confusion, shock, loss of self-esteem, sadness, and fear (Moore *et al.*, 2021). Multiple feelings, especially related to bodily changes, can be experienced within a day, or even an hour. Art therapists can encourage patients to identify, document, and express their emotions about their body changes through visual imagery. This tangible record of their experiences may provide therapeutic distance from overwhelming emotions and begin to identify patterns of negative thinking impacting their body image. Patients can learn healthy ways to externalize their emotions rather than holding them inside. The journal serves as a safe container for processing the medical journey and adjusting to permanent or temporary physical changes.

Altered book

Altered books can be appealing and useful to the adolescent population (Chilton, 2007). The metaphor of changing or retelling a story can be useful when a patient has experienced a life-changing medical event or diagnosis. Self-leadership of the narrative of one's experience is empowering and can give an adolescent a sense of mastery or feeling of control. To address a physical change due to a medical condition or trauma, an art therapist may encourage the patient to alter the book by creating art related to the narrative about their body or adapting a new self-image. Processing these visual adaptations serves as a metaphor for the changed body from a body-positive perspective.

Problem-solving comic strip

Problem-solving skills are useful when addressing changes in daily functioning. For example, the loss of a limb may require that the patient learns how to walk or get dressed differently, potentially impacting self-esteem and body image. Phang (2021) suggested that comic strips, or sequential art, can help people process past problems and challenges. The use of comic strips in art therapy is one way to help process challenges and strengthen a person's problem-solving skills. Using a pre-drawn series of comic strip boxes, the patient draws an image of the problem, challenge, or concern in the first box. Once this is completed, they draw what happens next in the following boxes. The phrase, "what happens next" can be used as many times as needed to encourage problem-solving skills in response to the prompt. Processing of the finished product focuses on what resources are needed to achieve the outcome and support systems.

Self-compassion mandalas

Practicing self-love and compassion can help manage body image issues, especially with adolescents with cancer (Moore *et al.*, 2021). The structure of a mandala provides a sense of containment, especially when exploring topics that can be emotionally charged. A wide range of materials can be used when creating mandalas, providing patients with choices and supporting autonomy in uncontrollable situations. Examples of prompts are, "How can you treat your body when it is struggling?", "What about your body makes you unique?", "How can you show love to your body?", and "What do you do well/are you proud of?"

The "New Me" video

Technology is an everyday part of life for teens. Finding art therapy directives and approaches that incorporate technology may increase participation, offer novelty within a restricted environment, and provide an age-appropriate avenue for self-expression. Video recordings are accessible with the wide range of devices that have recording features. A directive such as, "Create a short video that represents you and how you want to be treated" could give voice to an adolescent and provide a creative outlet for helping them to take control of their situation by encouraging verbal and visual documentation about how they want to be treated now that their life is different. Short videos can utilize storytelling and can provide a platform for adolescents to educate others on how to be supportive. In the therapeutic process, editing and compiling a video serves as a metaphor for compiling, editing, and reconstructing new ways of interacting with the world after a significant medical diagnosis or event. This type of project supports trial and error and abstract and concrete thought processes, and requires courage.

Family support

In addition to individual work, social support is extremely important at the adolescent stage of development, especially when they are faced with a life-altering medical diagnosis. Family support is crucial after a serious medical event or diagnosis because family is often most readily available due to the level of care necessitated by the medical situation. Adolescents with chronic illness are most likely to disclose their feelings and experiences to family members who are closely connected to the treatment or management of the illness (Kaushansky *et al.*, 2017). Family art directives addressing concerns, fears, or perceptions of the patient offer a supportive environment for the patient to communicate their struggles and voice their needs. Art therapists can normalize family sessions by offering them frequently and selecting directives in which the entire family can take part. Utilizing art therapy to establish a strong line of communication early in the medical event or diagnosis will provide long-term benefits for the adolescent.

Art media effective/appealing to the population

Art therapist Shirley Riley (1999) insists that each individual material that is offered to a client has a significant impact on the session, and materials offered to adolescents should be thoughtfully considered. Art therapists are trained in the breadth of art media and understand the impact of materials on clients. This knowledge is used to select specific materials at specific times with specific clients to achieve therapeutic goals. Art therapists working with adolescents find that there are preferred materials because of the nature and potential of the media. For example, many adolescents will select colored pencils, sharpie markers, pens, or other materials that provide a sense of control. Art therapists understand that the emotional turmoil experienced in adolescence can be balanced with the choice of a controllable media. "The use of classical art materials... allows distancing, denial, projection, or symbolic handling of this stressful [body image issue]" (Cameron *et al.*, 1984, p.112). In addition to traditional art materials, the materials described below have been successful with the adolescent population.

Collage

Collage materials offer pre-made images or phrases which can make the sharing process easier because the image or word is already externalized. Adolescents who may struggle to identify thoughts and emotions or be hesitant to openly reveal their inner thoughts and feelings are often drawn to this media. Collage provides an opportunity to have a bit of separation and to be selective about what is shared. Collage also provides a tangible way for patients to practice rearranging, organizing, or exploring various compositions, which can reflect how they are rearranging or reorganizing their lives after a shocking medical scenario or experience. Or rather, they have an opportunity to create order out of something that can feel chaotic.

Photography

Photography is accessible for many, with the ability to snap photographs and the technological advancements of cell phones. With social media sites that promote visual expression through image sharing, using imagery to express oneself has become a cultural norm. Using digital photographs for expressive purposes to create collages, digital stories, or comic books takes advantage of this interest.

Fiber arts

Adolescents are often attracted to fiber arts, which can include fabrics, ribbons, yarn, thread, and wool. The opportunity to create a functional piece of clothing or headcover can empower a patient who faces a temporary or permanent visible bodily change. When an adolescent experiences a bodily change that affects their perception of the usefulness of their body, the ability to create functional and useful items can help alleviate feelings of worthlessness. Learning a skill such as knitting or crocheting helps one feel a sense of mastery and accomplishment, while also providing opportunities to create gifts and objects to give to others. The ability to give something to others when one is typically on the receiving end of gifts can help build confidence, self-worth, and self-esteem. Many fiber arts projects such as needle felting, cross-stitching, knitting, and crocheting require repetitive movements that can become self-soothing, healthy coping mechanisms.

Clay

Clay is a sensory, tactile, three-dimensional material for creating one's own body image; it allows for play and reflection in ways that other two-dimensional materials do not. It can be cut, pulled apart, and then repaired and put back together, becoming a metaphor for injury, trauma, and making whole again (Crocker & Carr, 2021, p.9).

The energy required to manipulate clay can be therapeutic and offer an expressive outlet appealing to adolescents. The tactical sensations of working with wet clay and the resistive nature of clay can be cathartic experiences. Through metaphor, Crocker and Carr (2021) relate life and the human condition to the clay-firing process. Similar to working with clay, life can be dangerous and unpredictable, but the result can be a solid, stronger final product that retains some fragility.

SPECIAL CONSIDERATIONS

Art therapists working with this population may work in outpatient services, schools, or a wide variety of other settings. In some cases, opportunities to work with this specific population may be limited to short-term medical settings. If a hospital is where one encounters a patient, the art therapist must learn to work quickly and effectively to begin addressing body image issues within a limited timeframe due to the unknown length of time a patient will be hospitalized. Art therapists may also need to work collaboratively with other health professionals, such as occupational therapists and physical therapists, to help develop adaptive tools and methods of working with art materials so that patients can find ways to engage in artmaking in the hospital or at home. Maintaining a solid referral list for outside mental health professionals to provide services to patients who are discharged from the hospital is vital to helping them continue to address the challenges of body image post-hospitalization. Art therapists can help educate parents about the potential for body image issues to arise in adolescents after a bodily trauma, injury, or diagnosis and encourage them to proactively seek support outside the hospital.

Art therapists who work with adolescents who have chronic illnesses should advocate for all medical professionals working with a patient to monitor for and discuss body image issues promptly after diagnosis so that patient concerns can be addressed as early as possible (Helms *et al.*, 2017). Helping a patient develop a healthy body image early on will establish a solid foundation for when concerns about appearance become more intense during the adolescent years. Finally, art therapists should be self-aware of any body image issues they may themselves have and be mindful of how this may impact the work they do.

FUTURE PLANNING

Self-esteem, body image, and body confidence are heavily influenced and impacted throughout adolescence; thus, a body-altering medical experience can further complicate these challenges. There is not currently an art therapy assessment specifically designed to assess body image. An assessment of this nature would be beneficial to this population and others, especially one that could be administered quickly and over time to monitor changes. There are also no standard protocols or evidence-based interventions developed to address body image issues with hospitalized adolescents who experience body image disturbance. Art therapists are uniquely positioned to provide healthy outlets for this population and help address body image issues; however, there is a deep need to document and expand information in this area of practice so that art therapists are better equipped to address the body image concerns that are intensified with chronic illnesses and other life-changing medical diagnoses or events.

REFERENCES

Berk, L. E. (2004). *Development through the Lifespan* (3rd ed.). Pearson.

Bhatt-Poulose, K., James, K., Reid, M., Harrison, A., & Asnani, M. (2016). Increased rates of body dissatisfaction, depressive symptoms, and suicide attempts in Jamaican teens with sickle cell disease. *Pediatric Blood & Cancer, 63*(12), 2159–2166. https://doi.org/10.1002/pbc.26091

Cameron, C. O., Juszczak, L., & Wallace, N. (1984). Using creative arts to help children cope with altered body image. *Child Health Care, 12*(3), 108–112. https://doi.org/10.1207/s15326888chc1203_1

Chilton, G. (2007). Altered books in art therapy with adolescents. *Art Therapy, 24*(2), 59–63. https://doi.org/10.1080/07421656.2007.10129588

Ciucci, A. (2021). Advocacy through Innovation. In M. Itczak (ed.), *Pediatric Medical Art Therapy* (pp.129–146). Jessica Kingsley Publishers.

Compas, B. E., Jaser, S. S., Dunn, M. J., & Rodriguez, E. M. (2012). Coping with chronic illness in childhood and adolescence. *Annual Review of Clinical Psychology, 8*(1), 455–480. https://doi.org/10.1146/annurev-clinpsy-032511-143108

Councill, T. (2003). Medical Art Therapy with Children. In C. A. Malchiodi (ed.), *Handbook of Art Therapy* (pp.207–219). Guilford Press.

Crocker, T. & Carr, S. M. D. (2021). *Clay Work and Body Image in Art Therapy: Using Metaphor and Symbolism to Heal.* Routledge.

Corbett, T. & Smith, J. (2020). Disordered eating and body image in adolescents with type 1 diabetes. *Diabetes Care for Children & Young People, 9*(3), 53. https://diabetesonthenet.com/

diabetes-care-children-young-people/disordered-eating-and-body-image-in-adolescents-with-type-1-diabetes

Çubukçu, D. & Bilir, İ. (2022). Quality of life and perception of visual deformity in adolescents with mild idiopathic scoliosis. *Turkish Journal of Osteoporosis, 28*(3), 200–205. https://doi.org/10.4274/tod.galenos.2022.00821

Darukhanavala, A., Merjaneh, L., Mason, K., & Le, T. (2021). Eating disorders and body image in cystic fibrosis. *Journal of Clinical & Translational Endocrinology, 26*, 100280. https://doi.org/10.1016/j.jcte.2021.100280

Davis, A. (2021). Infection Control and Art Supplies. In M. Itczak (ed.), *Pediatric Medical Art Therapy* (pp.25–37). Jessica Kingsley Publishers.

Dhawan, M., Sudhesh, N. T., & Kakkar, S. (2021). Body image issues and self-concept dilemmas in adolescents living with thalassemia. *Psychology, Health & Medicine, 27*(3), 598–612. https://doi.org/10.1080/13548506.2021.1903050

Falvo, D. (2005). *Medical and Psychosocial Aspects of Chronic Illness and Disability* (3rd ed.). Jones and Bartlett Publishers.

Hartman-Munick, S. M., Gordon, A. R., & Guss, C. (2020). Adolescent body image: Influencing factors and the clinician's role. *Current Opinion in Pediatrics, 32*(4), 455–460. https://doi.org/10.1097/MOP.0000000000000910

Helms, S. W., Christon, L. M., Dellon, E. P., & Prinstein, M. J. (2017). Patient and provider perspectives on communication about body image with adolescents and young adults with cystic fibrosis. *Journal of Pediatric Psychology, 42*(9), 1040–1050. https://doi.org/10.1093/jpepsy/jsx055

Huang, Y.-K. & Su, Y.-J. (2021). Burn severity and long-term psychosocial adjustment after burn injury: The mediating role of body image dissatisfaction. *Burns, 47*(6), 1373–1380. https://doi.org/10.1016/j.burns.2020.12.015

Kail, R. V. & Cavanaugh, J. C. (2010). *Human Development: A Life-Span View* (5th ed.). Wadsworth, Cengage Learning.

Kaushansky, D., Cox, J., Dodson, C., McNeeley, M., Kumar, S., & Iverson, E. (2017). Living a secret: Disclosure among adolescents and young adults with chronic illnesses. *Chronic Illness, 13*(1), 49–61. https://doi.org/10.1177/1742395316655855

Lacroix, E., Atkinson, M. J., Garbett, K. M., & Diedrichs, P. C. (2022). One size does not fit all: Trajectories of body image development and their predictors in early adolescence. *Development and Psychopathology, 34*(1), 285–294. https://doi.org/10.1017/S0954579420000917

Lee, S. B., Chae, H. W., Kwon, J. W., Sung, S., *et al.* (2021). Is there an association between psychiatric disorders and adolescent idiopathic scoliosis? A large-database study. *Clinical Orthopaedics & Related Research, 479*(8), 1805–1812. https://doi.org/10.1097/CORR.0000000000001716

Malchiodi, C. A. (1999). Introduction to Medical Art Therapy with Children. In C. A. Malchiodi (ed.), *Medical Art Therapy with Children* (pp.13–32). Jessica Kingsley Publishers.

Moore, J. B., Canzona, M. R., Puccinelli-Ortega, N., Little-Greene, D., *et al.* (2021). A qualitative assessment of body image in adolescents and young adults (AYAs) with cancer. *Psycho-Oncology, 30*(4), 614–622. https://doi.org/10.1002/pon.5610

Phang, C. (2021). *Individual versus Sequential: The Potential of Comic Creation in Art Therapy* [Master of Arts in Marriage and Family Therapy, Dominican University of California, San Rafael, CA]. https://scholar.dominican.edu/art-therapy-theses-dissertations/2

Ricciardelli, L. A. & Yager, Z. (2016). *Adolescence and Body Image: From Development to Preventing Dissatisfaction*. Routledge.

Riley, S. (1999). *Contemporary Art Therapy with Adolescents*. Jessica Kingsley Publishers.

Schattie, A. (2018). *Art Therapy and Body Image: Developing Positive Art Therapy Interventions for Adults with Body Image Concerns* [Master's thesis, Florida State University]. ProQuest. www.proquest.com/docview/2121115826?pq-origsite=primo https://diginole.lib.fsu.edu/islandora/object/fsu%3A650604

Troncone, A., Cascella, C., Chianese, A., Zanfardino, A., *et al.* (2020). Body image problems and disordered eating behaviors in Italian adolescents with and without type 1 diabetes: An examination with a gender-specific body image measure. *Frontiers in Psychology, 11*(2020), 1–15. https://doi.org/10.3389/fpsyg.2020.556520

CHAPTER XIII

Effective Methods for Art Therapists Partnering with Breast Cancer Survivors to Improve Body Image and Quality of Life

A Literature Review

— HEIDI MOFFATT —

BREAST CANCER

A lump, swelling, redness, scaling, flaking, thickening, or other physical change of the breast; back pain; shortness of breath; cough; and fatigue are some of the symptoms which may occur during initial stages of breast cancer. Medical treatment for breast cancer may include surgery and lumpectomy (removing part of the breast) or mastectomy (removing the entire affected breast), radiation, chemotherapy, and hormonal treatments. Following breast amputation, patients may experience pain or swelling in the breast or limb (lymphedema) or changes in sensation of the breast or chest wall (Effa *et al.*, 2020). Physical effects from radiation or chemotherapy may include changes in weight, loss of hair, skin discoloration, and hot flashes. And hormonal treatment for breast cancer may impact sexual functioning of the patient. Significant fatigue that often accompanies cancer and medical treatments impacts the patient's life. It may limit the ability to engage in physical and social activities important for the mental health and body image (BI) of breast cancer survivors (BCS), which is defined in this chapter as those who have been diagnosed with breast cancer, from time of diagnosis and beyond.

BODY IMAGE AND QUALITY OF LIFE

Body image transcends objective physical traits and is multifaceted, including how people see themselves (perceptual), feel about themselves (affective), think about and are aware of themselves (cognitive), and interact in the world (behavioral and social). Additional contributors to BI include: self-schema, sense of self, body self-concept, perceptual accuracy of the body, overall body satisfaction, and embodiment, which is aware-ness of and attunement between inner states, social relatedness, and the body. The inner and outer experiences of the individual are entangled.

Body image and quality of life (QoL) have a reciprocal relationship. Disturbed BI impacts QoL, and BCS with poor BI are likely to experience psychosocial, physical, functional, and social issues. Resultant lowered self-esteem, depression, or anxiety may further lessen QoL. Jalambadani and Borji (2019; citing the World Health Organization) identify QoL as multidimensional and consisting of mental, physical, social, cognitive, and sexual functions; working ability; and lifelong pleasure.

Studies indicate the importance of addressing BI to improve the QoL for BCS (Chow *et al.*, 2016; Davis *et al.*, 2020; Effa *et al.*, 2020). Post-treat-ment for breast cancer may be a particularly important time to address BI, as reports of BI disturbance and QoL deterioration are higher (Chow *et al.*, 2016). Additionally, Davis *et al.* (2020) found in their systematic literature review that BI is important to the BCS, regardless of age. BI and QoL are crucial to address to reduce or eliminate suffering of the individual and enhance meaning-making and life-legacy. Further, QoL is a vital consideration in survivorship and understanding the long-term impact of cancer and medical treatment.

ART THERAPY

Art therapy is a profession that promotes well-being, quality of life, insight-orientation, and empowerment through artmaking, creative pro-cess, and psychotherapy, within a therapeutic partnership with a pro-fessional art therapist. Involving emotional processing by way of visual artmaking, art therapy has been useful for expression and communication and has been linked to symptom reduction in individuals with cancer (Czamanski-Cohen *et al.*, 2020). Art as a means of communication is accessible. And when art therapy is made available in the community, healing is possible. For BCS, art therapy is beneficial in improving mental health and QoL as well as managing symptoms related to diagnosis. Art therapy combined with attention to the body's sensations and movement as well as thoughts, emotions, perceptions, and drives promotes self-awareness, mind-body connection, transformation, emotional and physical balance, self-regulation, and self-compassion, and harnesses life-force energy and creativity. The depth that creative process offers in combination with a supportive, therapeutic relationship lends itself to development and strengthening of resiliency for adult breast cancer survivors.

LITERATURE REVIEW

A literature review on current (2012 to present) research and data about the topics of breast cancer, BI, and art therapy was completed to:

- identify, describe, summarize, and evaluate the extensiveness of knowledge on these topics in the field

- synthesize the interconnection of these topics

- offer a distilled compilation of assessment tools, art therapy treatment approaches, directives, and art media notable for clinical support for BCS.

This will help art therapists make efficient and informed treatment decisions with BCS and continue to expand research and applied science.

LITERATURE REVIEW METHODS

In collaboration with Indiana University Health Medical Library research services, relevant studies were identified through Ovid MEDLINE, CINAHL, and EBSCO Host using search terms: "art therapy," "breast cancer," and "body image." Articles were included if they were written from 2012 to 2023, English language, and accessible full-texts. Articles were excluded if they involved non-adult populations or non-art therapy services. The review included a screening of the title and abstract, followed by full-review of the article. (See Appendix for full details of search strategies.)

The data was abstracted from the selected articles and is presented in Table 13.1: author, year, country; study design, sample size; objectives related to BI; assessments tools that measure impacts on components related to BI; therapeutic approach, treatment duration; art therapy aim, directive, art media; study results; and study considerations.

LITERATURE REVIEW RESULTS

Eighty-one articles were identified; 26 were initially screened (abstract review), and 20 were fully reviewed (abstract and full text). Eleven texts met the full criteria.

Data study designs

Table 13.1 organizes the 11 articles and their study designs. Body image was a secondary outcome only in the scoping review (Effa *et al.*, 2020). Quality of life was a primary outcome in four of the six randomized controlled trials (RCTs). One of the RCTs with a primary outcome of QoL also measured anxiety and depression, and another measured stress. The remaining studies assessed mental, emotional, physical, and spiritual components of QoL, including stress, psychological distress, anxiety, depression, pain, fatigue, cerebral blood flow as related to stress and anxiety, other cancer-related somatic symptoms, self-efficacy, and spiritual well-being.

Body image and corresponding outcome measures

The scoping review by Effa *et al.* (2020) sought to examine how BI is defined and measured across the studies. The researchers found that none of the studies defined BI or provided details of what BI aspect they were attempting to measure. Additionally, they found that the instruments to measure BI varied. The single art therapy study from the scoping review utilized the European Organization for Research and Treatment of Cancer Quality of Life Questionnaire (EORTC QLQ-BR23) that includes questions related to BI, sexual functioning, sexual enjoyment, and future perspective (Svensk *et al.*, 2009; as cited in Effa *et al.*, 2020).

Assessment tools measuring quality of life and psychosocial health

When considering BI and QoL, it is important to identify what specific components or domains are relevant for BCS to select the most appropriate assessment tool.

Similar to quality of life, body image affects the cognitive, physical, emotional, social, and behavioral health of the BCS, demonstrating the multidimensionality of the construct. As such, specifically defining the aspect of body image of interest—whether it be all aspects or in the realm of positive body image psychology, subjective satisfaction, perceptual, affective, cognitive, or behavioral components of body image—will provide clarity on the selection of the measurement tool. (Effa *et al.*, 2020, p.432)

Two studies utilized the World Health Organization Quality-of-Life-BREF questionnaire (WHOQOL-BREF, 2023) that is divided into domains of physical health, psychological health, social relationships, and the environment (Svensk *et al.*, 2009, as cited in Effa *et al.*, 2020; Jalambadani & Borji, 2019). And two studies utilized the EORTC QLQ (2023) which summarizes the overall feeling of health and QoL of the cancer patient and evaluates physical, emotional, and social functions (Svensk *et al.*, 2009, as cited in Effa *et al.*, 2020; Jang *et al.*, 2016).

Assessment tools are important to identify and address specific needs of BCS, and understanding the types of assessment tools enables the clinician to make informed decisions for patient needs. Table 13.1 lists all assessment tools from the primary review of literature. Practitioners understand the importance of quickly discerning an appropriate assessment tool when supporting a patient.

Art therapy approaches

Six of the 11 studies included mindfulness-based art therapy (MBAT) to treat BCS. In the systematic review by Kievisiene *et al.* (2020), they found four out of nine involved MBAT. MBAT pairs a core mindfulness-based stress reduction curriculum with artmaking (Jalambadani & Borji, 2019; Jang *et al.*, 2016; Joshi *et al.*, 2021; Kievisiene *et al.*, 2020; Monti *et al.*, 2012, 2013). In MBAT, the participant engages in the creative process as a way of exploration while observing the body's natural physical functions and sensations and addressing BI with compassion and non-judgment. MBAT encourages rest and repair of the body and is beneficial for improving quality of life QoL and stress and anxiety. Joshi *et al.* (2021) found the following:

Mindfulness-based interventions are found to be effective in reducing psychological distress and other symptoms in cancer patients. They have shown significant improvements in existential well-being, the number of self-identified losses, grief scores, as well as mental adjustment styles in breast cancer patients. Enhanced mindfulness is shown to partly mediate the association between increased daily spiritual experiences and improved mental health-related QoL. Changes in spirituality and mindfulness were shown to be significantly associated with improvement in mental health. (p.552)

Four of the 11 studies used MBAT in group therapy. The remainders included open art studio and bodymind model of art therapy paired with focusing therapy. Individual art therapy approaches included brief art therapy and phenomenological-inspired art therapy.

Art therapy aims, directives, and art media

Mindfulness-based art therapy

Jalambadani and Borji's (2019) 12-week intervention study of MBAT aimed for mindful exploration of the present moment experience and mind-body relationship, creative problem-solving and imaging self-care, understanding the physiology of stress and communication, and visualizing health and healing.

Monti *et al.* (2006; as cited in Jang *et al.*, 2016) used a restructured version of MBAT with a focus on progress in each session and encouraged participants to share their inner pain or feelings. The aim of the intervention was "to learn self-awareness methods through directed observation (mindfulness practice), express their thoughts and feelings creatively (art therapy), and accept things on their own through verbal or non-verbal relations or societal support (group therapy)" (Jang *et al.*, 2016, p.338). Jang *et al.* (2016) outlined the session structure in a table (p.337).

Monti *et al.* (2013) implemented MBAT to study the effects of the mindfulness exercise paired with artmaking. The program involved drawing a picture of oneself, building awareness of sensory stimuli, envisioning self-care, producing art to foster mindfulness, creating stressful and pleasant event pictures, and exploring creative expressions.

The aims for MBAT in the study by Monti *et al.* (2012) were to provide opportunities for self-expression, facilitate coping strategies, and improve self-regulation. Standardized tools were provided to help participants observe, assess, and negotiate their objective and subjective experiences of the illness process. Body scans, awareness of breathing, awareness of emotions; and mindful yoga, walking, eating, and listening were all paired with artmaking (Monti *et al.*, 2012).

In the intervention by Joshi *et al.* (2021), an emphasis was made on kindness, curiosity, and non-judgment of the art process. The directive involved mindfulness meditation for 15 minutes including a body scan, anchor breathing, and non-judgmental awareness of physical sensations, thoughts, and emotions. Art media included mindfulness-based coloring sketches with 12 colored pencils or crayons. Participants were encouraged to mindfully explore art materials with an awareness of sensory stimulus and response during artmaking. The week of daily guided (voice recording in facilitator's voice) home practice involved 30 minutes of mindful coloring and 15 minutes of guided mindfulness meditation along with a diary of the daily MBAT practice.

Based on these studies, MBAT as a path and a process is equipped to address the multifacets of BI by affording the breast cancer survivor with the opportunity to become uniquely in touch and present with the inner sensations and experience as well as the relationship with the external world. Emphasis on curiosity and non-judgment aids the individual with tuning in to the experience of the body and self in a safe and compassionate way. Being in touch in this way impacts the ability to communicate this experience. In partnership with an art therapist with proper training and ongoing practice in mindfulness, insight, healing, reconciliation, and joy are possible.

Open Art Studio

The approach by Reilly *et al.* (2021) aimed for communality and deep engagement with the individual creative processes. Participants were asked to complete a brief feelings check-in and a guided visualization exercise for relaxation and focus at each session. Then they began open art studio, in which artistic process is central to the therapeutic work, and no directives or interpretations are made by the art therapist. To conclude the sessions, facilitators in this study invited participants to have a short feelings check-out and a grounding exercise. Weekly topics included addressing a changing mind-body relationship; processing challenging emotions, thoughts, and relationships; highlighting one's strengths and capabilities; building talismans and amulets (for protection); and increasing one's self-awareness of the realities of living with cancer. Art media offered included oil or chalk pastels, pencils, tempera or acrylic paints, brushes, high-quality paper, tissue paper, boxes, mirror tiles, beads, glitter, fabric, yarn, photo collage materials, glue, clay, wire, and an assortment of natural materials such as leaves, twigs, sand, shells, and seeds.

Bodymind model of art therapy and focusing therapy

The intervention administered by Czamanski-Cohen *et al.* (2020) involved a theoretical framework based on the bodymind model of art therapy aimed at building body awareness and the application of focusing therapy to art therapy, which is "being friendly, accepting, non-judgmental and welcoming to one's inner felt sense" (p.4). Sessions began with rapport-building and check-ins, then artmaking, followed by processing and discussion. With art materials on the table, the art therapist provided a brief explanation of the use of materials, and participants were encouraged to explore and experience as they wished. Conversation was limited, and instrumental music was played to encourage introspection. The art therapist created a calming environment, attuned to the participants' verbal and non-verbal expressions, offered a *third hand* ready to guide and assist without imposing, and maintained a group experience that was respectful and non-judgmental (Czamanski-Cohen *et al.*, 2020).

Phenomenological-inspired art therapy

One study included five weekly, hour-long individual art therapy sessions aimed at offering time and space for expression and reflection, giving support in the process of restoring BI, reducing stress, and supporting agency (Svensk *et al.*, 2009; as cited in Effa *et al.*, 2020). Sessions were inspired by the phenomenological method of art therapy, in which the artwork is observed more objectively by participants and the art therapist and discussed based on formal elements of the artwork. Thus, the subjective experience of artmaking is integrated. The same art media were offered at all sessions: sheets of paper, a roll of paper, oil pastels in 48 colors, oil paints, paintbrushes, tempera fluid, pencils, charcoal, adhesive tape, and scissors.

Brief art therapy

In another study, individual, standardized, hour-long art therapy sessions were administered to engage the mind, body, and spirit connection (Elimimian *et al.*, 2020). Participants were directed to engage their creativity

— 246 —

and given full freedom to art media: painting, drawing, clay, and collage construction. The art therapist guided participants to self-reflect on their art at the end of the session.

OUTCOMES OF ART THERAPY TREATMENT FOR BREAST CANCER SURVIVORS

The outcomes from the literature review indicate that art therapy is a viable treatment approach for supporting breast cancer survivors. Six of the 11 studies found that the QoL of BCS was improved from art therapy (Effa *et al.*, 2020; Jalambadani & Borji, 2019; Jang *et al.*, 2016; Kievisiene *et al.*, 2020; Monti *et al.*, 2013; Xu *et al.*, 2020). The therapeutic approaches from the studies that showed significant improvements in QoL included MBAT and Korean MBAT as well as phenomenological-inspired art therapy.

Improvements in the level of stress and distress were also indicated as results of art therapy for BCS from four of the studies (Elimimian *et al.*, 2020; Jalambadani & Borji, 2019; Joshi *et al.*, 2021; Monti *et al.*, 2012). The therapeutic approach in three of these studies involved MBAT. In the study by Monti *et al.* (2013), outcomes indicated that art therapy may have a more enduring effect for distressed cancer patients than emotional support alone.

Art therapy was found to have positive effects on improving depression in three of the studies (Elimimian *et al.*, 2020; Jang *et al.*, 2016; Xu *et al.*, 2020). Depression symptoms were notably reduced for younger BCS, aged 55 and under, in the meta-analysis by Xu *et al.* (2020) that included three studies of art therapy utilizing drawing and painting media.

Anxiety symptoms were also positively impacted by art therapy, as seen in three of the studies (Elimimian *et al.*, 2020; Jang *et al.*, 2016; Xu *et al.*, 2020). Elimimian *et al.* (2020) found that art therapy is likely to be beneficial when administered repeatedly and frequently. Improvements in anxiety were significant for women aged 55 and over in the meta-analysis by Xu *et al.* (2020).

Additional significant results include improvement of emotional symptoms (Kievisiene *et al.*, 2020; Monti *et al.*, 2012, 2013); reduction in pain (Elimimian *et al.*, 2020); provision of a safe context to process change and re-story losses (Reilly *et al.*, 2021); and enhancement of future perspective (Effa *et al.*, 2020).

Table 13.1: Extracted data from literature review: Objectives, assessment tools, therapeutic approaches, directives, and art media

Czamanski-Cohen *et al.*, 2020/Israel, Australia, United States

Study design, sample size

RCT, n = 240 adult, female BCS (50% Jewish and 50% Arab) who entered study within 24 months of diagnosis and who have completed chemotherapy, surgery, and/or radiation therapy 3–18 months before intervention.

Objectives related to body image

Increase emotional processing to alleviate psychological symptoms and reduce physical complaints, improve body awareness, develop a Focusing approach (being friendly, accepting, non-judgmental, and welcoming to one's inner felt sense).

Assessment tool

AE, BCPT, CES-D, FSI, LEAS, PROMIS Pain Intensity and PROMIS Pain, Interface, PVQ-RR, Resting EEG data for HRV.

Therapeutic approach, treatment duration

Group AT: Bodymind model of AT and application of focusing therapy.

Weekly sessions for eight weeks: 90-minute sessions.

Art therapy aim, directive, and art media

Aim: To reduce depression, pain, and fatigue in Jewish and Arab BCS. To develop body awareness and focusing therapy skills.

Directive: With art materials on the table, art therapist provides brief explanation of use of materials, and participants are encouraged to explore and experience as they wish. Art therapist is present to guide and assist (third hand). Conversation is kept to a minimum, music is played for introspective experience. During processing, group participants can respond/provide support respectfully and non-judgmentally.

Art media: Not specified.

Study results

Website created to disseminate information about the study to participants: http://repat.haifa.ac.il/en.

Considerations

Since this reference is a protocol for a study, considerations were not included.

Effa *et al.*, 2020/United States (citing Svensk *et al.*, 2008/Sweden)

Study design, sample size

Scoping review of eight articles; one of eight studies was AT. RCT, n = 41; AT, n = 20; Control group, n = 20 (as cited in Svensk *et al.*, 2008).

Objectives related to body image

Influence the mind and body to promote health and well-being, QoL, and self-image.

Assessment tool

EORTC QLQ-BR23, WHOQOL-BREF.

Therapeutic approach, treatment duration
Individual AT: Phenomenological-inspired.

Weekly sessions for five weeks: one-hour duration.

Art therapy aim, directive, and art media
Aim: Offer time and space for expression and reflection, give support in process of restoring BI, reduce stress and support agency.

Directive: Not specified.

Art media at each session: Sheets of paper, roll of paper, oil pastels in 48 colors and oil paints, tempera fluid, lead pencils, charcoal, adhesive tape, scissors, paintbrushes.

Also, weekly diary about experiences, thoughts, and feelings concerning their life situation with breast cancer during the study.

Study results
Significant improvement by six months in AT group for overall QoL and general health, domains of BI, and future perspectives.

Considerations
Specifically defining the aspect of BI of interest—whether it be all aspects in the realm of positive BI psychology, subjective satisfaction, perceptual, affective, cognitive, or behavioral components of BI will provide clarity on selection of measurement tool.

Future studies should consider alignment of definition, study objectives, and the chosen measurement tool, to facilitate better understanding of meaning of results. Choose measurement tools that are brief and easy to administer to minimize patient burden.

Elimimian *et al.*, 2020/United States

Study design, sample size
Pilot study, n = 50 adult patients receiving chemotherapy for BC (44%), gastrointestinal cancers (22%), hematological malignancies (18%), or other malignancies (20%).

Objectives related to body image
To enhance physical, mental, and emotional well-being; evaluate personal or social influences which might contribute to QoL; and evaluate changes in patient distress, depression, anxiety, and pain.

Assessment tool
NCCN Distress Management Screening tool and Problem Checklist, UPAT.

Therapeutic approach, treatment duration
Individual AT.

Single session: one-hour duration.

Art therapy aim, directive, and art media
Aim: To engage the mind, body, and spirit of the participant.

Elimimian *et al.*, 2020/United States *cont.*

Directive: Employed consistent, standardized AT practices. Participant was encouraged to engage their creativity. Participant had full freedom of art media selection at each session. Session concluded with art therapist guiding patient to reflect on their own art.

Art media: Participants had freedom to choose painting, drawing, mandala, collage, and clay work.

Study results

AT improved the emotional distress, depression, anxiety, and pain among all cancer patients. AT is likely to be beneficial when administered repeatedly and frequently. AT may have greater benefit for Hispanic patients with depression.

Considerations

Discovering simple, effective, therapeutic interventions to aid in distress relief in cancer patients is important for ensuring clinical efficacy of treatment and improved QoL.

Jalambadani & Borji, 2019/Iran

Study design, sample size

RCT, women with BC, aged 40–60; MBAT group n = 50; Control group n = 50.

Objectives related to body image

Promote QoL.

Assessment tool

WHOQOL-BREF.

Therapeutic approach, treatment duration

MBAT group.

Weekly sessions for 12 weeks.: 90-minute duration.

Art therapy aim, directive, and art media

Aim: Promote QoL, self-exploration, and understanding.

Directive and art media:

Session 1: Intro to artmaking; "Draw a complete picture of yourself" self-picture assessment (SPA) task.

2: Mindful exploration of art materials (colored pencil, marker, pastel, watercolor crayon, and paint); awareness of sensory stimulus and response; body scan meditation, attitudinal foundations of mindfulness; anchoring attention with breath.

3: Exploring the mind-body relationship: pre-post assessment of mind-body relationship before and after gentle yoga.

4: Creative problem-solving, imaging self-care; transforming mental, emotional, and physical pain; introducing self-care imagery into the picture.

5: Exploring meditation practice experience: art productions, using collage element serving as the basis for increasing skills with mindfulness practice in the realm of thoughts and feelings.

6: Stressful and pleasant event pictures as introduction to physiology of stress, including stressful communication and non-reactive communication skills.

7: Open Studio: free artmaking.

8: Guided imagery to a place of healing.

9: Drawing a complete and healthy picture of yourself based on this visualization of health; care of mind consciousness, focusing on your complete and healthy image.

10. SPA task.

11 & 12: Group discussion and sharing of member experiences and summaries on the content of all sessions.

See Jalambadani & Borji, 2019, p.195.

Study results
MBAT interventions had significant effects on decreasing symptoms of distress and improving QoL.

Considerations
The post-intervention data is not sufficient to predict long-term effects of the intervention. The results cannot be generalized to all women with BC.

Jang *et al.*, 2016/Korea

Study design, sample size
RCT, n = 24 women with BC over age 50; MBAT group n = 12; Control group n = 12.

Objectives related to body image
Promote QoL and improve depression and anxiety.

Assessment tool
EORTC QLQ-C30, PAI.

Therapeutic approach, treatment duration
MBAT group. 12 sessions: 45-minute duration.

Korean mindfulness-based stress reduction (K-MBSR) psychological intervention applied to mindfulness activities.

Art therapy aim, directive, and art media
Aim: To understand the treatment effects of MBAT on breast cancer survivors' depression, anxiety, and QoL.

Directive: See Jang *et al.*, 2016, Table 2., p.337, for Stage-Wise Goals and Curriculum of MBAT Intervention.

Art media: Drawing, collage, paint (body).

Study results
Significant improvement in health-related QoL and decrease in anxiety and depression.

Considerations
Evaluation of treatment effects using program development and large-scale research for future clinical application are needed.

Future studies should observe a large number of patients to evaluate the effects of MBAT and observe ways to clinically apply MBAT.

Joshi *et al.*, 2021/India

Study design, sample size

Single group, pre-test post-test study, n = 30 patients with BC, aged 20–70, undergoing chemotherapy.

Objectives related to body image

Enhance psychosocial health, spiritual well-being, QoL.

Assessment tool

DT, FACIT-SP12 Version 4, Psycho-oncology assessment questionnaire.

Therapeutic approach, treatment duration

MBAT.

First session in-person: 15 minutes of mindfulness meditation and 30 minutes of mindful artmaking.

Then, one week, daily guided home practice: 30 minutes of mindful coloring and 23 minutes of facilitator-guided mindfulness.

Art therapy aim, directive, and art media

Aim: Reduce psychological distress and improve spiritual well-being.

Directive: First in-person, supervised session conducted by facilitators, followed by one week of daily guided home practice.

Mindfulness meditation: Body scan, anchoring attention with the breath, and non-judgmental awareness of physical sensations, thoughts, and emotions.

Mindful art: Mindful exploration of art materials with awareness of sensory stimulus and response during coloring; and home practice: mindful coloring and facilitator-guided mindfulness meditation and diary of daily MBAT practice.

Daily telephonic follow-up of participants.

Art media: Mindfulness-based coloring prints or sketches with 12 colored pencils or crayons.

See Joshi *et al.*, 2021, p.558, Table 4.

Study results

One week of MBAT significantly decreased the psychological distress and significantly improved spiritual well-being.

Considerations

Further validation is required by conducting RCTs with a larger sample size.

Kievisiene *et al.*, 2020/Lithuania

Study design, sample size

Systematic review of RCTs with BCS, n = 9 studies of AT involving 540 participants.

Objectives related to body image

Overall QoL and stress, anxiety, depression, pain, fatigue, other cancer-related somatic symptoms.

Perceived self-image (as cited in Thyme *et al.*, 2009).

Assessment tool

AE; BCPT; BSI-18; CES-D; EORTC-QLQ-BR23; EORTC-QLQ-C30; LEAS; PAI; SASB; SCL-90-R; SF-36; The fMRI imaging protocol; WHOQOL-BREF.

Therapeutic approach, treatment duration

MBAT (four studies): AT + relaxation techniques.

Individual AT sessions (two studies).

Brief AT sessions (one study).

"Traditional AT framework" (two studies).

Art therapy aim, directive, and art media

Aim, directive, and art media varied by referenced studies. See Kievisiene *et al.*, 2020, p.4, Table 1.

Study results

AT was oriented towards the effects on QoL and emotional symptoms.

Improvements were made in stress, anxiety, depression reduction, pain, fatigue, and cancer-related somatic symptoms.

Considerations

More detailed and highly descriptive single therapy and primary mental health outcome-measuring RCTs are necessary to draw evidenced-based advice.

Monti *et al.*, 2012/United States

Study design, sample size

RCT, n = 18 patients with BC diagnosed six months to three years prior to enrollment.

MBAT group n = 8, Control group n = 10.

Objectives related to body image

Improve QoL.

Assessment tool

SCL-90-R; The fMRI imaging protocol.

Therapeutic approach, treatment duration

Group MBAT.

Eight weeks of (one) two-and-a-half-hour session per week.

Art therapy aim, directive, and art media

Aim: Provide opportunities for self-expression, facilitate coping strategies, and improve self-regulation. Provide standardized tools to help participants observe, assess, and negotiate their objective and subjective experiences of the illness process.

Directive: Artmaking paired with formal meditational practices: body scan, awareness of breathing, awareness of emotions, and mindful yoga; walking, eating, and listening.

Art media: Not listed.

See Monti *et al.*, 2012, Table II, p.400, of study for MBAT eight-week programme curriculum.

Monti *et al.*, 2012/United States *cont.*
Study results
Significant improvements in psychosocial stress and QoL post-intervention and at six months in MBAT group.
MBAT intervention helped mediate emotional responses in women with BC.
Considerations
Future studies might ask subjects to perform either the meditation or neural condition first in a randomized manner.
Monti *et al.*, 2013/United States
Study design, sample size
RCT, n = 191 women, aged 21+, with BC; MBAT group n = 98; Control group n = 93.
Objectives related to body image
Improve QoL and reduce psychosocial stress and stress-related somatic complaints.
Assessment tool
SCL-90-R, SF-36.
Therapeutic approach, treatment duration
Group MBAT.
Eight weeks of (one) two-and-a-half-hour session per week.
Art therapy aim, directive, and art media
Aim: Address the needs of cancer patients for stress reduction, emotional support, and meaningful modes of expression.
Specific AT directives complement the MBSR curriculum by providing an additional non-verbal mode of identifying and organizing internal and external representations of stressors and related emotions in a non-judgmental format.
Directives: Draw a picture of the self, awareness of sensory stimuli, imaging self-care, art production to foster mindfulness, creating stressful and pleasant event pictures, and free expression.
Art media: Not listed.
Study results
MBAT may be particularly effective for distressed cancer patients and may have a more enduring effect than standard emotional support.
Considerations
Future studies should focus on additional therapeutic advantages specific to MBAT program, compared with MBSR program alone, and to further assess the generalizability of the intervention.
Reilly *et al.*, 2021/Canada
Study design, sample size
Pilot study, qualitative cross-case comparative case; n = 10 women living with BC.

Objectives related to body image
Address QoL, self-efficacy, emotional enhancement, insight, communication.

Assessment tool
Not applicable. This study involved interpretivist paradigm, which assumes reality is socially constructed and accessed through language and shared meanings.

Therapeutic approach, treatment duration
Open Art Studio.

Nine weeks of (one) two-hour session weekly.

Art therapy aim, directive, and art media
Aim: Communality and deep engagement with individual creative process.

Directive:

Session structure: Brief check-in about feelings at onset of session; guided visualization exercise for relaxation and focus; beginning of Open Studio where no directives or interpretations are given by the facilitating art therapist who participates in session; short check-out on feelings and grounding.

Weekly topics: Addressing a changing mind-body connection; processing challenging emotions, thoughts, and relationships; highlighting one's strengths and capabilities; building talismans and amulets (protection), and increasing one's self-awareness of the realities of living with cancer.

Art media: Oil and chalk pastels, pencils, tempera and acrylic paints, brushes, high-quality paper, tissue paper, boxes, mirror tiles, beads, glitter, fabric and yarn, photo collage materials, glue, clay, wire, and an assortment of natural materials (leaves, twigs, sand, shells, and seeds).

Study results
AT provides a safe context to reflect on personal changes and to re-story losses following adversity through creative practices as dimensions of care.

Considerations
More research is needed to identify the healing components of art therapy.

Xu *et al.*, 2020/United States (one study), Sweden (one), Korea (one)

Study design, sample size
Meta-analysis, n = 446. Of the nine studies with women with breast cancer, three involved art therapy; Sub-group meta-analyses according to AT domain, age, and ethnicity.

Objectives related to body image
Address anxiety, depression, and multiple aspects of health-related QoL.

Assessment tool
PAI; POMS; SCL-90.

Therapeutic approach, treatment duration
Varied by studies.

Art therapy aim, directive, and art media
Aim: To reduce anxiety and depression in BCS.

> **Xu *et al.*, 2020/United States (one study), Sweden (one), Korea (one)** *cont.*
>
> *Directive:* Varied by study.
>
> *Art media:* All studies referenced involved drawing or painting media.
>
> **Study results**
> AT has positive effects on improving depressive symptoms, enhancing QoL, and increasing survival for younger (aged < 55) patients with BC. AT had a favorable effect on improvement of anxiety for women age 55+.
>
> **Considerations**
> Further studies should include age as a factor. Long-term effects of AT should be investigated for future studies.
>
> **Note abbreviations used:**
> Acceptance of Emotions Scale (AE)
>
> Art therapy (AT)
>
> Body image (BI)
>
> Body Image Self-Rating Questionnaire for Breast Cancer (BISQ-BC)
>
> Breast cancer survivors (BCS)
>
> Breast Cancer Prevention Trial (BCPT) Symptom Checklist
>
> Brief Symptom Interview-18 (BSI-18)
>
> Center for Epidemiologic Studies-Depression scale (CES-D)
>
> Distress thermometer (DT)
>
> European Organization for Research and Treatment of Cancer Quality of Life Questionnaire (EORTC QLQ)
>
> Fatigue Symptoms Inventory (FSI)
>
> Functional Magnetic Resonance Imaging (fMRI)
>
> Functional Assessment of Chronic Illness Therapy-SWB Scale 12 (FACIT-SP12) Version 4
>
> Heart rate variability (HRV)
>
> Korean mindfulness-based stress reduction (K-MBSR)
>
> Medical Outcomes Study Short-Form Health Survey (SF-36)

SUMMARY OF FINDINGS

Literature defining BI and examining the effects of art therapy when addressing BI with BCS is sparse. However, positively indicated for BCS are treatments that emphasize the bodily felt sense, such as MBAT and bodymind model with focusing therapy, which helps the individual compassionately attune with self and its relationships.

Studies that evaluated the effects of art therapy on the domains of QoL of BCS are more extensive, and art therapy is notable for its positive effects on QoL, including emotional and social factors as well as overall BI. Body image and QoL are interconnected topics, and disturbed BI negatively impacts QoL. Studies examined in this literature review reveal the importance of addressing BI for breast cancer survivors to improve QoL. Art therapy is a viable service to support BCS in addressing their various needs. Positive impacts on depression, stress and distress, anxiety, emotional symptoms, pain, and outlook were made for BCS participating in art therapy.

Assessment tools to evaluate BI varied. However, the single art therapy study referenced by Effa *et al.* (2020) that specifically examines BI utilized the EORTC QLQ-BR23 to assess BI, sexual functioning, sexual enjoyment, and future perspective. Secondary findings uncovered during the literature review include the Body Image Self-Rating Questionnaire for Breast Cancer (BISQ-BC) and the Quality of Life Questionnaire (SF-36v2 Health Survey, 2023) for Chinese patients (An *et al.*, 2022). An *et al.* (2022) utilized the BISQ-BC to evaluate the BI of 354 Chinese BCS. This tool assesses key aspects of BI-related changes with five subscales: BI-related behavior change, BI-related psychological change, BI-related sexual activity change, BI-related role change, and BI-related social change. Additionally, the Chinese version of the Quality of Life Questionnaire (SF-36v2 Health Survey, 2023) was used to assess QoL domains, involving a multidimensional questionnaire of eight subscales: physical function, role-physical, bodily pain, general health, vitality, social function, role-emotional, and mental health (An *et al.*, 2022). The SF-36v2 Health Survey measures functional health and well-being from the patient's point of view and can be used across age, disease, and treatment groups (2023).

Various art therapy approaches were found beneficial for addressing QoL and improving cognitive, emotional, social, and behavioral functioning: MBAT, open art studio, bodymind model with focusing, and phenomenological-inspired art therapy. Both group and individual art therapy sessions were involved. Aims of art therapy interventions included mind-body relationship, self-compassion, creative expression, emotional and social support, visualizing healing, and self-efficacy.

DISCUSSION

This author encourages the continued examination of BI in general and for BCS and the continued study of the effects art therapy has on QoL as related to BI. For BCS, a treatment approach that influences a compassionate relationship with felt sense and attunement with self in relation to the body and outer world is beneficial and important. Wisdom is felt, not just thought or learned. When BCS stay curious and open to what arises in mind-body practice, insight is developed with regard to the relationship between inner and outer experience and the interconnected facets of BI. Embracing and trusting the wisdom of the body involves a process that is worthwhile for the healing and peace which follow.

The relationship between the breast cancer survivor and professional art therapist is very important to the healing process. Careful consideration should be given to compatibility prior to embarking on the therapeutic journey. The stage of cancer must be taken into consideration when collaborating with the breast cancer survivor for treatment goals and objectives. Additionally, details involving treatment setting and treatment duration impact the therapeutic experience. Intentional communication about potential benefits and limitations with respect to these details as well as the therapeutic approach and therapy format is required. Supportive care involves multidisciplinary collaboration for the physical, psychological, social, and spiritual needs of the patient, and this necessitates strong communication directly related to the breast cancer survivor's unique needs and goals. Co-treatment sessions between art therapists and yoga therapists utilizing mind-body approaches, particularly MBAT, are suited for survivors. Outcomes from new MBAT studies will support healthcare providers with further understanding of survivorship and the long-term impact of cancer and medical treatment.

LIMITATIONS

Only two databases were searched exhaustively for this literature review, and some articles may have been missed. However, the two databases were carefully selected with the help of the library services manager at the Indiana University Health Medical Library to ensure that the searches were relevant and comprehensive. Despite the extensive search, only one study was clearly specific to art therapy for BI with BCS.

The findings are also limited by the wide variability in assessment tools and art therapy approaches, restricting the ability to make extensive recommendations. Additionally, no male participants were included in the studies, restricting the ability to make recommendations for this population.

CONCLUSIONS

Based on current research, this study developed a reference of assessment tools, art therapy treatment approaches, and directives relevant to addressing BI and QoL with BCS. Body image is clearly related to QoL as well as behavioral, social, cognitive, affective, and perceptual domains. Joining with the BCS to build trust in the wisdom of the body by way of effective art therapy practice enhances QoL during survivorship. The BCS' ability to attune to somatic and visceral information helps to create a feedback loop for the survivor and their healthcare partners. Art therapy is a proven treatment option for BCS that offers a creative channel for attunement to mind-body-spirit and an opening for healthcare partners to gain knowledge and wisdom in working with this group. Expanded research on the components of BI and QoL in relation to BI would be beneficial to continue to define BI. Additionally, further utilization and study of the assessment tools, therapeutic approaches, and directives presented in this study with BCS would build on research done so far. Additionally, further utilization and study of the assessment tools, therapeutic approaches, and directives presented in this study with BCS should be documented and shared to build on research done so far.

REFERENCES

An, J., Zhou, K., Li, M., & Li, X. (2022). Assessing the relationship between body image and quality of life among rural and urban breast cancer survivors in China. *BMC Women's Health, 22*(1), 1–10. https://doi.org/10.1186/s12905-022-01635-y

Chow, K. M., Hung, K. L., & Yeung, S. M. (2016). Body image and quality of life among breast cancer survivors: A literature review. *World Journal of Oncology Research, 3*, 12–20. https://doi.org/10.15379/2413-7308.2016.03.02

Czamanski-Cohen, J., Wiley, J., & Weihs, K. L. (2020). Protocol for the REPAT study: Role of emotional processing in art therapy for breast cancer palliative care patients. *BMJ Open, 10*(11), 1–11. https://doi.org/10.1136/bmjopen-2020-037521

Davis, C., Tami, P., Ramsay, D., Melanson, L., *et al.* (2020). Body image in older breast cancer survivors: A systematic review. *Psycho-Oncology, 29*(5), 823–832. https://doi.org/10.1002/pon.5359

Effa, C. J., Dolgoy, N. D., & McNeely, M. L. (2020). Resistance exercise and art therapy on body image in breast cancer: A scoping review. *Women's Health Reports, 1*(1), 424–435. https://doi.org/10.1089/whr.2020.0058

Elimimian, E. B., Elson, L., Stone, E., Butler, R. S., *et al.* (2020). Assessing the relationship between body image and quality of life among rural and urban breast cancer survivors in China. *BMC Women's Health, 22*(1), 1–10. https://doi.org/10.1186/s12885-020-07380-5

EORTC QLQ (2023). Questionnaire. https://qol.eortc.org

Jalambadani, Z. & Borji, A. (2019). Effectiveness of mindfulness-based art therapy on healthy quality of life in women with breast cancer. *Asia-Pacific Journal of Oncology Nursing, 6*(2), 193–197. https://doi.org/10.4103/apjon.apjon_36_18

Jang, S.-H., Kang, S.-Y., Lee, H.-J., & Lee, S.-Y. (2016). Beneficial effect of mindfulness-based art therapy in patients with breast cancer—A randomized controlled trial. *EXPLORE, 12*(5), 333–340. https://doi.org/10.1016/j.explore.2016.06.003

Joshi, A. M., Mehta, S. A., Pande, N., Mehta, A. O., & Randhe, K. S. (2021). Effect of mindfulness-based art therapy (MBAT) on psychological distress and spiritual wellbeing in breast cancer patients undergoing chemotherapy. *Indian Journal of Palliative Care, 27*(4), 552–560. https://doi.org/10.25259/ijpc_133_21

Kievisiene, J., Jautakyte, R., Rauckiene-Michaelsson, A., Fatkulina, N., & Agostinis-Sobrinho, C. (2020). The effect of art therapy and music therapy on breast cancer patients: What we know and what we need to find out—A systematic review. *Evidence-Based Complementary and Alternative Medicine*, 1–14. https://doi.org/10.1155/2020/7390321

Monti, D. A., Kash, K. M., Kunkel, E. J., Brainard, G., *et al.* (2012). Changes in cerebral blood flow and anxiety associated with an 8-week mindfulness programme in women with breast cancer. *Stress and Health, 28*(5), 397–407. https://doi.org/10.1002/smi.2470

Monti, D. A., Kash, K. M., Kunkel, E. J., Moss, A., *et al.* (2013). Psychosocial benefits of a novel mindfulness intervention versus standard support in distressed women with breast cancer. *Psycho-Oncology, 22*(11), 2565–2575. https://doi.org/10.1002/pon.3320

Reilly, R. C., Lee, V., Laux, K., & Robitaille, A. (2021). Creating doorways: Finding meaning and growth through art therapy in the face of life-threatening illness. *Public Health, 198*, 245–251. https://doi.org/10.1016/j.puhe.2021.07.004

SF-36v2® Health Survey (2023). Quality metric. www.qualitymetric.com/health-surveys/the-sf-36v2-health-survey

Thyme, K. E., Sundin, E. C., & Wiberg, B. (2009). Individual brief art therapy can be helpful for women with breast cancer: A randomized controlled clinical study. *Palliative and Supportive Care, 7*(1), 87–95. https://doi.org/10.1017/S147895150900011x

WHOQOL-BREF (2023). Physiopedia. www.physio-pedia.com/WHOQOL-BREF

Xu, L., Cheng, P., Wu, Y., Zhang, J., Zhu, J., Cui, J., & Yu, R. (2020). The effects of art therapy on anxiety and depression in breast cancer patients: An updated meta-analysis. *European Journal of Cancer Care, 29*(5), 1–8. https://doi.org/10.1111/ecc.13266

CHAPTER XIV

Exploring Male Body Image and Considerations for Men with Cancer in Art Therapy

—— CHARLIE MARSHALL ——

AUTHOR'S PERSPECTIVE

I am a cisgender, male art therapist who has had the privilege of working for more than 30 years with adults in the continuum of care from inpatient to outpatient services. Understanding the root of my biases has informed my clinical practice; I continuously remind myself how beliefs, perspectives, and limitations of awareness stemming from my cultural and personal experiences influence my perspective. These lenses can enhance or inhibit the therapeutic relationship with my clients.

I grew up as the fifth child and third son in a family of ten children in a multi-cultural and multi-generational household. I was influenced by the masculine ideals of the 1940s and 1950s, as well as media exposure from television shows, cartoons, magazines, and newspapers of the 1960s and 1970s. My role models of masculinity were my father, grandfather, church leaders, coaches, and scout leaders. My adolescent experience differed from many of my peers who seemed to be concerned with body hair, height, and shoe size as measurements of masculinity.

My father's lifestyle and image were traditional in terms of the male role model of his time. He kept his hair neatly groomed, wore a suit and necktie, and consistently left for work early in the morning for his day job. He worked hard, attended church, socialized with friends, regularly visited his mother, fixed the household appliances, played French horn in a big band orchestra, took my mother to regular social events, and enjoyed watching sports while drinking cold beer and having snacks. He also ironed clothes and fixed Sunday brunch wearing my mother's apron, both of which aligned with the image of the male role models of his time.

Specific body image discussions in my family centered on body size, good hygiene, and being clean cut. It was considered important to not be "too big" or "too skinny," to keep hair and nails trimmed, to wear clean clothes, to keep skin clear of blemishes, and to smell good. These were all qualities that my mother found attractive. My father did not exercise regularly or focus on a muscular physique. I saw this mirrored on television with the characters of a Superman, Batman, and professional wrestlers who had thick mid sections as they demonstrated feats of heroism and physical strength. I grew up with male role models that influenced my understanding of the male body image as not fixated on a certain body type or strict demarcation of masculine/feminine duties at home.

My personal indoctrination of male body image included having a strong work ethic, using my abilities to support others, and having an internal sense of strength of character. These traits also accompanied the unspoken rules of not talking about emotions, not asking for help, and obeying rules. This still influences my self-image and can impact my ability to connect and help others who may be struggling with their body image. It is my experience that the awareness of my perspectives can allow me to be present to the needs of my clients.

MALE BODY IMAGE

England (2022) reports that male body image research has been focused on how young men formulate their concept of self, related to their body, as influenced by social media, movies, and images of superheroes. Today's youth are flooded with images of hyper-muscular, lean bodies doing adventurous acts and lacking vulnerability, seemingly equating this appearance with the ability to be a rescuer, defender of others, and someone who saves the day. This unrealistic standard may lead to feelings of shame, anxiety, and/or depression related to struggles with self-acceptance or body image. I have seen in my practice that a lack of vulnerability, as influenced from an early age, can manifest as a desire to fix others, a lack of language to express emotions or not knowing one's own needs, as well as a difficulty reaching out for help. These outcomes often lead to a sense of isolation, depression, anxiety, addiction, or an avoidance of physical concerns.

In a study of the male body image through the centuries, Ricciardelli (2016) found that western cultures currently have internalized body ideals which reflect an "overemphasis on competition and winning, the objectification of women and an underrepresentation of gay men" (para. 2). Ricciardelli further elaborates that male body ideals are associated with body image including muscularity and low body fat. There are many articles which echo this point as they focus on studies of young men (Central Coast Treatment Center, 2021; England, 2022; Jones, n.d.; Millar, 2021).

In their research article, Thornborrow *et al.* (2020) describe studies that show a current drive for muscularity as fueled by media exposure and media internalization. The study found that social cultural influences may influence the male body image in many cultures around the globe. Social cultural influences include family, peers, and media. It also speculated that less exposure to media may relate to fewer body image concerns. This suggests that media exposure could increase a sense of dissatisfaction with body image as men internalize the idealized male image.

In a study by Millar (2021), a survey was used to measure the degree of males being judged on body shape or size. The survey found that 60% of respondents desired a "lean and athletic" body and 87% agreed that social media put pressure on males to attain and maintain an ideal body. This can be related to increased anxiety, feelings of isolation, and non-acceptance of self. Pope *et al.* (2000) studied body image in three different cultures and hypothesized that vulnerable males may be more likely to have a variety of issues "as body ideal moves steadily away from the body reality…" (para. 24). I have noticed in my practice that this can affect men of all ages and cultures as they struggle with body image during times of stress.

Although male body image can be negatively impacted by bullying, superheroes, and advertising, there are ways to improve it. Instead of focusing on hair loss, weight, skin issues, and other imperfections, men can develop skills that focus on health, being vulnerable with thoughts and feelings, and finding ways to celebrate themselves, inside and out (Central Coast Treatment Center, 2021; Jones, n.d.). England (2022) writes, "Male body image issues might be under-reported right now, but that's something that we can all help to change" (section 4, para. 5). This offers hope that, even if a man is conditioned not to accept his body image, this may be brought out in the open and addressed in order to build resilience and cope in times of stress, including when facing cancer.

CANCER AND THE MALE BODY IMAGE

Diagnosis and treatment of cancer can deeply impact how a man sees himself, his perception of the human body, and how he fits into the world. In their study, Brederecke *et al.* (2021) state:

> ...many patients experience not only physical complaints but also psychosocial problems such as anxiety and depression, sleep disturbances, post-traumatic growth, the impact of cancer on relationships and fear of cancer recurrence...the body image construct in the domain of psycho-oncology can generally be conceptualized as multidimensional, including thoughts, feelings and perceptions towards the own body, sexuality, and functionality and thus affecting a person's quality of life. (para. 2)

Many studies about body image in men with cancer focus on prostate cancer (Alexis & Worsley, 2018; Chambers *et al.*, 2017; Green, 2021; McInnis & Pukall, 2020; Langelier *et al.*, 2018; O'Shaughnessy *et al.*, 2013; Rosser *et al.*, 2020; Skwirczynska *et al.*, 2022; Ussher *et al.*, 2017). The review by Bowie *et al.* (2022) states that worldwide, prostate cancer is the second most found cancer in men. Their review discusses how men with prostate cancer may experience changes in body image, self-esteem, and ideas of masculinity. The majority of men from the study reported the effects of depression and anxiety symptoms during the diagnosis process, and pre- and post-treatment. Bowie *et al.* (2022) share that this will affect a man's body image, which is defined as "an affective-cognitive-behavioral concept encompassing not only appraisal of physical appearance but also avoiding others, feeling less sexually attractive, and self-consciousness" and having historical, social, and cultural influences (p.97). This highlights the intertwine of medical health of male sexuality, body image, and a sense of well-being. This may also put into jeopardy a man's hopes for relationships, possibility of fathering children, and their ideas of what it means to be a man. Art therapy is uniquely able to address all of these issues in the presence of a knowledgeable, skilled, and empathetic art therapist.

ADDRESSING ISSUES WITH ART THERAPY

Art therapy is psychotherapy involving visual expression and art media choices. For art therapists, goals can focus on the specific needs of a man with cancer at any stage of survivorship. As an example, diagnosis and treatment can have an impact on one's perception of body image, relationships, and roles in life. It is important for the art therapist to assess these aspects and formulate goals appropriate for the individual. Due to the combination of verbal and non-verbal exploration and processing, art therapy is uniquely suited to help individuals dealing with overwhelming diagnoses and is well suited to match a man's method of processing information, to address maladaptive perceptions of self, and to create new ways of processing emotions related to life changes.

In becoming a licensed professional art therapist practicing in a mental health setting, I learned more about myself and became more conscious of how my biases can influence how I interact with a client. Being aware of this helps me be present to the client's struggles while limiting distortion from my own issues. I learned two important concepts which still help me as a therapist today. These are "meet the client where they are" and "you can't take someone where you haven't been." In order to meet the client where they are without judgment, I need to be aware of their needs, get an idea of their perspective, and understand the way they are processing their situation which may be holding them back from getting what they need to cope. Their perspective may be a strength when redirected to their benefit in meeting their needs. Building rapport with the client will help inform the art therapist what is most concerning to the client. The art therapist can identify how the client processes their experiences and chooses art materials and themes to echo their way of processing their experience. With the established trust in the art materials and the art therapist, the client can be guided to explore new perspectives and new ways of coping. The Expressive Therapies Continuum (ETC) and the Media Dimension Variables (MDV) as designed by Lusebrink and Kagin (Lusebrink, 1990) guide the art therapist in the process of appropriate selection of art materials and themes.

EXPRESSIVE THERAPIES CONTINUUM

Lusebrink (1990) described in her book a framework for understanding imagery and visual expression which can guide a therapist in understanding a client's needs, perception, and how they process their circumstances. This is called the Expressive Therapies Continuum (ETC) (Lusebrink, 1990). She wrote, "In order to make intelligent choices, the therapist has to be familiar with the expressive qualities of the media." She collaborated with Kagin who created a continuum for describing media properties, ranging from fluid to resistive (p.84). This is called the Media Dimension Variables (MDV) (Hinz, 2006, p.31). These qualities can correspond to the degree of felt control and freedom of emotional expression while using the material. The ETC's multi-level framework maps out the processing of information in a way which the art therapist can utilize in assisting the client as they are introduced to alternative ways of processing events and expressing emotions safely. It can also be used as a guide when meeting the client on the processing level they use most, and encouraging creativity to enhance self-awareness and coping skills. This may include first introducing media and tasks that reflect the current way they are coping and then introducing media and tasks that allow a new way of expression and seeing themselves.

ART THERAPY APPROACHES

Art therapy includes exploring and creating images as a means of communication and expression, along with verbal processing, structured within psychological theories appropriate to the client's needs. The therapeutic approach needs to be aligned to the client's needs. For clients who intellectualize their experience with cancer and changes in the body and sense of self, the art therapist can begin by focusing on the facts of the diagnosis and treatment and meet the client on the cognitive-symbolic level of the ETC by using resistive art media, as described by the MDV. Implementing humanistic and cognitive-behavioral psychological theories may help the client experience additional ways of processing the situation, enable them to be safely introduced to emotional expression, and practice new ways of coping. Guided by the ETC and MDV, the art therapist can help the client safely explore affective-perceptual ways of processing their circumstances. The benefit to the client could include acquiring a different perspective of their experience, developing an outlet for the emotions related to the changes in their life, and exploring their own creativity in developing new coping skills.

Important goals for clients with cancer include improved coping during the medical journey, addressing the effects of cancer on body image, and management of side-effects of diagnosis and treatment. A skilled art therapist will continually assess the needs of the client by selecting the appropriate theoretical approach and adjusting the level of the ETC and art media. The aim is for the client to build and maintain a sense of safety and trust with the therapist, the art media, and their own ability to use personal strengths to create a stronger sense of self and body image.

CLINICAL EXAMPLE: John Doe

I met with a male client who sought help after family and friends became concerned about his low energy, restricted affect, and obsessions over the recent side effects of treatment for his cancer. He reported that the cancer had been in remission and that the medical staff told him the side effects of the treatment would subside. He had difficulty believing this as he had read that in some cases it did not get better. He ruminated on the cases he read, and his perspective became fixated. This contributed to racing thoughts and an inability to feel connected to friends and family. He agreed to art therapy sessions although he described not liking art in school.

In the first session, he was given a choice of materials to visually explore his thought patterns. The material choices included magazines for collage, pencils, pens, markers, and oil-based clay. He chose the magazines to create a collage. He described his collage as what was inside his head and symbolized his feelings related to how cancer had changed his perspective on his life. The images included a winter landscape with a frozen lake and a black and white image of a home destroyed by a hurricane. When verbally processing the collage, he pointed these two images out as most important. He then described the feeling that his body had been changed and he felt a need to protect others in his life by not being emotional. This indicated to me that it was still crucial to continue the therapeutic approach within the cognitive-symbolic level of the ETC to promote a feeling of safety. Later, more fluid media were introduced to have him recreate the images. This media change allowed for the affective-perceptual level of processing and the experience of expressing emotions in a different way.

Humanistic and cognitive behavioral approaches were used to facilitate ways to build trust and develop goals. This allowed the client to safely focus on incremental changes of behavior. Throughout several sessions, he worked on goals to be more vulnerable with loved ones, and acceptance of changes in his body. The creative process helped in providing a safe way to explore different perspectives and fostering hope in reconnecting to friends and family.

The concept of "you can't take anyone where you haven't been," as applied to therapy, involves my own willingness to experience the changes in perception, different ways of expression, and how my own creativity has helped me in coping with difficulties. This involves experiencing a wide variety of art media, experiencing different ways of processing information on all the levels of the ETC, and taking a risk to be vulnerable with others. Understanding my own internalized body image and ideas of masculinity helps me be present to my clients' needs, remain curious and open to how they view their own body image, and understand what influences them to the positive or negative.

ART THERAPY INTERVENTIONS

As an art therapist, I help clients in individual and group settings. Each of the interventions presented here may be adapted to an individual or group setting. This is a short list of examples, in no particular order, of what a trained art therapist may use to help men develop trust, learn how to process emotions associated with the changes in roles and self-perception, learn better ways to cope, gain insights, and connect with feelings of empowerment and hope.

Body outlines

Purpose

This intervention meets the client on the cognitive-symbolic level of processing information, as described in the ETC, and safely introduces the affective-perceptual level of processing. The low level of complexity will enhance a sense of mastery and a feeling of safety. The goal is to visually and verbally debrief their experience with cancer, allow for discussion of how the illness affected the body, and provide a way to make connections to body image, sense of self, and emotional reactions to the illness.

Materials

Two 8.5" x 11" pieces of white paper with an outline of the human body on each and a set of colored pencils. A sense of safety and control is emphasized with the familiar size of paper and the resistive nature of the colored pencils.

Process

The client is provided with colored pencils as he is given one of the body outlines. He is then asked to show where in the body the cancer has been diagnosed and show locations of any discomfort or pain associated with the illness. Following this, the client is presented with the other body outline and asked to show where emotions are felt in the body. The client may be encouraged to create a key to indicate what each color represents to him. Using open-ended questions, the therapist then encourages the client to verbalize the information on the body outlines.

Observations

As I encourage verbalization of the information, I keep away from interpreting the colors or marks for the client. My goal is to provide an environment of non-judgment and allow a higher sense of control for the client. The use of open-ended questions helps the client to share his experience. These questions allow the client to share what he knows about the cancer and how he first learned about the diagnosis. A sense of control can be further built, acknowledging that the client is the expert of his experience. This debriefing process can help the client build more trust in me as the therapist and disclose more difficult information. After processing the second body outline, open-ended questions are used to learn about somatic responses to emotions, which emotions are dominant, and see if the two body outlines relate to each other. This allows for building awareness of how emotions are felt in the body, discussing ways to channel the energy in the emotion, and explore how his body image has been affected. Retelling the story of the diagnosis and describing the emotions associated to life changes can be very intimidating and difficult, especially if the client had been conditioned to ignore emotions and had limited understanding of emotions before the diagnosis.

Self-expression mandala

Purpose

This mandala intervention can promote a feeling of containment of overwhelming emotions, help focus on inner aspects of the self, and visually explore being aware of the present moment to become conscious of body sensations. These skills are directly related to learning to face and cope with the changing body issues men with cancer may encounter.

The low complexity of the intervention allows for expressing personal experiences safely. Therefore, this intervention may be used to build trust in the therapeutic process. Goals for this intervention include safely exploring thoughts and feelings about changes in self since having cancer, gaining awareness of the body, exploring ideas of masculinity while dealing with the illness, and learning a creative way to communicate emotions.

All levels of processing information, as described by the ETC, can be accessed with this intervention. This flexibility can help with providing a safe place to share overwhelming feelings as well as exploring the expression of unfamiliar emotions.

Materials
Materials used include an 8.5" x 11" piece of paper with a large outline of a circle, and a variety of art media. The art media would best represent a range of properties from resistive to fluid, as described by the MDV. Examples are pencils, markers, oil pastels, and watercolor paints.

Process
The process of this intervention is to first make all the material available, ask the client to think of emotions related to the body and cancer, instruct him to represent the thoughts and feelings using lines and shapes within the circle shape, and then verbally process the image and experience.

Observations
I have experienced great respect for my clients as this intervention has allowed them to share difficult topics and express reduced anxiety while creating. I find therapeutic curiosity can be important in helping the client share this inner world and be aware of maladaptive behaviors, as well as their strengths. This awareness is important in finding new ways of dealing with cancer, the ongoing changes in the body, and the after effects of treatment.

Body image collage
Purpose
Most clients I have helped have connected with this directive as the ready-made images reduce any self-imposed pressures to create images, and reduce anxiety about using images to communicate. The primary level of the ETC experienced with this intervention is the cognitive-symbolic level. It also allows for creative integration of this level with both the kinesthetic-sensory level and the affective-perceptual level, which can provide a meaningful experience for the client.

The complexity of the collage is in the medium range as it integrates multiple levels of processing information with a low number of steps in the process. The goals include providing the client with a safe mode of exploring external and internal expectations of the masculine role, sharing changing perspectives of self since the diagnosis of cancer, and creating an opportunity to start processing emotions about life changes. This can reveal important information about the client's perspective and serve as a guide to developing healthy coping skills.

Materials

Materials used for this intervention include 12" x 18" paper, magazine pages, colored paper, and a choice of adhesives, including glue and tape. Scissors are also provided but not necessary since tearing the paper can add to the kinesthetic-sensory aspect of the experience.

Process

After the client has been presented with the materials, he is asked to create a collage describing two aspects of body image. The therapist can choose which two contrasting aspects would be most beneficial to explore. The client may be asked to create a two-part collage describing body image and roles from external sources compared to body image and roles related to internal pressures. Another focus could be a contrast of how the client viewed body image and roles before the cancer diagnosis and how these are seen since the diagnosis. This intervention could take place in one session or over the course of several sessions.

Adaptations

Besides adapting this intervention to span over several sessions, it can also be adapted to the client who is suffering from a lack of energy and/ or the inability to hold the materials. In this case, the art therapist can act as the hands for the client as he chooses the images and indicates where to place the image in the collage.

Observations

I have been in awe many times as I have watched and heard clients openly share about themselves after finding images which seem to be tailored to their needs. I am careful not to impose my meanings onto the images as I listen to the client, and I help guide the discussion of the images on the collage. I have helped clients explore contrasting parts, identify emotions associated with the images, and choose the most important aspects of the collage. This has helped the client with self-awareness and to identify aspects they would like to address in therapy.

Battle drawing

Purpose

This intervention may be used to help the client to express anger at the cancer, gain a sense of control, and use imagination to envision power over the illness. This intervention can reflect all of the ETC levels of processing information and creativity. The degree of this depends on how much the client connects with the process.

This intervention is low in complexity as the directive instructs the client to visualize a literal fight with cancer. Goals of this intervention include expression of emotions about fighting cancer, separating the body and sense of self from the illness, exploring the role of guilt, shame, or helplessness associated with the diagnosis, identifying support, and gaining a sense of power, control, and mastery over the illness.

Materials

A variety of art materials may be offered to the client in order to create two-dimensional images on several 12" x 18" sheets of paper. The more resistive materials could allow for an increased sense of control.

Process

The process starts with the art therapist asking the client to create a representation of the illness outside the body in the form of a creature(s). The client is asked to create a battle scene between the creature and the client, and any resources needed to fight the illness creature. This can be in one large battle scene or a series of battle images. The therapist can help emphasize themes of externalizing the illness, use of support, asking for help, and working with a team to fight the cancer. This line of discussion about the images can be directly associated with coping skills used to deal better with the effects of cancer and the treatments.

Adaptations

This intervention could be adapted to use a fluid material, such as paint, to simulate an increased kinesthetic-sensory experience and promote emotional expression. Another adaptation is to use Sandtray. Sandtray is an expressive intervention and allows the use of a choice of figures in a container of dry sand. This provides a symbolic and dynamic way of experiencing the battle and feeling a sense of control. A third adaptation is the use of clay. The client is instructed to create the creature representing cancer in clay. The battle could then be acted out in the clay.

A more cognitive-symbolic approach asks the client to write a conversation with the creature. This can reveal to the client and the therapist the relationship with the illness, the degree of power the client feels at the time, and any negative self-talk that may be affecting the client's self-image and ways of coping. This can allow for a sense of safety as the emotional content may be explored in the writing.

Observations

I have witnessed how the expression and insights experienced by clients using the battle drawing can be transformative. In my experience, it is moving to see how the externalization of the illness from the body and sense of self frees energy previously blocked by denial, blaming the self, and feeling helpless.

Losses and gains collage

Purpose

If the treatment needs to be terminated, one way to prepare for ending therapy sessions is to facilitate a review of their journey. At this time, a sense of safety and control is important. Using a more resistive material, such as magazine images, can help achieve this. The goals of this collage include the expression of grief for the past losses, building a sense of empowerment, and acknowledging gain in the experience.

This collage has a medium range of complexity as it has a few steps in the process and allows for multiple levels of processing information. This intervention focuses on the cognitive-symbolic level of processing information to promote a feeling of safety, empowerment, and hope. The affective-perceptual level is also a factor as the topic is laden with emotion, and creating the collage uses perceptual ways of thinking.

Materials

Materials for this intervention include magazine pages, a variety of adhesives, scissors, and 12" x 18" sheets of paper.

Process

As a first step, the client is asked to create a collage using magazines, showing images of the losses related to the illness on one part of the collage. Losses could include the changes in body function, changes in functioning as a man in a variety of roles, and changes in perceptions of the body. On the other part of the collage, the client is asked to focus on the gain, which is singular, from the cancer experience. The emphasis on body image in processing this collage allows the client to recognize that the many losses experienced during the diagnosis and treatment could lead to some meaningful gain in self-perceptions and relationships.

Observations

This collage is best used after the art therapist has determined how the client is coping and processing the changes in body image and male roles. I have seen how this intervention allows for a safe experience to grieve losses and celebrate a gain in self-awareness.

CONCLUSION

Body image is a multi-layered issue unique to each man, involving his background, culture, and experiences. Art therapy is uniquely suited to address the body image of the male client with cancer. Many of today's body image concepts come from visual sources, such as magazines, movies, and social media. Art therapy visually and verbally targets the needed changes in maladaptive internalized imagery related to body image and masculine roles. It also enhances coping with a cancer diagnosis, its treatment, and the after effects of the treatment. My hope for the future is that art therapy is further recognized for its power to be tailored to the individual needs of the client, for the non-judgmental way it provides a safe pathway to insight and better coping, and how it can leave the client with new internalized imagery, which enhances their life.

REFERENCES

Alexis, O. & Worsley, A. J. (2018). A meta-synthesis of qualitative studies exploring men's sense of masculinity post-prostate cancer treatment. *Cancer Nurse, 41*(4), 298–310. https://doi.org/10.1097/NCC.0000000000000509

Bowie, J., Brunckhorst, O., Stewart, R., Dasgupta, P., & Ahmed, K. (2021). Body image, self-esteem, and sense of masculinity in patients with prostate cancer: A qualitative meta-synthesis. *Journal of Cancer Survivorship, 16*(1), 95–110. https://doi.org/10.1007/s11764-021-01007-9

Brederecke, J., Heise, A., & Zimmermann, T. (2021). Body image in patients with different types of cancer. *PLoS ONE, 16*(11), 1–20. https://doi.org/10.1371/journal.pone.0260602

Central Coast Treatment Center. (2021). *Male body image problems are real—and they're really complicated.* Central Coast Treatment Center. www.centralcoasttreatmentcenter.com/blog-1/male-body-image-problems-are-real

Chambers, S. K., Chung, E., Wittert, G., & Hyde, M. K. (2017). Erectile dysfunction, masculinity, and psychosocial outcomes: A review of the experiences of men after prostate cancer treatment. *Translational Andrology and Urology, 6*(1), 60–68. https://doi.org/10.21037/tau.2016.08.12

England, A. (2022). *Where do men fit into the body positivity movement?* Verywell Mind; Dotdash Media, Inc. www.verywellmind.com/where-do-men-fit-into-the-body-positivity-movement-5496295

Green, R. (2021). Maintaining masculinity: Moral positioning when accounting for prostate cancer illness. *Health (London), 25*(4), 399–416. http://doi.org/10.1177/1363459319851555

Hinz, L. (2006). *Expressive Therapies Continuum: A Framework for Using Art in Therapy.* Routledge.

Jones, G. (n.d.). *Male body positivity: Overcoming male body image issues.* Ape to Gentlemen. www.apetogentleman.com/male-body-image-struggles

Langelier, D. M., Cormie, P., Bridel, W., Grant, C., *et al.* (2018). Perceptions of masculinity and body image in men with prostate cancer: The role of exercise. *Support Care Cancer, 26*(10), 3379–3388. https://doi.org/10.1007/s00520-018-4178-1

Lusebrink, V. B. (1990). *Imagery and Visual Expression in Therapy.* Plenum Press.

McInnis, M. K. & Pukall, C. F. (2020). Sex after prostate cancer in gay and bisexual men: A review of the literature. *Sexual Medicine Reviews, 8*(3), 466–472. https://doi.org/10.1016/j.sxmr.2020.01.004

Millar, J. (2021). *Men in the mirror: A closer look at body image.* Men's Health. www.menshealth.com/uk/mental-strength/a38033712/men-in-the-mirror-body-image

O'Shaughnessy, P. K., Ireland, C., Pelentsov, L., Thomas, L. A., & Esterman, A. J. (2013). Impaired sexual function and prostate cancer: A mixed method investigation into the experiences of men and their partners. *Journal of Clinical Nursing, 22*(23–24), 3492–3502. https://doi.org/10.1111.jocn.12190

Pope, H. G., Gruber, A. J., Mangweth, B., Bureau, B., *et al.* (2000). Body image perception among men in three countries. *American Journal of Psychiatry, 157*(8), 1297–1301. https://doi.org/10.1176/appi.ajp.157.8.1297

Ricciardelli, L. (2016). Masculine norms and internalization of body ideals on body image. *Eating Disorders Catalogue.* www.edcatalogue.com/masculine-norms-and-internalization-of-body-ideals-on-body-image

Rosser, B. R. S., Kohli, N., Polter, E. J., Lesher, L., *et al.* (2020). The sexual functioning of gay and bisexual men following prostate cancer treatment: Results from the Restore study. *Archives of Sexual Behavior, 49*(5), 1589–1600. https://doi.org/10.1007/s10508-018-1360-y

Skwirczynska, E., Wroblewski, O., Tejchman, K., Ostrowski, P., & Serwin, N. (2022). Prostate cancer eligible for radical prostatectomy: Self-esteem of patients and forms of coping with stress. *International Journal of Environmental Research and Public Health, 19*(11), 6928. https://doi.org/10.3390/ijerph19116928

Thornborrow, T., Onwuegbusi, T., Mohamed, S., Boothroyd, L. G., & Tovée, M. J. (2020). Muscles and the media: A natural experiment across cultures in men's body image. *Frontiers in Psychology, 11*(495). https://doi.org/10.3389/fpsyg.2020.00495

Ussher, J. M., Perz, J. Rose, D., Dowsett, G. W., *et al.* (2017). Threat of sexual disqualification: The consequences of erectile dysfunction and other sexual changes for gay and bisexual men with prostate cancer. *Archives of Sexual Behavior, 46*(7), 2043–2057. https://doi.org/10.1007/s10508-016-0728-0

Appendix: Search Strategies

CINAHL

1. (MH "Art Therapy (Iowa NIC)") OR (MH "Art Therapy")

2. art therapy or art psychotherapy or creative arts therapies or expressive arts therapy

3. S1 OR S2

4. (MH "Breast Neoplasms+")

5. breast cancer or breast neoplasm or breast carcinoma or breast tumor

6. S4 or S5

7. S3 and S6

OVID MEDLINE
Preliminary search: art therapy-oncology-body image, 1946-2022

1. exp Body Image/(19204)

2. body image*.mp. [mp=title, abstract, original title, name of substance word, subject heading word, floating sub-heading word, keyword heading word, organism supplementary concept word, protocol supplementary concept word, rare disease supplementary concept word, unique identifier, synonyms] (25366)

3. body representation*.mp. [mp=title, abstract, original title, name of substance word, subject heading word, floating sub-heading word, keyword heading word, organism supplementary concept

APPENDIX: SEARCH STRATEGIES

word, protocol supplementary concept word, rare disease supplementary concept word, unique identifier, synonyms] (1006)

4. self-image.mp. [mp=title, abstract, original title, name of substance word, subject heading word, floating sub-heading word, keyword heading word, organism supplementary concept word, protocol supplementary concept word, rare disease supplementary concept word, unique identifier, synonyms] (3892)

5. body image disturbance*.mp. [mp=title, abstract, original title, name of substance word, subject heading word, floating sub-heading word, keyword heading word, organism supplementary concept word, protocol supplementary concept word, rare disease supplementary concept word, unique identifier, synonyms] (725)

6. self esteem.mp. [mp=title, abstract, original title, name of substance word, subject heading word, floating sub-heading word, keyword heading word, organism supplementary concept word, protocol supplementary concept word, rare disease supplementary concept word, unique identifier, synonyms] (23634)

7. ((perception* or thought* or attitude* or feeling* or belief*) adj5 (body or bodies or appearance)).mp. (9615)

8. 1 or 2 or 3 or 4 or 5 or 6 or 7 (55935)

9. exp Neoplasms/(3706536)

10. (cancer* or carcino* or oncolog* or tumor* or tumour* or neoplasm*).mp. (4570774)

11. exp Art Therapy/(1683)

12. art-making.mp. [mp=title, abstract, original title, name of substance word, subject heading word, floating sub-heading word, keyword heading word, organism supplementary concept word, protocol supplementary concept word, rare disease supplementary concept word, unique identifier, synonyms] (129)

13. art therap*.mp. [mp=title, abstract, original title, name of substance word, subject heading word, floating sub-heading word, keyword heading word, organism supplementary concept word,

protocol supplementary concept word, rare disease supplementary concept word, unique identifier, synonyms] (2530)

14. 9 or 10 (4987655)

15. 11 or 12 or 13 (2606)

16. exp Breast Neoplasms/(328471)

17. breast cancer.mp. [mp=title, abstract, original title, name of substance word, subject heading word, floating sub-heading word, keyword heading word, organism supplementary concept word, protocol supplementary concept word, rare disease supplementary concept word, unique identifier, synonyms] (315133)

18. exp Mammaplasty/(16236)

19. exp Mastectomy/(35656)

20. breast carcinoma in situ/or carcinoma, ductal, breast/or carcinoma, lobular/or inflammatory breast neoplasms/or unilateral breast neoplasms/or triple negative breast neoplasm.mp. [mp=title, abstract, original title, name of substance word, subject heading word, floating sub-heading word, keyword heading word, organism supplementary concept word, protocol supplementary concept word, rare disease supplementary concept word, unique identifier, synonyms] (19571)

21. 16 or 17 or 18 or 19 or 20 (430151)

22. 14 or 21 (4998556)

23. 15 and 22 (345)

24. 8 and 23 (12)

25. limit 24 to English language (10)

Subsequent search

1. exp Art Therapy/(1683)

2. art-making.mp. [mp=title, abstract, original title, name of substance word, subject heading word, floating sub-heading word, keyword heading word, organism supplementary concept word,

APPENDIX: SEARCH STRATEGIES

protocol supplementary concept word, rare disease supplementary concept word, unique identifier, synonyms] (129)

3. art therap*.mp. [mp=title, abstract, original title, name of substance word, subject heading word, floating sub-heading word, keyword heading word, organism supplementary concept word, protocol supplementary concept word, rare disease supplementary concept word, unique identifier, synonyms] (2530)

4. 1 or 2 or 3 (2606)

5. exp Breast Neoplasms/(328471)

6. breast cancer.mp. [mp=title, abstract, original title, name of substance word, subject heading word, floating sub-heading word, keyword heading word, organism supplementary concept word, protocol supplementary concept word, rare disease supplementary concept word, unique identifier, synonyms] (315133)

7. exp Mammaplasty/(16236)

8. exp Mastectomy/(35656)

9. breast carcinoma in situ/or carcinoma, ductal, breast/or carcinoma, lobular/or inflammatory breast neoplasms/or unilateral breast neoplasms/or triple negative breast neoplasm.mp. [mp=title, abstract, original title, name of substance word, subject heading word, floating sub-heading word, keyword heading word, organism supplementary concept word, protocol supplementary concept word, rare disease supplementary concept word, unique identifier, synonyms] (19571)

10. 5 or 6 or 7 or 8 or 9 (430151)

11. 4 and 10 (68)

12. limit 11 to (English language and last 10 years) (40)

Subject Index

acceptance
  positive rational 31
  self-accepting body talk 32
adaptive art therapy 177–9
adolescents with illness
  altered books 232
  art media for 234–6
  body appreciation
    collage/image 231–2
  body image issues
    arising 227–8
  body sculpture 231
  cancer 225
  clay art therapy 236
  collage 235
  directives appropriate
    for 230–4
  family support 234
  fiber arts 235
  goals related to the
    population 228–30
  impact of medical
    experiences 225–7
  "New Me" video 233–4
  no protocols for body
    image work 224–5
  overview 224–5
  photography 235
  problem-solving
    comic strip 233
  psychological
    consequences 227–8
  self-compassion
    mandalas 233
  self-esteem 230
  special considerations
    236–7
  visual body feelings
    journal 232
adrenaline 97

Adverse Childhood
  Experiences
  (ACEs) 99–100
alexithymia 62
altered books 64–6, 65f, 232
And the Rain Wouldn't
  Come (poem) 129, 130f
anorexia nervosa
  role of body image
    in 48–50
  subtypes 48
appearance comparison 29
appearance fixing 31
appearance investment 32
archetypal images 213
attachment 206
attachment injury 78–80, 157
Attuned Representational
  Model of Self 44
attunement 29–30, 206
avoidance (as response to
  body image threat) 31
awareness of breath scan 71

battle drawing 272–3
beauty standards 33, 192
binge eating disorder
  co-occurring mental
    conditions 51
  reward system activated 47
  role of body image in 51–2
biological domain 42–3
black-out poetry 65, 66f
body acceptance 32
body appreciation
  33–4, 231–2
body attention scan 70–1
body betrayal 118
body concept 17–8
body dysmorphia 124

body functionality 30
body image
  art therapy and
    (overview) 63
  biological domain 42–3
  continuously evolving
    development of 26
  flexibility 30–1
  multidimensional
    construct of 26
  neuroscience of 58–62
  personal definition of 67
  psychological domain
    46–8
  and quality of life (QoL)
    26, 117–8, 240
  as result of collection of
    lived experiences 18
  in social domain 43–5
  trauma and 102–5
  trauma survivor's
    perception 77–80
  see also positive
    body image
body image distress 138
body image disturbance 57
body outlines 268–9
body perception 17, 175
body pride 34
body sanctification 34
body schema 60, 207
body sculpture 231
body shaming 52
body terrorism 79
body tracing 107, 168
body-checking
  behaviors 28–9
bodymind model of art
  therapy 246, 248
breast cancer 239

— 280 —

SUBJECT INDEX

breast cancer survivors
(literature review)
art directives 244–7
art media 244–7
art therapy aims 244–7
art therapy approaches
243–4
assessment tools 242–3
body image and
corresponding
outcome measures
242
bodymind art therapy
246, 248
brief art therapy 246–7
data study design 242
discussion 258
limitations 258–9
methods 241–2
mindfulness-based art
therapy (MBAT)
243–5, 250–4
open art studio 245–6, 255
outcomes of art therapy
treatment for 247–56
phenomenological-
inspired art
therapy 246, 249
quality of life (QoL)
247, 257
summary of findings 256–7
breastfeeding 197–8
breath awareness scan 71
brief art therapy 246–7
bulimia nervosa (role of
body image in) 50–1

C-section 199–200
cancer
adolescents 225
children 213, 216
see also breast cancer;
breast cancer survivors
(literature review);
men with cancer
Cash, Dr. Thomas 25
cephalopod 207
check-ins 86
chemotherapy 216–7
child life work 218–9
childhood abuse 78
children (development of
body image in) 206–7
children with illness
age-appropriate
understanding 208–9

artmaking to reduce
stress 219
body image in children's
art 212–5, 214f, 215f
body image evaluation
of 207–9
body image perceptions
and chronic illness
215–7, 216f, 218f
body memory 212
body satisfaction 208
calming/soothing
activities 219–20
cancer 213, 216
case study: Janie 214, 215f
case study: Margaret 210–1
case study: Thomas 212
case study: Veronica
213–4, 214f
chemotherapy 216–7
embodiment of 208
grief 211
hospitalization 205–6
pain 217
skin as threshold 209–10
special considerations for
medical setting 220–1
spontaneous art 220
vitality and play in 210
circles of closeness 110
clay art therapy 144–50,
150f, 231, 236
closeness (circles of) 110
cognitive dissonance 192
collage 67, 106–7, 183–5, 184f,
231–2, 235, 270–2, 273–4
comfort collage 106
comic strips 233
complex post-traumatic
stress disorder 100, 116–7
conceptualization of
beauty (broad) 33
controllable identity
(body of) 47
coping
body of emotional 46–7
maladaptive 159
positive rational
acceptance and 31
cortisol 97
Covid-19 pandemic
impact 91–2
cross-cultural identities 44
cultural humility 121
cultural identities
(multiple) 44

culture (body of society
and) 44–5
cystic fibrosis 227

depersonalization 124
derealization 124–5
developmental trauma and
body image 102–4
diabetes 228
dialoguing with the body 64
digital art tools 178, 183
disconnecting from the
body 78–9, 118
discriminatory stress 45
dissociation 100–1
dissociative fugue 124–5
dissociative identity
disorder (DID) 122–3
domestic violence *see*
intimate partner
violence (IPV)

eating disorders
altered books as
metaphor 64–6, 65f
art therapy in treatment
of (overview) 53–4
awareness of breath
scan 71, 73–4
biological domain 42–3
body attention scan
70–1, 73–4
client example: Ellie 72
control/no control
dynamic 47
dialoguing with
the body 64
exploring internal
sensations
directives 69–74
goals unique to
population 80–2
guilt 47–8
heartbeat identification 70
identifying emotions
within the body 71–2
identifying smells 68–9
lack of training in 74
media literacy 66–7
neuroscience of 59–62
personal definition of
body image 67
pervasiveness of 62
psychological domain 46–8
shame 47–8
in social domain 43–5

eating disorders *cont.*
  special considerations 74–5
  traits linked with 58
  and trauma experience 77–80
  see also anorexia nervosa; binge eating disorder; bulimia nervosa
Edinburgh Postnatal Depression Scale (EPDS) 193
embodiment of children with illness 208
emotional coping (body of) 46–7
emotions (identifying within the body) 71–2
European Organization for Research and Treatment of Cancer Quality of Life Questionnaire (EORTC QLQ-BR23) 242, 243
Expressive Therapies Continuum (ETC) 84, 265–6
extrastriate body area (EBA) 60, 61

family dynamics (and eating disorders) 51, 79
family support (for adolescents) 234
fat talk 32
Felitti, Dr. Vincent 99
felted brain 73f
fetishization 159
fiber arts 235
fight, flight, or freeze response 97
filter (protective) 35–6
fitsporation 45
flexibility (body image) 30–1
fusiform body area (FBA) 60, 61

gender dysphoria 157–8
good-enough mother theory 188
grief (children with illness) 211
grounding meditation 83, 86–7
group work
  check-ins 86
  fears evoked by 81

in nature-attuned art therapy 82–5, 86–91
guilt (eating disorders and) 47–8

haiku 194–200
heartbeat identification 70
homeostasis 97
hysteria 98, 191

identifying emotions within the body 71–2
identifying smells 68–9
implicit body memory 212
implicit relational knowing 206
improvisation 84
inclusivity 121
infection control 220, 231
inferior parietal lobe (IPL) 60
insula 43, 58–61, 62
internal family systems 163–4
interoceptive awareness 17, 42, 43, 60–1, 69–74, 72
interoceptive signals (from food) 59
interpersonal stressors (and bulimia nervosa) 50–1
intersectionality 44
intimate partner violence (IPV)
  case example: Tina 149–51
  clay art therapy 144–50, 150f
  counselling service providers 142–3
  creative journalling 144–8
  cultural standards and 141–2
  definition 135–6
  dynamics of 139–41
  harmful stereotypes about 141
  reluctance to leave relationship 139–41
  research 137–9
  terminology around 136–7
invisible diagnoses 227

journalling 144–8, 232

knowledge (clinicians' lack of) 26–7, 74

labels (impact of) 136–7
learned helplessness 140

male body image
  cancer and the 264
  overview 262–3
  see also men with cancer
mandalas 233, 269–70
marginalized groups 45
Media Dimension Variables (MDV) 266
media literacy
  eating disorders 66–7
  impact of 34–5
medical equipment 220
medical trauma 158
men with cancer
  addressing issues with art therapy 264–5
  art therapy approaches 266–8
  art therapy interventions 268–74
  author's perspective 261–2
  battle drawing 272–3
  body image collage 270–2
  body outlines 268–9
  clinical example 267–8
  losses and gains collage 273–4
  prostate cancer 264
  search strategies 276–9
  self-expression mandalas 269–70
  see also male body image
military sexual trauma (MST) 176
mindfulness-based art therapy (MBAT) 243–5, 250–4
minority stress theory 156
misattuned relationships 79
miscarriage 196–7
mother-baby bonding 192
motivational salience 29
mourning and remembrance 108–9

nature-attuned art therapy
  approaches 82–5
  art process 87
  authentic connection in 82
  example participants 85
  examples of art response 87–90, 89f, 90f

— 282 —

SUBJECT INDEX

goals (eating disorders) 80–2
grounding meditation 83, 86–7
group work in 82–5, 86–91
outcomes 90–1
session example 86–91
special considerations 91–2
needlesticks 209
neurobiological body 42–3
neuroscience
adolescents' brain development 58
of body image 58–62
trauma and the brain 104–5
"New Me" video 233–4

objectification theory 158–9
open art studio 245–6, 255
overcomer (label of) 136

pain (in children) 217
parasympathetic nervous system (PSNS) 97
Partial Hospitalization Program (PHP) 92–3
partner violence see intimate partner violence (IPV)
perfectionism 49–50, 81
peri/postpartum outpatient program
breastfeeding 197–8
C-section 199–200
case findings: Jennifer 196–8
case findings: Johanna 199–200
case findings: Vera 198–9
Edinburgh Postnatal Depression Scale (EPDS) 193
expectations (social) 189, 192–3
haiku 194–200
miscarriage 196–7
overview 189–90
pregnancy 190–3
strength-based approach 190
weight gain during pregnancy 193
phenomenological-inspired art therapy 246, 249
photography 235
play in children with illness 210

poetry
And the Rain Wouldn't Come 129, 130f
black-out 65, 66f
haiku 194–200
sex trafficking survivors 129, 130f, 131
poiesis 82, 84–5
positive body image
definition 27
development of 26–7
empowerment and 119–20
as holistic construct 19, 27
positive rational acceptance 31
post-traumatic growth 119–20, 126, 131
post-traumatic stress disorder 100, 138
Postpartum Mood and Anxiety Disorder (PMAD) 191
pregnancy 190–3
see also peri/postpartum outpatient program
problem-solving comic strip 233
process over product 195
prostate cancer 264
protective factors for body image 159
protective filter 35–6
psychoeducation 104
psychological domain 46–8

quality of life (QoL)
body image and 26, 117–8, 240
breast cancer survivors 247, 257
European Organization for Research and Treatment of Cancer Quality of Life Questionnaire (EORTC QLQ-BR23) 242, 243
World Health Organization Quality-of-Life-BREF questionnaire (WHOQOL-BREF, 2023) 243
queer community
art therapy directives with 168–9
art therapy goals 166–8

body image in the 154–5
case study: Emma 160–3, 161f, 162f, 163f
case study: Jane 163–5, 163f
gender dysphoria 157–8
maladaptive coping 159
media and materials 169
medical trauma 158
objectification and dehumanization 158–9
protective factors for body image 159
psychotherapy approaches 165–6
rejection and attachment trauma 157
special considerations 169
stigma 155–6
systemic oppression and discrimination 156
trauma and the body in 155–65
violence/bullying 156–7

"reconnection" 110
remembrance and mourning 108–9
resilience factors 101–2

safety
absolute vs. relative 91
as therapeutic goal 105–8
Salience Network 59
sanctification of body 34
schemas 17
scoliosis 228
self with other (images of) 110–1
self-accepting body talk 32
self-compassion mandala 233
self-esteem 138, 230
self-expression mandala 269–70
self-identity 138
self-image 17, 42
self-perception 17
self-portrait 109
self-schemas 17
sense of self 17, 207
sex trafficking
art mediums 125–6, 128–30
art therapists as advocates for change 121–2
art therapy approaches 127–8

sex trafficking *cont.*
  art therapy theory/
    goals 120–1
  body image and quality
    of life 117–8
  case example: Amy
    Anna 126–31, 129f
  case example: Veronica
    122–6, 124f, 125f
  introduction to 115–6
  post-traumatic growth/
    future goals 126, 131
  predominantly females 115
  ramifications of 116–8
  survivor-informed
    psychotherapy 123–5
  treatment for survivors
    of 118–9
shame (eating disorders
  and) 47–8
sickle cell disease 228
size privilege 52
skin as threshold 209–10
smells (identifying) 68–9
social action (art
  therapists and) 121–2
social domain 43–5
social media
  comparisons on 29, 34
  powerful influence of 35
  selective body
    representation on 45
spice paintings 68–9, 68f
spiritual significance
  of the body 34
state body image work 28
state and trait body image
  (trauma and) 102
state-based body image
  assessments 28
stigma
  in the queer community
    155–6
  weight 52
strength-based
  approaches 190
stress hormones 97
survivor identity 137
survivor (label of) 136–7
survivor-informed
  psychotherapy 123–5

sympathetic nervous
  system (SNS) 97
symptom-focused body
  images 107–8
symptoms collage 106–7
systemic oppression and
  discrimination 156
systems approaches 165–6

technology
  digital art tools 178, 183
  "New Me" video 233–4
  virtual sessions 86,
    91–2, 178
terminology
  debates around 136–7
  queer community 154
thriver (label of) 136
trait constructs 28
trait and state
  interactions 28, 102
trait-level disturbances
  in body image 28
trauma
  Adverse Childhood
    Experiences
    (ACEs) 99–100
  associated disorders
    100–1
  and the body 103
  and body image 102–5
  and body perception
    78–80
  and the body in the queer
    community 155–65
  and the brain 104–5
  children with illness 211
  circles of closeness 110
  comfort collage 106
  complex post-traumatic
    stress disorder
    100, 116–7
  definition 97
  developmental 102–4
  and eating disorders 77–80
  historical perspectives
    98–9
  images of self with
    others 110–1
  post-traumatic growth
    119–20, 126, 131

post-traumatic stress
  disorder 100
prevalence of 100–1
remembrance and
  mourning 108–9
risk factors 101–2
safety and 105–8
self before and self
  after 108
self in the moment
  of 108–9
self-portrait 109
symptom-focused body
  images 107–8
symptoms collage 106–7
Trauma Symptom
  Inventory Alternate
  Version (TSI-A) 103
trauma-informed models
  of art therapy 104

United States military
  173–4

veterans
  adaptive art therapy 177–9
  body image within the
    population 175–6
  ethos of active-duty
    individuals 174
  reasons for joining
    military 173
  role of art therapy 176–85
  Steve's story 179–85,
    182f, 184f
  United States
    military 173–4
victim (label of) 136–7
virtual sessions 86, 91–2, 178
vitality/play in children
  with illness 210

weight gain during
  pregnancy 193
weight stigma 52
World Health Organization
  Quality-of-Life-
  BREF questionnaire
  (WHOQOL-BREF,
  2023) 243

Author Index

Abas, M. 116
Ackard, D. M. 117, 118
Ahadzadeh, A.S. 34
Alexis, O. 264
Allan, J. 208, 220
Allen, K. L. 51
Alpers, J. 205, 208, 211, 213, 214, 216, 217, 220
Alvy, L. M. 159
Amatruda, K. 220
American Art Therapy Association 176
American Psychiatric Association 42, 43, 47, 48, 50, 51, 57, 100, 101, 116, 124, 138, 190
American Psychological Association 97
An, J. 257
Anand, K. S. 104
Anda, R. F. 99, 103
Antonie, L. 192
Anzani, A. 159
Armstrong, M. T. 103
Arnold, C. 43, 48, 49, 62
Arseniev-Koehler, A. 45
Attias, R. 102, 105, 106, 111
Augustus-Horvath, C. L. 32
Avalos, L. C. 32, 33
Avery, J. A. 59

Bach, S. 208, 213, 214, 220
Backos, A. 104, 105, 108
Bacon, L. 120
Bargai, N. 140, 141, 142
Barton, J. 217
Berk, L. E. 225
Bertoia, J. 208, 220
Bhatt-Poulose, K. 228
Bibring, G. L. 193

Bilich, M. 120
Bilir, Ý. 228
Bischoff-Grethe, A. 59, 61, 70
Bloom, S. 117
Bogousslavsky, J. 98
Bohner, G. 136
Boone, L. 49, 50
Borji, A. 240, 243, 244, 247, 250
Bowie, J. 264
Bowlby, J. 205
Brederecke, J. 264
Breiner, S. 74
Brewster, M. E. 158
Briere, J. N. 100, 104
Brownstone, L. M. 52
Bryson, B. 206, 209
Buchholz, L. J. 51
Burns, R. C. 110

Cabrera, R. 141, 142, 147
Caldwell, C. 78
Calhoun, L. G. 119
Cameron, C. O. 228, 230, 234
Camp, J. 156, 157, 166, 167
Cane, F. 104
Carmel, T. C. 156, 157, 158, 159
Carpenter, J. 97
Carr, S. M. D. 231, 236
Cash, T. 25, 30, 31, 63, 74
Cavanaugh, J. C. 225
Centers for Disease Control and Prevention 99, 211
Central Coast Treatment Center 263
Ceunen, E. 61, 71, 107, 108
Chambers, S. K. 264
Channa, S. 46, 52
Chapman, L. 123, 128

Chilton, G. 232
Chmielewski, J. F. 165, 167, 168
Choudhary, P. 175, 176
Chow, K. M. 240
Churruca, K. 46, 47, 51, 52
Cirlot, J. E. 213
Ciucci, A. 229
Cleveland Clinic 97
Cohen, B. M. 105, 109
Coleman, S. R. 116, 117
Compas, B. E. 225
Conti, J. E. 47, 49
Cook-Cottone, C. 29, 30, 32, 44, 46, 48, 51, 79, 80, 105
Corbett, T. 225, 228
Corning, A. F. 32
Councill, T. 205, 211, 217, 219, 220, 221, 225, 229, 230
Courtois, C. A. 116
Crane, J. L. 211
Crocker, T. 231, 236
Çubukçu, D. 228
Czamanski-Cohen, J. 240, 246, 248

Dahlenburg, S. C. 48, 49
Dalzell, H. 154, 166, 167, 168, 169
Dana, D. 80
Danylchuk, L. 120
Darke, K. 156, 157, 159, 160, 165, 166, 167, 168, 169
Darukhanavala, A. 225, 226, 228
Davids, C. M. 45
Davidtz, J. 117
Davis, A. 231
Davis, C. 211, 240
Dawson, N. 48, 49

— 285 —

DeLucia, J. M. 185
Dhawan, M. 225
Dhikav, V. 104
Dieguez, S. 98
Doley, J. R. 52
Drosdick, C. 120
Duarte, C. 51
DuFrene, T. 69
Dunn, J. L. 136, 137

Effa, C. J. 239, 240, 242, 243, 246, 247, 248, 257
Elimimian, E. B. 246, 247, 249
Elkis-Abuhoff, D. 178
England, A. 262, 263
Erickson-Schroth, L. 156, 157, 158, 159
Erikson, E. H. 209
Esposito, R. 59, 62

Fallon, P. 117, 118
Falvo, D. 226
Fardouly, J. 29
Farmer, K. 120
Fay, D. 79
Felitti, V. J. 99, 103
Fernlund, A. 196
Festinger, L. 192
Findlay, J. C. 109
Finlay, H. 78, 104
Fitzsimmons-Craft, E. E. 29
Flores, A. R. 156
Ford, J. D. 116
Frank, G. K. 43
Franko, D. L. 44, 47
Franzoni, E. 62, 103
Fredrickson, B. L. 27, 117, 118
Freud, S. 98, 196
Freysteinson, W. M. 176
Frisén, A. 119
Fuchs, T. 41, 46, 49, 50
Fuller-Tyszkiewicz, M. 26, 28, 29, 31, 35, 58, 102
Furth, G. M. 208, 220

Gabriels, R. L. 216
Gaete, M. I. 41, 46, 49, 50
Gao, X. 60, 61
Garrett, M. 74
Garrod, T. 197
Gaskill, R. L. 211
Gattario, K. H. 119
Gavron, T. 146, 151
Gaydos, M. 181
Geilhufe, B. 155, 157, 159, 167

Gerassi, L. B. 116
Goodill, S. W. 208, 210
Goodwin, J. 102, 105, 106, 111
Green, M. A. 45
Green, R. 264
Grilo, C. M. 47, 48, 50, 51, 52
Groth, T. 78
Groves, K. 61
Guarda, M. 48
Guillaume, S. 78
Guyton, V. D. 131

Hammack, P. L. 156
Hanna, B. 103
Hartman-Munick, S. M. 226
Hartzell, M. 206
Hass-Cohen, N. 104, 109
Heiderscheit, A. 73
Helms, S. W. 236
Herbert, B. M. 42, 43, 49
Herman, J. 98, 105, 108, 110, 116
Hetherington, R. 167, 168
Hill, A. 97, 104
Hill, M. L. 166, 167
Hinz, L. 49, 53, 84, 266
Hodgkinson, E. L. 192
Homan, K. J. 30
Hook, J. N. 121
Huang, Y.-K. 225
Hyde, J. S. 30

International Labour Organization 115
Itczak, M. 211

Jackson, L. 121
Jacobson, H. L. 34
Jalambadani, Z. 240, 243, 244, 247, 250
James, S. 158
Jang, S.-H. 243, 244, 247, 251
Jarry, J. L. 25, 26, 29
Jax 192
Jones, B. A. 167
Jones, G. 263
Joshi, A. M. 243, 245, 247, 252

Kail, R. V. 225
Kaplan. F. F. 121
Kaushansky, D. 234
Keeling, M. 175
Kelly, A. C. 64
Kessler, R. C. 100
Kievisiene, J. 243, 247, 252

Kilpatrick, D. G. 101
King, J. L. 104
Klorer, P. G. 109
Koch, S. C. 208, 210
Koeppel, C. J. 59, 68
Kometiani, M. K. 120, 131, 132
Kopytin, A. 177
Kossak, M. S. 208, 219
Kramer, E. 104
Kubany, E. S. 143

Lacroix, E. 224
Langelier, D. M. 264
Lazar, A. 178
Lebedev, A. 177
Lee, S. B. 228
LeFranc, B. 63
Leonidas, C. 46, 49, 51
Levine, S. 80
Levy, B. 194
Levy, C. E. 178
Linde, K. 197
Linehan, M. 30
Lobban, J. 177
Longobardi, C. 99
Losada, M. F. 27
Lucid, N. 129
Ludy-Dobson, C. 206
Lusebrink, V. 84, 265

McCabe, J. E. 192
McCarthy, D. 207, 211
McCue, K. 205
McDonald, M. C. 102
McHugh, T. L. 168
McInnis, M. K. 264
McKinley, N. M. 30
Mahoney, A. 34
Makin, S. 41
Malchiodi, C. 104, 108, 137, 195, 205, 211, 212, 218, 229, 230
Malivoire, B. L. 104
Marie, G. O. 123, 126
Markey, C. H. 206, 207, 208, 215, 217
Marlatte, H. 105
Martin, K. M. 46, 47
Matheson, F. I. 136, 138, 139, 140, 141, 142, 147, 151
Merriam-Webster 207
Metzl, E. 167, 169
Meyer, I. H. 156
Mijas, M. 159
Millar, J. 263
Millen, M. 160, 167, 168, 169

AUTHOR INDEX

Mills, A. 105, 109
Mischel, W. 190
Misluk-Gervase, E. 53
Mitchell, L. 157
Moayedi, M. 60, 61, 63
Monti, D. A. 243, 244, 245, 247, 253
Moon, B. L. 194
Moon, C. H. 144
Moore, J. B. 225, 226, 232, 233
Moore, T. M. 120
Morrissey, R. A. 29, 34, 36, 62, 63
Murphy, D. 177
Mustanski, B. 166, 167, 168

Nagata, J. M. 156, 158, 168
National Coalition Against Domestic Violence 135, 139
National Human Trafficking Hotline 115
National Institute of Mental Health 101
Naumburg, M. 98, 104
Nichols, A. J. 116
Nomination of Ruth Bader Ginsburg 188

Ogden, P. 98
Ohannessian, C. M. 34, 58
O'Hara, M. W. 192
Oral, R. 211
Oram, S. 116
O'Shaughnessy, P. K. 264

Pachankis, J. E. 166
Palmisano, G. 47, 48
Papendick, M. 136
Pascal, J. 197
Pattoni, L. 190
Paxton, S. J. 35
Perry, B. 206, 211, 212
Petrucelli, J. 30, 32, 35
Phang, C. 233
Piaget, J. 42
Pinto-Gouveia, J. 51
Piran, N. 35
Pivnik, B. 207
Polaris 118
Pope, H. G. 263
Press, S. A. 60, 61
Protos, K. 154, 158, 166, 167, 168, 169
Psychology Today 175

Pukall, C. F. 264
Pylvanainen, P. 41, 43, 52, 83

Rabin, M. 42, 120
Rabinor, J. R. 120
Rae, W. A. 209
Rakovec-Felser, Z. 135
Reilly, R. C. 245, 247, 254
Ressler, K. J. 206
Reyes-Haro, D. 60
Ricciardelli, L. 103, 224, 263
Riley, S. 234
Roberts, T. A. 117, 118
Rochat, P. 207
Rode, D. 211, 218
Rodgers, R. F. 175
Roe v. Wade 188
Romito, B. 218
Ross, B. 194
Rosser, B. R. S. 264
Rowling, J. K. 86

Sáez, G. 138, 139, 142, 143
Saguy, A.C. 52
Saleebey, D. 119
Saltzman, L. E. 135, 136
Sandoz, E. 31, 69
Santos, M. A. 46, 49, 51
Scarce, J. 42, 117
Schattie, A. 224
Schilder, P. 42
Schneider, S. 46
Schore, A. N. 206
Scott, C. 100, 104, 169
Scott-Miller, S. 156, 157, 159, 160, 165, 166, 167, 168
Sevelius, J. M. 159
SF-36v2 Health Survey 257
Shaw, L. 160, 168
Shoda, Y. 190
Sholt, M. 146, 151
Sidorova, V. 80
Siegel, D. J. 206
Simmons, W. K. 59
Simpson, W. 193
Skwirczynska, E. 264
Smith, A. 177
Smith, J. 225, 228
Smith, M. L. 159
Smolak, L. 117, 118, 119
Soulliard, Z. A. 167
Spring, D. 117, 120
Stern, D. 206, 207, 210
Su, Y.-J. 225
Sukach, T. 118
Sundaram, R. 217

Suputtidada, P. 144, 146
Sweeney, A. 100

Talwar, S. 104, 121
Tan, L. A. 120
Tan, W. 30, 31
Tangney, J. P. 199
Tankersley, A. P. 157
Tasca, C. 98
Tasca, G. A. 78
Taylor, S. 45, 52, 54, 79
Tedeschi, R. G. 119
Terr, L. 211
Thornberry, T. 48, 49
Thornborrow, T. 263
Thyme, K. E. 252
Ticen, S. 50
Tiggemann, M. 120
Totenbier, S. L. 41
Towne, M. 218
Tripp, T. 106
Troncone, A. 225, 228
Tsutsumi, A. 116
Turner, J. C. 205
Tylka, T. L. 25, 26, 27, 30, 31, 32, 33, 34, 35, 36, 69, 71, 102, 110

United States Census Bureau 189
U.S. Department of Defense 173, 174
U.S. Department of Health and Human Services 115, 116
U.S. Department of State 116, 119
Ussher, J. M. 264

van der Kolk, B. 103, 105, 143, 155
Vander Wal, J. S. 167
Vanderlinden, J. 47, 48
Vannucci, A. 34, 58
Vende, K. 50
Verschueren, M. 43, 44, 46, 47
Victims of Trafficking and Violence Protection Act of 115
Volpe, U. 103

Wadeson, H. 106
Walloch, J. C. 166, 167
Wanchena, V. C. 122, 125

Ward, A. 52
Waring, S. V. 64
Warschburger, P. 69, 70, 106, 107
Watson, B. 190
Weaver, T. L. 137, 138, 140
Webb, J. B. 26, 29, 30, 31, 33, 34, 44, 45, 102, 168
Wiederman, M. W. 118
Wierenga, C. E. 59, 61
Williams, G. A. 74

Williams, L. 64, 69
Williamson, C. 116
Wilson, C. 116, 117
Winnicott, D. W. 188
Wood-Barcalow, N. 25, 27, 30, 31, 32, 33, 34, 35, 36, 69, 71, 102, 110
World Health Organisation 100, 116, 240
Worsley, A. J. 264
Wu, S. 103

Xu, L. 247, 255

Yager, Z. 103, 224
Young, L. 103

Zeankowski, J. 210
Zimmerman, C. 117
Zullig, K. J. 159, 167